PICKING THROUGH THE PIECES

Web: HVSaviation.com
Contact: contact@HVSaviation.com

Paperback edition
ISBN 978-1-7752834-4-7

Typesetting and Cover Design by FormattingExperts.com

Visit HVSaviation.com/pieces for easy access to all videos referenced in this book and additional material.

To my wife Charlotte – and to our children Tanya, Laraine, and Andrew

To our grandchildren, who are so incredibly precious to us

To all of our relatives, near and far

And to all the generations who will follow them

FOREWORD

There is an old saying in the aviation safety business, it goes like this: "Learn from the mistakes of others, because you will not live long enough to learn them all yourself". Larry has made a few mistakes in his years as an aviation safety professional, but as he explains in this book, he has taken each of them to heart and learned from them. He has gained so much knowledge and experience that others can now learn from him. Some of those experiences presented unique problems that he had to resolve, dilemmas not only new to Larry, but never before undertaken in the world of accident investigation. If you're a budding or experienced accident investigator, there are plenty of lessons to learn from in this book. If you are not an accident investigator, but are curious as to how things work during an accident investigation, you will find these stories very interesting.

I have worked with Larry for over two decades and I am still learning from him, including his lighthearted jokes, of which there are many in this book. He has entertained not only me, but the hundreds of investigators he has worked with over the years. His approach to humour not only makes serious and challenging work less stressful, but has the effect of bringing everyone together to work towards a common goal. That elusive goal of figuring out what has happened and why, not only to prevent it from happening again, but to give families, loved ones and survivors involved in the accident some desperately needed answers.

Larry is dedicated to providing answers to those suffering or even grieving from a loss as a result of an accident or incident. It means so much to him, that he makes it a huge part of his teaching to other accident investigators. Not only does he teach it, he wrote the book! Larry was responsible for writing the guidelines that are used by Transportation Safety Board (TSB) of Canada investigators of all modes of investigation (Air, Rail, Marine, and Pipeline). This document has been in use for over 20 years and various parts of it are used all over the world. There are many good examples in this book that illustrate Larry's ability to go out of his way to comfort those that need answers.

If you are seeking answers, Larry will give them to you, not only in this book, but also in his first book titled *MH370: Mystery Solved*. Larry wrote this book about his theory on the missing MH370 flight that disappeared in the vast Indian Ocean in 2014. Leveraging his years of experience as a pilot, accident investigator and consultant, he put together some very compelling arguments as to what happened and why. I highly recommend this book because it not only provides some insight into this accident, but some insights into solid accident investigation work in general.

In *Picking Through the Pieces*, Larry shares his life's work in aviation and aviation safety in a style that reads like he is talking to you as a friend, teacher and colleague. He has been all of those to me and I will always be grateful for that. There is another saying in aviation that goes like this: "There are old pilots, and bold pilots, but there are no old bold pilots".

Larry is an old pilot and a bold accident investigator, we can all learn from him.

Mark Clitsome, TSB Director of Investigations (Ret'd)

INTRODUCTION

Two weeks before I started writing this book, I was in court testifying as an expert witness. The case involved the crash of a single-engine Cessna Caravan aircraft. The primary cause of the crash was poor decision-making by the pilot. Even though he knew that his aircraft was overweight, and also covered with ice from freezing precipitation, he taxied out and took off anyway. Not surprisingly, the aircraft crashed soon after takeoff. All ten people on board were killed.

My testimony was part of a litigation case that was finally being heard in court an incredible fifteen years after the accident. I was there to help the court understand the circumstances of the event. As is standard when testifying as an expert witness, I was asked about my background and experience. The questioning took me back to my start in aviation 53 years earlier, and followed through my time as a flight instructor, flight test examiner, civil aviation inspector, training pilot, aircraft accident investigator, and consultant. I answered questions about investigating accidents, and about teaching investigation courses in various parts of the world.

Later, during a break in my testimony about the accident circumstances, a court officer came over to chat. He led off with, "you have lived a very interesting life". I responded with something like, "you work every day in this courtroom, I think it's you who has lived an interesting life". As we chatted, he told me that to him, life stories like mine are intriguing and unique, and worth telling.

Following my testimony, family members of one of the victims of the crash approached me. They thanked me for my testimony. They said they had been waiting for 15 years to hear the analysis that I provided to the court. They also said they found the testimony about my career to be compelling. The conversations in that courtroom made me think that my story is worth telling, and after I had time to reflect on all of that, I committed to giving this book a try.

I have written one other book – *MH370: Mystery Solved*. The writing of it consumed my life for 15 months. It's not easy to write a book, or to make that kind of time commitment, but now that I've started this one, I am all in. To the best of my ability, I'll tell my life story openly and honestly. None of what I say will be fiction.

MY DESCRIPTION OF ME

To be fully open and honest in this undertaking, I need to start with a candid description of myself. My investigation work has helped me polish my skills in assessing other people – or at least I like to think so. But it's quite different and challenging to attempt an honest self-assessment, and to write it down. Try it sometime and you'll see for yourself.

So here we go with some honesty about me. I am, by nature, a very optimistic person. My default is to look first at the positive side of every situation, and I have to work hard to recognize the negative. I trust people instinctively, and it takes more than one bad action for me to recognize my instinct was wrong.

I have a good sense of humour. I love to laugh, and I can break into a belly laugh even when I'm all by myself. I'm naturally wired to look for the funny side of situations, and to weave together those elements that make a story its funniest. I use humour to disarm, to de-stress, and to try to make others feel good.

My laugh threshold is right at the surface. I'm one of those people who easily start to laugh, and sometimes I have a hard time stopping. Those who share that affliction will know how it can be overpowering, and at times very embarrassing. That's especially true in my line of work. I love to share funny stories and to laugh with others. Jokes are good fun, but I especially enjoy the more subtle stuff, like stories about events and circumstances that happen along the way, especially things that involve me. Self-deprecation can be lots of fun, especially when everyone knows you're not serious. In this book I will sprinkle in some funny stories, and I hope you get a laugh out of them.

My default is always to avoid conflict, and to try to make peace. I am big on compromise. I have a keen desire for fairness, and a huge dislike for bullying. I very much dislike it when people in positions of power are unfair to those who have less power or are vulnerable.

I have been cursed with an overly strong desire to be liked. I have an instinctive need to be viewed as a nice person. This can be a real liability, emotionally. Sometimes I look back and get frustrated with how far I've gone to satisfy that desire. I've worked at becoming less sensitive and more "thick skinned". Getting older has helped, but I still slip too easily into hurt feelings and a somber mood when I see or sense negativity towards me.

I'm big on finding and relying on the truth. I have no time for people who purposefully lie, or intentionally avoid seeking or recognizing the truth, especially for their own gain. I have trouble dealing with people who are phoney – those who present themselves as something they're not. I especially dislike braggers, and the egotistical, and the arrogant. I have learned how to tolerate them where I have to, but in reality, I have little time or respect for them. In my experience, they inevitably turn out to be the phoniest, and the least trustworthy.

I get uncomfortable when people display anger. I have almost no temper myself, and I have a hard time dealing with people who do. When tensions raise, my immediate instinct is to be a calming influence, and never a primary antagonist. I have absolutely no appetite for physical conflict. No doubt I fit the classic definition of "chicken" (i.e., to cower in fear). This has kept me out of a few scrapes over the years, which is a good thing, but I've looked back at some situations where I wish I had had the fortitude to step up more aggressively. Basically, mother nature has caused me to be this way – in any type of conflict situation, I am quite content when someone else is willing to take the lead.

Thankfully, my natural chicken tendencies do not surface in places like investigation meetings, or litigation proceedings. Those are controlled environments where "conflict" is frequently part of the process. I've got to where I almost enjoy that kind of engagement. When it comes to arguing my case, or sharing my opinions, I've evolved to where I have no hesitation in going toe-to-toe with anyone, no matter how big the stage.

It's funny how aging works. I find that my "stand up and be counted" attitude is changing as I get older. I observe that I'm getting braver, even as I get slower and weaker. I observe the same thing in other aging men.

I have an aversion to the feeling of embarrassment. I don't mind so much being directly embarrassed myself – I can make a joke out of that. It's more the uncomfortableness of being in the presence of embarrassment. For example, as much as I'd like to enjoy the humour in the television show Seinfeld, I can't force myself to watch it in full episodes because it's so full of what I see as embarrassment.

When embarrassment starts to happen, I have a powerful "you have to fix this" instinct. I need to disperse or shift the blame or guilt away from whoever is being embarrassed. I'll even accept responsibility that's not mine in order to ease someone else's embarrassment. That might seem like a noble action, but in truth I'm simply trying to relieve my own embarrassment phobia, no matter what it takes.

Mother nature has given me compensation for my nice-guy tendencies. An active part of my long-term memory makes injustices unforgettable. When someone intentionally and maliciously sets up someone else to embarrass them, or take advantage of them, I never forget it. It gnaws at me when things don't get closed out properly. I can't rest easy when individuals or institutions get away with wrongs they've committed. This is particularly true for investigations. Fairness is important to me. I'm driven to make things right, no matter how long it takes. You'll recognize some of this "making it right" happening in this book.

I'm about midway on the scale of laziness. I've always had to guard against an abundance of procrastination. On the other hand, once I get started on something, such as an investigation or writing this book, I have a drive that kicks in and I want to get it done no matter what, and to the best of my ability. If I say I am going to do something, then it's going to get done. I'm not saying that I don't procrastinate, but I'll finish what I set out to do and give it all I have. I strive for "perfection", even while knowing that I'll not achieve it. To me, if you are not trying to make something as close to perfect as you can make it, it's not worth doing.

I could be wrong, but I believe I have more natural curiosity than average. I think that extra curiosity is something I was born with, but it could be that it has developed because of my work. When I'm curious about something, I can't let it go. For example, I wake up at night thinking about unresolved investigation issues. Thankfully, my natural laziness and procrastination keep me from becoming obsessed. My fallback action is to enter into deep thought. I achieve a reasonable work/life balance because my deep thought results in idle time, and idle time is something I enjoy. I spend a lot of time in deep thought, running evidence and events through different potential accident scenarios, all because I'm too curious to not do that.

Like everyone else, my nature forces me to self-assess, both overall, and for singular events and interactions. My go-to tool for self-assessing is the giver versus taker scale. To be content, I need to see myself solidly on the giver side. If I assess that my actions or inputs could have been interpreted as selfish, I get very uncomfortable – similar to my embarrassment feeling.

To be clear, I have no problem being a receiver. That's totally different than being selfish. It's only fair that I get my share – I deserve that, like everybody else. And it gives me great joy when someone intentionally gives me more than my share. It makes them feel good, which makes me feel good for them. And it doesn't hurt that I get more of the stuff.

I feel a great responsibility to take care of myself, physically and mentally. I see it as selfish to not do that. I cringe at the thought of ever being a burden in any way – to be in a circumstance where I have to take more than I can give. It would be unbearably cringeworthy if I had made lifestyle choices that helped put me there – to where I had to be a taker. I'm not a health nut – far from it, but I exercise, and I try valiantly to eat right, with varying degrees of success. I have never been a user of anything not medically prescribed.

A quick anecdote – I had a turning point in my life when I was only five years old – I had not yet started school. I remember being in the kitchen with my mother while she was making breakfast for everyone. Something happened that made her upset; I can't remember what, but maybe she dropped something. She told me she had to stop and make herself a cup of tea – she said that she couldn't function until she had that tea. She said that if she didn't have tea, she would get a headache.

I loved my mom, and that scared me. I remember doing a lot of thinking about it. I came to believe that tea was the problem, because somehow it had made my mom need it – it had power over her. I made a vow that I would never touch it. To this day I have never had even one sip of tea. Same for coffee – not one sip.

As I got older, I got really headstrong about not getting dependent on anything. I saw (and still see) dependency as the opposite of independence, and I was going to have none of it – no dependence on cigarettes, alcohol, recreational drugs, coffee, tea – nothing like that.

It follows that I react negatively to compulsive takers and selfish acts. Of course, I recognize that good people can occasionally commit selfish acts. They can be forgiven. But I have no tolerance or respect for people who seem genetically wired to be takers. These are the ones who have no compunction about knowingly taking from others to their own benefit. They are not to be trusted.

These are some of the basic traits that mother nature gave me, or that my nurturing and upbringing implanted. More will be revealed along the way. I think that these traits have helped me to be a better accident investigator. This book is my attempt to describe how I got to be who and what I am – for better or worse.

For those who might be curious about my family life, as of the year 2020 I've been married for 49 years, all to the same woman – my wife Charlotte – she continues to tolerate me. Our roots are in the eastern Canadian province of New Brunswick – specifically in our original hometown of Sackville, and in our moved-to hometown of Riverview/Moncton – but for the past 30 years we have lived in our nation's capital, Ottawa. We are fortunate to have our three children, and their spouses, and our five grandkids, all living nearby in our adopted hometown.

As you can imagine, accident investigations can be stressful. It's critical to have ways to dial things back a bit, to break the tension, and to give people a mental pause. In this book, when you come to a "let's take a pause" section like this one, I'll present you with some of the stories and banter that I've used over the years for this purpose. You'll see that it's just simple stuff, but in times of stress these little stories can be invaluable in keeping people healthy. When times are tough, it doesn't take too much to get some back-and-forth going – everyone needs it, and it makes everyone feel better.

Kids and grandkids are always good sources of fun stuff, and stories involving them are especially helpful for people who have some of those – it's easy for co-workers to relate, and they can conjure up stories of their own. I'll give you two examples of such stories.

When we first moved to Ottawa, I was driving my youngest daughter to her skating practice when we had to stop at an intersection for a red light. For the first time, my daughter heard one of those audible signals – beep, beep, beep – away back then, they hadn't yet made their way to Moncton. She asked me what that beeping sound was for, and I told her it was for the blind people. "Oh", she said. "I didn't know they could drive".

Another time, I was with my son and his family at a big box store. As they were looking at appliances, I wandered off with the two little ones to keep them occupied. After a while, they got nervous about not knowing where their parents were. The older sister said we should go one way, and I said we should go the other. The little brother had the best observation – "we should have an adult with us". His sister agreed. What a great confirmation it was for me that I was viewed as an equal playmate – that's exactly what I wanted to be.

Larry at the Twin Otter accident site
in the Mealy Mountains near Goose Bay – October 1984

Larry at the CASB Regional Office in Moncton – circa 1986

2

INTRODUCTION TO THE
REAL WORLD OF ACCIDENT INVESTIGATION

Since this book will focus primarily on my career as an aircraft accident investigator, I'll start off telling you about my first experience out in the field. My accident investigation career started in October 1984 when I joined the Canadian Aviation Safety Board (CASB) in their Atlantic regional office in Moncton, New Brunswick.

A housekeeping item here – just to keep the logistics clear – later on, in 1990 (the same year I moved to Ottawa), CASB morphed into the Transportation Safety Board (TSB), and their Atlantic regional office eventually moved from Moncton, New Brunswick, to Halifax, Nova Scotia.

On my very first accident investigation, I encountered something uniquely stressful. In fact, in all the years since I've never encountered it again – what are the odds of that? When I moved into accident investigation, I knew it could happen, and now it was here for real. This would be a test, and how I was able to handle this test would tell me whether or not I was suited for this type of work.

I was part of the response team investigating the crash of a de Havilland Twin Otter aircraft on a mountaintop in the wilderness of Labrador, a remote part of eastern Canada. All four occupants had been killed in the crash. The aircraft had struck a rock outcropping just below the level summit of a 2,050-foot mountain. After it struck, the aircraft careened up the short slope to the summit, and there it left a trail of broken wreckage over some 200 feet.

This accident was incredibly tragic. They had struck the very last bit of high ground on their route home. Had they made it past that last high ground in the Mealy Mountains, it would have been a routine descent to the airport less than 20 miles away. For some reason, on their approach to the airport the pilots had descended too early.

Along with the two pilots, the dead included a doctor and a nurse from the local hospital. They were on their way home from a medevac flight where they had transported patients from the Goose Bay hospital to St. Anthony, Newfoundland, a community some 1 hour and 20 minutes flying time away. News of the crash had devastated the isolated community of Goose Bay.

CASB's regional manager, my new boss Dave Owen, was the Investigator-In-Charge (IIC). One of my new workmates, a veteran technical investigator (an aircraft maintenance technician), was there to lead the wreckage examination. I was there to help investigate the operational and piloting issues, but mostly I was there to take it all in. I was new, and I needed to be trained, and the best accident investigation training is done on the job.

The first task in accident investigation is to gather up the initial "boilerplate" information. For starters, we obtain things like the flight plan information, the crew and passenger manifest, the weather forecast and the actual weather conditions, and the aircraft's maintenance records.

What a shock it was for me to discover that the deceased captain of the Twin Otter was someone who I knew. In fact, he had been a student of mine back when I was a flying instructor. I remembered him as a really nice guy and a good student. And now, here I was headed to the place where he had lost his life, and my job would be to investigate how and why.

For an accident response, we had priority access to the government's fleet of aircraft. We took one of their Beechcraft King Airs and flew it to Goose Bay from our home base in Moncton. On the way, we stopped in St. Anthony where the Twin Otter had dropped off the medevac patients. We checked out the pilots' pre-flight activities in St. Anthony.

My logbook shows 4 hours, 30 minutes total flight time from Moncton to Goose Bay via St. Anthony. During the flight, Dave and I had lots of time to review the investigation process ahead of us. I told Dave about my previous contact with the pilot. Nothing much needed to be said about that. It would be a part of the dynamic, and that was that.

I was 35 years old. To that point in my life I had not had any first-hand experience with accidental loss of life. In fact, I had precious little experience with anything to do with death. My wife and I had gone through the devastating loss of our second child, a full-term baby boy – he had died five days before his birth. Other than that, no one I was close to had ever died unexpectedly or tragically. I had been to memorials and funerals where the casket was open, but I had never viewed an accident site where there were bodies or human remains.

I had spent nine years as a flying instructor, and another six years as a inspector/pilot for Transport Canada (TC). I felt ready to be trained in accident investigation, but nothing in my personal or professional background provided a framework to put the human tragedy aspect into perspective.

We arranged to have a helicopter meet us when we landed in Goose Bay. The police and coroner had their own chartered helicopter. They had done the work at the site to identify the boundaries of the wreckage, and to photograph everything. We had given them permission to remove the bodies, and I was relieved about that. In this accident circumstance we assessed that we could do our investigation without physically viewing the bodies in situ. Instead, we could use the photos and autopsy results.

Being on that mountaintop was surreal. You could see forever. Looking down into the expanse of forested wilderness, it felt like a place where no one had been before. There was nothing man-made in view. But we were focused on the localized area that contained the wreckage. We found the initial impact point, noted the paint transfer onto the rock surface, and took our own photographs and measurements to document the wreckage.

Part of my tasking was to inspect the remains of the cockpit to document anything that could provide evidence. Nothing is overlooked for documenting; you never know what might become important in the analysis to follow. I went through the investigation checklist, looking for evidence of things like engine throttle settings, and flap selector position. I looked for readings on the flight instruments, and indicator positions captured on gauges. I took photos and notes and measurements, all standard actions for an on-site investigation.

I examined the pilot's seats, and the controls and instrument panels in front of each pilot position. Sometimes it's possible to determine which pilot was active on the controls by matching damage on the control wheel and rudder pedals with physical damage to the hands and feet of the pilots. Doing this type of detailed work slaps you with direct evidence about the violence of the impact; these are things that stay with you.

It was surreal, I was examining the seat that my former student had been sitting in when he flew into the side of that mountain. Everything in the remnants of that cockpit showed the intensity of his last moments, and the last moments of the others. How I reacted to this would let me know if I could have a career in aircraft accident investigation. I would find out whether I was physically and mentally capable of being there. As mentioned earlier, thankfully, this was the only instance in my entire career where I encountered this specific circumstance.

As I write this in 2020, more than 35 years have passed since I was on that mountaintop. I can tell you that it took me a long time to put the above description of that accident into words. Writing about it now, and describing it as you see it, revived in me some familiar emotions – similar to those I had felt back then. When recalling accident sites, it's all but impossible not to relive the sights and smells. As I wrote this, it all came back to me. Along with that, I very clearly recalled the tension of being new to the job, and how hard I tried to get things right. I find it quite amazing that after such a long time those recollections and emotions can come back so readily.

Now I will tell you what I know has allowed me to keep doing this type of work. For me, remembering that accident from so long ago took an intentional mental effort. I had to purposefully kick my memory into gear. One great blessing I have is that my memory of accident sites does not activate randomly, or overpoweringly.

Fortunately for me, throughout my career I have never been confronted with flashbacks, either awake or asleep. For whatever reason, my brain is not wired that way. I have never had to worry about sudden or disturbing memories popping up. That part of my makeup was revealed to me after that first investigation, and nothing has changed through all these years.

Here is what we found out about why that Twin Otter crashed. The aircraft had been updated with a relatively new piece of navigation equipment. It was based on an emerging technology called Loran C, which was a pre-cursor to the GPS based navigation we use today.

Loran C had well known accuracy limitations. Therefore, in aviation it was certified to be used only as a supplement to more basic and time-tested (albeit less efficient) navigation equipment. But as they got more used to it, pilots increasingly relied on Loran C for "accurate" location information.

The accident pilots had been flying in accordance with visual flight rules (VFR). As such, they were required to stay clear of cloud, and maintain visual contact with the terrain below them. As they approached Goose Bay, the visibility became marginal for VFR flight. They had to descend in order to maintain visual contact. We concluded that they were primarily using Loran C for position information. They mistakenly calculated that they had already flown past the high ground, and that there were no obstructions between them and the airport. This navigation error was directly attributable to their reliance on this new Loran C technology – something they were not fully familiar with.

We studied the impact marks on the rocks, the positions of the flight controls at the time of initial impact, and the trajectory of the aircraft after the initial impact. That evidence showed us that at the last instant the pilots saw the high ground ahead of them. They tried to pull up, but it was too late. That investigation near Goose Bay was the start of my training. There was much more to come.

3

DEALING WITH DEATH, TRAUMA AND TRAGEDY

For on-site investigators, it's part of the job to deal with death, trauma and tragedy. It's the same in other professions; examples would be crime scene investigators, paramedics, medical workers and firefighters. You either develop coping mechanisms, or you don't last. Earlier, I told the story about working at a site where my former student had died. I found out that I'm not susceptible to flashbacks. That's a fortunate happenstance, but it is not a coping mechanism.

I've interacted with investigators for decades, and I've seen how they cope. Essentially, it's by internalizing the following key realities: the losses that have been suffered are not their losses; the grief is not theirs to take on; their detached professionalism is not cold-hearted; and, they know they'll be able to help people the most by simply doing their job.

Nothing in these four coping strategies points to a lack of compassion. Career professionals are among the most compassionate people out there. I can tell you through first-hand knowledge that they feel the grimness and sorrow, and it all sticks to them, but they channel their emotions into motivation. They help ameliorate the suffering by bringing order to the chaos. For accident investigators, their objective is to figure out what happened, and to deliver valid information to those who crave it.

Fatal accident sites are places of great human tragedy. You are exposed to sights and smells that most people never encounter. It's your job to pick through the pieces. Media photos and video can give you a sense of what it looks like, but nothing compares to actually being there. For me personally, the smells are more overpowering than the sights.

A searing stressor can come from anywhere. You can move a piece of wreckage and find somebody, or a piece of somebody, or a coveted personal item or photograph, or a backpack that looks just like the one your child has. Imagine how difficult it would be for you to cope if those scenes returned in flashbacks. I am so thankful that for me, they don't.

I have done a lot of this work, but I think I'm none the worse for wear. I don't think I've been adversely affected, or emotionally scarred. I started out with my "normal mental state", and I don't think my work has done much to change it. From what I've seen, maintaining their "normal state" is common among the other career investigators I've worked with. A few might not be at the mid-point on the overall normal scale, but that's not because of their work – that's where mother nature originally placed them.

When doing this kind of stressful work, you need to strive to maintain your own "normal". It's the same for an investigation team that needs to function as a unit. Everyone on the team has to buy in to a common effort to normalize things at the interaction and relationship level. A particularly important ingredient for maintaining normalcy is humour. When working around human tragedy, humour, and shared laughter, are fundamental tools for counteracting the potential negative effects.

Needless to say, what I'm talking about here is humour that is kept exclusively within the team. There is nothing funny about the circumstance of the tragedy, or the losses suffered. They are never a source for humour.

As is normal, the humour comes from the funny things that naturally happen along the way. Someone does or says something that has a funny twist to it. Someone else picks up on it, and it escalates into an even funnier exchange. It's all normal stuff, normal banter – the only thing different is that it's taking place in this unnatural setting. In even the direst of circumstances, it's not at all uncommon for someone to purposefully break the tension by being comical. Quite frequently, that person is me. In all my years, I've never seen this backfire. In these stressful situations, there are two choices for emotional release – you can laugh, or you can cry. When working as part of an investigation team, most people would rather laugh.

Let me give you an example of how this works. Back in the early days I did an accident with old Charlie, a technical investigator who was there when I first joined CASB. We flew in a helicopter out to a remote site where a single engine aircraft had crashed – the two occupants had been killed. It was winter, and the mangled aircraft was resting upside down in the snow, surrounded by trees. The two people were still inside, frozen in position. It was gruesome.

Charlie was trying to get a photo looking into the cockpit from an angle where his camera would be down low, right down at the surface of the snow. He bent over and tried a couple of times, but somehow it wasn't working out. He struggled in the deep snow to take a couple of steps backwards to try again. He managed to back up, but that put him so close to a tree trunk that when he bent over, he pushed his butt hard into a sharp little nub left by a broken branch. It was sticking out at just the right height and angle to get him where it hurt the most.

The shock of it caused him to try to bolt forward, but the snow wouldn't let his feet move, so down he went. He came to rest in a prone position – this was a full-on face plant. On his way down he flung his arms out in front and managed to keep the camera above the snow. I watched his head raise, and I watched him blink the snow out of his eyes, and I watched him check the camera angle. He now had the perfect angle for taking the photo he wanted. I heard the click of the camera shutter. This was pants-wetting funny. That short visual sequence, with accompanying grunts and groans from Charlie, is one of the funniest pieces of slapstick I have ever witnessed.

Here is where this story fits. We were at the site of a gruesome tragedy. Two people had lost their lives. They had loved ones who were shocked and grieving, and we would have to deal with all that later. Our first job was to figure out what happened. This accident site was not a place for laughter, but laughter was there in great abundance. How could it not be? As an investigator, if you get to an emotional state where you can't laugh at something like that Charlie incident, then you're too mentally vulnerable to be doing the job.

Here's how this quick story connects with the long-term mental stability of investigators. The Charlie story is what I recall most about that particular investigation. It all but drowns out the other stuff. That's a very positive thing. When people who have these shared experiences get together and reflect on past experiences, they spend most of their time reviving and embellishing the stuff that made them laugh. They can go to those comical events and stories because they gave themselves permission to "create" them in the first place. Imagine how incredibly different it would be if everyone's memories were full of only the trauma. Needless to say, that wouldn't work.

When I first get to an accident site, I make a pact with the dead. I tell them I'll do my best to figure out what happened, and I'll let their loved ones know. For their part, they need to recognize that for me to be at my peak performance I need to stay detached from the loss and grief. Everyone on the investigation team needs to be normal. We'll be doing some joking and laughing, but none of it will be related to their demise. I explain that being normal helps every-one do their best work, but more importantly, it gives them their best shot at staying healthy in both the short and long term.

An investigation team can include individuals with varying levels of ex-posure to the customary team dynamic. The experienced people know that it will soon settle into where they can be normal. For the uninitiated, they need to see it happening, and through that they're given permission to be normal. The presence of humour in these circumstances is important to solidify the team. New members are socialized and accepted through participating in the humour, and they come to recognize how the experienced people negotiate the emotional demands of the work.

I don't want to give anyone the impression that tragic sites are places of merrymaking and hilarity. Nothing could be further from the truth. It's because of the dire circumstances that there needs to be a counterbalance. Laughter is the best antidote to gloom and doom. During an investigation, you can tell how well the team is coping by how much joking and humour is happening among them, both at the site, and in the down times.

You have to keep monitoring for this. If the normal joking and humour slows down or stops, something is wrong. Your team is under psychological threat. You have to figure out what's happening, and you have to make changes – and you need to do that quickly. Maybe people are pushing too hard, and they need some downtime. Maybe there is some kind of disagreement or conflict, or maybe people have lost track of where the overall investigation is going. Maybe there has been some specific new trauma that has been introduced. Whatever it is, it needs to get fixed.

There is an emotional burden that can't be managed through humour. That's when an investigation has to focus on the loss of a child – then, there's no joking or laughing. There's only the task in front of you, and you need to focus on that and get through it. Over and above the loss of others, the loss of a child is crushing and heartbreaking. There's no way to put it in perspective. The one emotional release that's available is crying. That's the go-to for both seasoned and novice investigators. Crying has none of the benefits of laughing, either short-term or long-term. Every investigator knows that this type of loss, with no opportunity to be "normal", puts the emotional strain at an entirely different level.

One thing that stands out about the people from my home area on the east coast is their easy going way of life. It's common to hear things described in an understated way – that's their nature. Here are two examples.

When I was about nine years old, I was allowed to go to the barber-shop on my own. I overheard this exchange between the barber and the guy who was getting his hair cut.

Barber   So, is there anything new?

Client   No – not much.

(Pause)

Client   Come to think of it there is one thing – you remember my brother Brian – he comes here.

Barber   Oh, sure I remember Brian – he's been coming here for years, maybe longer than you – how's he doing?

Client   Well, not too good really.

Barber   Oh, that's too bad.

Client   Yea, he died last night.

(Pause)

Barber   What'd he die of?

Client   Oh, nothing serious.

Many decades later, when I was on the east coast for the Swissair 111 investigation, I was in another barber shop where I overheard this exchange between the barber and two old guys waiting for their turn in his barber chair.

One old guy	I think that Willie Arnold took a turn for the worse.
Barber	Yea, I heard that he might have.
(Pause)	
Barber to the other old guy	What do you think Jeb – do you think Willie took a turn for the worse?
Other old guy	I'm not sure – I guess he might have.
(Pause)	
Barber	Are you guys going to the funeral?
Old guys mumbling a reply	Yea I probably will – yep, I expect so.
A thought by me	There's not much question about whether he took a turn for the worse – he's dead.

4

ACCIDENTAL LAUNCH INTO AN AVIATION CAREER

I have been blessed with an insignificant predisposition to think about the past. I'm grateful for this, because it leaves me more time to think about the now, and the future. And it gives me an excuse when my memory is deficient.

A book like this requires a lot of thinking about the past, not only to tell the stories, but to delve into why I think and function the way I do. Like everyone else, my approach to life comes from a combination of the inherent characteristics I was born with, and the ongoing interventions and experiences that elasticize those characteristics.

My career in aviation came about because of two chance happenings when I was a teenager growing up in the small town of Sackville, New Brunswick. The first one happened when I was fourteen years old, and in grade nine. A guy in grade 10 named Doug, who was in the local Air Cadet Squadron (681 Tantramar Squadron), came into our classroom (dressed in his uniform) to make a recruitment pitch. I wasn't really interested in his talk, and I never paid much attention. When he finished, he asked if anyone wanted to sign up. Only one guy, Carl, put his hand up. And then came the part that changed my life. For whatever reason, Carl spoke up with something like "is there no one else in here who has guts enough to raise their hand?". For whatever reason, that triggered me, and my hand went up. If Carl hadn't said that, there's no chance I'd be writing this book.

The second unplanned happening was a follow-on from the first, but it was just as influential in my life. A good friend of mine in the Air Cadets wanted to try for one of their coveted flying scholarships. In all the previous years, only two of those scholarships had ever been given to cadets from our tiny squadron. If you got chosen, you would train to get your private pilot's license – all expenses paid.

This flying scholarship program was not even remotely on my radar. In fact, at the time I didn't even know it existed. The cadet leaders needed to have two candidates in order to justify asking someone to prepare us for the selection testing. I volunteered to be the second candidate, just so my friend wouldn't miss out. We were tutored by the father of another friend of ours, a gentleman who had been a navigator in World War II. We both wrote the qualifying exams and, as you might have already guessed, I passed, and my friend didn't. I got the flying scholarship, and he went on to a long career in the Royal Canadian Mounted Police (RCMP).

It cannot be overstated just how much those two serendipitous events shaped the rest of my life. I'm not sure where I would have ended up, but there's no way that I would've ever become involved in aviation if those two events hadn't happened.

I've never been one of those pilots with an overwhelming passion for flying. I know pilots who would rather fly than eat. I would rather eat. As explained above, I started into flying quite by accident. Before any of this flying scholarship talk came up, I had been in an airplane only once. At an Air Cadet summer camp, they took us for a short flight on a hot and turbulent day in a loud and smelly old military Beechcraft Expeditor with no air conditioning. Sixteen of us had to sit sideways on benches, facing inward where we could watch each other turn green. Within fifteen minutes, only three of us had not thrown up. I'm sure the military pilots were trying for 100%. It didn't scare me to go airborne, but I never found it thrilling, or even enjoyable.

It was in late June of 1967 when my father drove me the 30 miles from Sackville to Moncton and dropped me off at the Moncton Flying Club to start my pilot training. Little did I imagine then that I would soon be instructing there, and that I would later become their Chief Flying Instructor, and that I would end up working there for nine years. We were a class of some twenty Air Cadets, and the instructors had six weeks to put us through our training. We stayed at a nearby military barracks, and we were training seven days a week, either flying or in ground school.

The instructor for my first three flying lessons was the legendary Don McClure. I had no idea that he was legendary at the time. I only found that out after I started working for him and he told me. During my first lessons, I quickly discovered that flying an aircraft felt very natural to me. Before long, I was in the circuit being trained on touch-and-goes, and after only 6 hours and 50 minutes of flight time I did my first solo. That was close to a record for shortest time to solo, as I recall.

During that summer of flying training, I came to believe that being a flying instructor would be a good way to make a living. That wasn't because I fell in love with flying, it was more because it seemed like an achievable path forward that wouldn't involve any more classic schooling. I was very good at flying an aircraft, and not at all good at being a school student. The only parts about school that I enjoyed were outside the classroom.

After finishing that flying scholarship training, I went back for one more year of high school, but I failed to graduate. To this day I don't have a high school diploma. I had no interest in applying myself to schoolwork. Thankfully, my parents decided they would finance my training to get my commercial pilot license and instructor rating. I don't remember asking them to do that, it just evolved that way after I told them what I wanted to do. They certainly weren't rich, and I'm not sure how they came up with the money, but I guess that as parents they were motivated by recognizing that flying seemed to be the only viable option for me. Otherwise, I had no plan.

As confirmed in my pilot logbook, I started my commercial pilot training at Moncton Flying Club on 31 July 1968. I took my check ride (flight test) on 3 December. That was followed by training with the legend himself, Don McClure – he would train me to be a flying instructor. I took my instructor check ride on 9 June 1969. Don hired me immediately, and I did my first work as a flying instructor on 11 June in a single engine Piper Cherokee.

Fast forward to 16 March 1978. On that day I did 5 hours and 45 minutes of instructing, again in a Piper Cherokee. That was my last day working at the Moncton Flying Club. I had worked there for eight years, nine months and six days. That was about seven years longer than the average instructor. I had accumulated over 8,200 hours of flight time, and over a thousand more teaching instrument procedures on our old simulators.

When I left the Flying Club, I was at the top of my game as a flying instructor. I had just turned 29 years old, and I had achieved a Class 1 instructor rating at a time when there were fewer than ten Class 1 instructors in all of Canada. I had been the Chief Flying Instructor for some six years. I was one of the first instructors in Canada to become a Designated Flight Test Examiner, with authorization to do private and commercial flight tests on behalf of TC.

By the end of my instructing career I was concentrating mostly on twin-engine instrument training, flight testing, and training instructors. Even with that, the wage I was earning was pitiful. Instructing wasn't viewed as a career. It was seen as a steppingstone – a way to build up flying hours before moving on.

Throughout my time as an instructor, I watched as most of my fellow instructors departed for airline jobs. Even many of my students had gone to the airlines. I decided early on that airline work wasn't for me. There were no airline jobs based in Moncton, and my instructing job allowed me to live close to my hometown and stay in touch with all my friends I grew up with. I was a small-town kind of guy, and that was important to me. But even more important was that I got married in 1971, and my wife had a good job as a schoolteacher, and we wanted to raise our kids in a small-town way, where there would be family nearby for support.

Also, I had a plan to get out of instructing, and into a more stable and better paying job. TC had their regional office in Moncton, and I figured that if I stayed where I was at the flying club long enough, eventually a job would open for me at TC. It would be a good paying government job with regular nine to five working hours. I'd have a steady income, and a great benefits package, and a solid pension plan. And I didn't have to move away to get that job. To me, that would be a perfect job for someone who wanted to be in aviation but still be a stay-at-home family man.

So, I stuck it out, for all those years. It wasn't all bad, of course. In fact, other than the poor wages and some oddball working hours, it was a great place to mature and learn life lessons. I got to work with some amazingly good people among my fellow instructors and coworkers.

Back then, the Moncton Flying Club was not only drawing students from across Canada, it was attracting significant numbers of international students. We had an interesting mix of different cultures, and we were actually hiring instructors from among our international student graduates. This culture mix was something I hadn't been exposed to growing up in a small town, and I learned a lot from it.

The foundation for my accident investigation career was actually built at the flying club. I got basic training in the three key investigation elements that are starting points for every investigation. You investigate 1) the Man; 2) the Machine; and 3) the Environment. Please excuse the non-gender-neutral terminology, but the man/machine/environment memory jogger rolls easily off the tongue. At the flying club, I was up to my neck in those three elements: observing and appraising aviation people, understanding airplane mechanics, and assessing environmental factors. To this day I go back to those 8+ years to help with my investigation analysis – those years at the flying club were invaluable.

The dominant influencer over everything at the Moncton Flying Club was Donald S. McClure, my first instructor, and my first boss in aviation. Don had started flying during World War 2 as an instructor in the Royal Canadian Air Force. He took over the flying club in 1959, and over time he transformed it from a local recreational club into the largest flying training facility in Canada, with a worldwide reputation.

Don had a great passion for aviation, and an incredible drive to be successful. He worked tirelessly, both at the club, and in his promotion of aviation in general. He was a man of his word, which I recognized and appreciated. He was especially passionate in his support of the Air Cadet League of Canada. Don retired from the flying club in 1989. He died in 2008 at the age of 85.

One highlight of Don's accomplishments was his winning of the Yorath Trophy. He won it an unprecedented 16 times, including nine times consecutively. Winning that trophy gave Don bragging rights as the best flying club manager in Canada. To many people, that claim was somewhat skewed though, because the award actually went to the manager of the club that "used its facilities to the best advantage". Don knew that he could win that trophy by using the least number of airplanes to fly the greatest number of overall hours. It was a mathematical calculation. Therefore, he was absolutely obsessed with getting our airplanes into the air. Every minute counted. They had to be up there, earning money and building up those flying hours.

Over the years, Don's accomplishments in flying training promotion were recognized through numerous awards. The awards came from the big names in aviation, both domestic and international. Don is highly revered, and rightfully so, by many of the thousands of students who passed through the club, and especially by the clan of aviation enthusiasts who stayed active around there.

I had a great personal relationship with Don, and we shared many laughs with all the other characters we worked with. But working for Don gave me much more than a good foundation in flying matters. Working there gave me tremendous reference points for how management style can influence the operating environment and safety culture of an organization. As I write more about all this below, I don't mean to diminish Don's accomplishments in any way. I'm simply trying to reveal how my accident investigation instincts took shape during my time there.

I remember Don as one of those bigger than life kind of guys. Everything he did was at least a little bit over the top. He loved to be the center of attention, and inevitably he was. In running the club, he pushed everything to the limit, and sometimes beyond the limit. He saw it as his mission to squeeze out every last drop of efficiency from both the aircraft and the instructors. He prided himself on being seen as a tightwad, in a whimsical kind of way, with a wink and a nod. The problem for us instructors was that in anything to do with running the flying club Don was an actual tightwad.

Don had full control over every aspect of operations. I had a "management" role as Chief Flying Instructor, but I never really controlled very much. With

23

Don's domineering presence, I was mostly just another flying instructor. As best I could, I tried to run interference for the other instructors, but for the most part everyone was on their own in dealing with Don.

Fortunately, for various lengths of time we had some very conscientious instructors join us. We worked together to elevate the training standards. We got great satisfaction in keeping the operation as safe as possible, and in trying to provide good value to the students. When it came to resisting Don's austerity programs, we viewed him like a "common enemy", and we used that for motivation. Everyone knew that it was Don who kept the operation viable financially, and we appreciated that, but we also wanted to produce the best training results, despite all the pressures that came from Don.

One constant gripe we had as instructors was that we were so poorly paid. That wasn't unique to our flying club, but we thought that because of our insane level of productivity and the quality we were giving that we deserved better. Of course, Don didn't see it that way. To him, he was helping us out by allowing us to build flying hours quickly at a place with an international reputation for producing first rate pilots. He was right about that, but it didn't help much in putting food on the table or paying the bills. That was one of the biggest factors in keeping the instructing profession transient. You simply couldn't afford to do it for very long.

As I said previously, in so many ways Don gave me a base line to use in investigations. I can put myself in the place of other pilots who have to work for someone with a domineering personality; someone who wouldn't hesitate to replace you for not toeing the line. Working environments like that can influence pilots and others to make unsafe decisions. Over the years I've investigated many accidents, big and small, where management issues have played a role.

Larry receiving his graduation certificate from Air Cadets

Phil Paquet, Jim Hughson, Don McClure,
Urban Murphy, Geo. Dewar Romaan Butler
Circa 1966
Don proudly displays "The Youth Trophy"
which he subsequently won 16 times,
an R.C.F.C.A record.

Don McClure holding the Yorath Trophy – 1966

Also in the photo Phil Paquet (on the far left), Jim Hughson (second from the left)

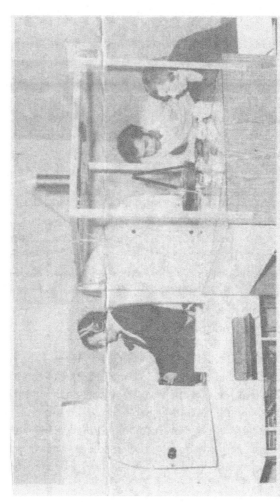

HIGH-FLYING GROUND SCHOOL — Students from all over the world learn the rudiments of flying in the recently installed Martin Flight Simulator at the Moncton Flying Club. Shown here being put through his paces is Tom Vatcher from Newfoundland while C. Pillai (left) from India and Assistant Chief Flying Instructor Larry Vance monitor his flight. (Arnold's Studio)

Larry teaching in the Simulator – Moncton Flying Club – 1973

My dad was very well known in our local community. He was one of those people who was into everything – lots of committee work, lots of volunteering, and lots of charity work. He spent many years in local politics, including a stint as deputy mayor. He was also a great story-teller, and he loved to set things up so that funny stories would result.

One evening he dropped my mom and my sister off at the start of the walking trail along the river – he was to pick them up later at the other end of the trail – he promised he would be there for sure, because it would be dark when they finished their walk. He arrived as planned. After a while he spotted the silhouettes of two ladies coming down the trail. He decided it would be fun to hide in the grass behind a bench so he could scare them by imitating the sound of a barking fox.

As they got closer, he started into his barking routine, and it scared them for sure. They stopped walking, and they wouldn't come any further. He barked a couple more times, just to give them a good scare – then he came out of hiding and went over to brag about how good he was at making animal sounds. When he got close, he found out that these ladies were not his wife and daughter – they were a couple of ladies he recognized from some committee he'd met with a time or two.

I've heard my dad tell the story quite a few times over the years – how he tried to explain that he didn't mean to scare them – how he actually meant to scare the two ladies walking behind them – how as deputy mayor it wasn't his habit to hide in the grass after dark and try to scare ladies – how he didn't normally bark like a fox when people were around – how he hoped to have their support in the upcoming election. Nobody could tell a story better than him.

5

INFLUENTIAL HAPPENINGS, SOME FUN, SOME TRAGIC

As discussed above, tragic accidents sites are places of great intensity and emotion. Investigators need to be mindful of how an atmosphere of gloom and doom can weigh on them. When it comes to "let's take a pause" stories, the characters and happenings at the flying club are great sources of material. I include in this chapter some stories that have stayed with me – the kinds of stories I can tell during investigations – when the time is right.

I tell the story about us instructors getting paid a base salary of $50 a week, and $2.50 per flying hour. That was my salary for a very long time. Even back then that was a subsistence wage. Some of us were at the same time taking additional training (I was taking multi-engine instrument training), and we paid for that out of our wages. Every two weeks we would go one at a time into Don's office to get our paycheck. Frequently there would be no paycheck, only a report from Don on how much we owed. He loved it when that happened.

I remember the time one of our instructors came out of Don's office staring at his paycheck in disbelief. As he stepped outside the wind blew it out of his hand and it went fluttering across the ramp. He never even bothered to chase it. Later he told us the check was for 82 cents, and that chasing after it wasn't worth the effort. That story always brings a chuckle at a "let's take a pause" break. There are many people in aviation who can relate to that one.

I tell stories about the happenings between Don and Jim Hughson. Jim was a grumpy character, and a comrade of Don's from back in their instructing days with the Air Force. Don brought him in to be the Chief Flying Instructor – Don was very loyal to Jim. I replaced Jim as CFI when Jim lost his medical – Don kept Jim on as a ground school and simulator instructor. Anyway, Don and Jim were close to the same age, but Don saw himself as much more youthful, and in fact, he was.

Don took great pleasure in taunting Jim, but rarely got the better of him. One day Don came prancing out of his office into the dispatch area to tease Jim about who had the best eyesight. Don stared intently across the ramp until everyone was watching. Then he said; "Look Jim, can you see that tiny spider away over on the fuel bowser?" Jim stared across the ramp for a few seconds, then replied,

"No, but I can hear him walking". Don retreated quickly to his office. That was how it went between those two – a constant banter like that. It was really fun.

Phil Paquet was our ground school instructor, and everybody loved him. He had flown transport aircraft during World War II. Toward the end of the war, his Douglas C-47 was shot down, leaving him with crippling leg injuries and a burn-scarred face. Phil was barely able to walk, but he bravely struggled his way around by using two canes.

Phil had an indominable spirit, a twinkle in his eye, and a huge laugh. I had incredible respect for him. He was another of the characters around there who loved to banter with Don. One day Don absentmindedly asked Phil to carry something with him on his way to the classroom across the hangar. Phil picked up his two canes and gave Don one of his classic responses – ok, and why don't you stick a broom up my butt so I can sweep the floor for you on the way across. And then came that gargantuan laugh.

At investigations, during down time, I have told this very interesting and tragic Phil Paquet story from the war. Phil had flown a disposal team to a newly liberated landing strip in North Africa. Their job was to clear the numerous booby traps left by the retreating enemy soldiers. They were keenly aware of the ever-increasing sophistication of the booby traps.

Phil watched from the airplane as the disposal experts checked the area around a small building. They spotted a pearl-handled Luger pistol lying on the ground. They knew, of course, that it would be booby trapped. There happened to be a spool of string by the building, and there was an earthen bunker nearby. They carefully tied the end of the string to the Luger's trigger. Phil watched as they spooled out the string, and he saw them shield themselves behind the earthen bunker. Then they pulled on the string, and the earthen bunker blew up. The entire disposal team was killed instantly.

I tell the story about Don's affinity for money. The instructors thought he had supernatural powers in the way he was able to shield it from them. One night, thieves broke in and stole our heavy metal safe. It had been under the dispatch counter, and it contained our petty cash. Don was distraught.

The police made no progress on the investigation until late in the winter, when they arrested two local guys for another crime. Somehow, they got them to confess to stealing our safe. The thieves said they had managed to carry the heavy safe quite a distance away from the hangar, across the infield. They had abandoned it after they broke it open to remove the contents.

After most of the snow had melted in the spring, the police brought in a tracking dog that was trained to sniff out money. To search for the safe, they asked a bunch of us to walk across the field line abreast in the direction described by the thieves. After we had walked for a while the tracking dog got excited and started to pull on its leash. The dog handler and the dog moved ahead, and then he let the dog loose.

It was then that we noticed that Don was already well ahead of us, and he was outsprinting the dog. We saw Don stop first, and then the dog caught up. When the rest of us arrived, we saw they had located our stolen safe. Don was triumphantly holding up a mangled old five-dollar bill that the thieves must have dropped. Don and the money sniffing dog had both picked up the scent of that five-dollar bill at the same time, and Don had outrun the dog to the spot. The dog handler was amazed, but it never surprised us instructors one bit.

Another of the colourful characters I worked with at the flying club was Raymond (not his real name). He was a dedicated instructor, and just a wonderful and fun guy to be around. He was an extrovert, with a quick wit and a great sense of humour. Nobody could be in a bad mood when Raymond was around.

Raymond was afflicted with stuttering. He had all the classic symptoms. He would repeat starting syllables and words, prolong certain sounds, and have extended silent pauses. When he got animated, his head would kind of puff up, and his eyes would get big like they were going to pop out. He loved to tell funny stories, and he made them all the funnier because he could use the rhythm of his stutter, and his animated body language, to turn them into the most wonderful side-splitting theatrics. He was a master at it.

One thing I admired about Raymond was that he never let his stuttering hold him back. He loved to fly, and he loved to teach, and he was good at both. He was never shy, and he was always the first to share his opinion about anything that needed discussing.

Raymond developed a unique relationship with the local tower controllers. Sometimes, especially for the early morning departures, the controllers would hear a microphone key open on the ground control frequency. To them, the open mike with the dead air meant it was Raymond, looking for taxi instructions. They would say, "good morning Raymond" and clear him to taxi out to hold short of the runway for his engine run-up. Later, when he got himself in gear, he would give them his specific request.

I had an interesting flight with Raymond back when Piper Aircraft were introducing the PA-38 Tomahawk to the market. Piper brought one to Moncton for us to evaluate. The design was a pretty radical departure compared to the more docile types we were using. They purposefully gave the Tomahawk more aggressive stall/spin characteristics, so students could learn how to recognize and recover from these deadly happenings.

Raymond and I took this demonstration aircraft up to about 5,000 feet. We cut the power, pulled the nose up to slow to stall speed, and then kicked in rudder to force it into a spin. In our trainers you could recover by simply applying opposite rudder and relaxing the back pressure on the elevator. The aircraft would automatically go nose down and accelerate out of the stall. The resulting spiral dive would give you some g-force, but the pull out of the dive was not a problem. You always made sure to enter the stall at a high enough altitude, because there would be some altitude loss.

So now we are in this stall/spin in the Tomahawk, and it feels different. Raymond was at the controls and he applied full opposite rudder and put the control column full forward to get the nose down. Despite this, the aircraft didn't go nose down into a dive. In fact, the nose never dropped much at all. It would go down some, and then come back up. This is what is known as a flat spin, and if you can't get out of a flat spin by getting the nose down to break the stall, the aircraft will go all the way to the ground that way. I had never been in a spin like that, and I'll admit that I was concerned.

We went around in this spin quite a few times with Raymond holding full opposite rudder and full nose down elevator. At one point I remember saying to Raymond, "this is different". After we went around a couple more times, and as we were approaching 2,500 feet, Raymond came out with words that I can recall like I heard them yesterday, "wa, wa, wa, wh-uut do you tha, tha, think – we should da, da, dooo, na, na, now?". There we were, in a real tight spot – life threatening, actually – and I had such an urge to laugh out loud.

I can't help it – honestly – I just laughed out loud right now as I was writing this. I can still see Raymond forcing a calm demeanour, but with his eyes bulging out in typical fashion. He was one of those guys who could make you laugh, no matter the circumstance.

To finish the story, we both knew that we had to do something to disrupt the equilibrium of the spin. We had to get the nose down to decrease the angle of attack and get unstalled. I was about to suggest that we slide our seats ahead to get the centre of gravity further forward. I was also thinking about opening the canopy to disrupt the airflow. Then, for some reason, the Tomahawk simply kicked itself out of that flat spin and the nose went down. Maybe the controls got more effective in the denser air, I don't know. When we got fully recovered, we were at about 1,500 feet.

We reported the happening to the Piper guy. I don't think we were the only ones with a story like that. I'm certain that they made some adjustments to the production versions of the Tomahawk to protect better against flat spins.

When I need a funny story in a stressful investigation scenario, I tell the one about when Don was trying to get a contract with a skydiving club. They were willing to pay for two aircraft so they could keep their flow of jumpers going. Each of our aircraft could take up to three jumpers at a time. Don figured he could double his profit by charging them for two aircraft while only using one.

He would be able to do this by quickly getting the one aircraft repositioned back on the ground after each jump. He convinced Raymond, and two other instructors (one of whom I will call Lawson) to be his guinea pig jumpers so he could time out his plan. For their jump, his only instruction to them was to count out loud to ten, and then pull the parachute's ripcord.

Lawson tells it like this. He jumped out first. He counted out loud to ten and pulled the chord. The parachute unfurled, and all was quiet as he was floating down, enjoying the view and the sensation. It was quite a while before all of a sudden there was a great swooshing sound as Raymond dove past. Lawson said he could see Raymond's eyes as big as dinner plates. He said that as Raymond's profile got smaller and smaller on his way down, he could still hear Raymond counting at the top of his lungs; ta-ta-ta-ta-ta-ta-TWO!!!

Don took pride in how good he was at displaying vanity. He was a natural. I remember the time he was going away on a trip somewhere, he had me drive him to the terminal like I was his butler or something. I carried his two suitcases to the check-in counter, and I was standing there when the lady said, "Mr. McClure, I'd like to switch you to a window seat, but there are none available". "That's okay dear", he said. "I expect we'll be flying too high for anyone to see me anyway." As the expression goes, that was Don in a nutshell.

For the most part, operations at the flying club were routine, in a hectic kind of way. There was no programmed focus on safety, but everyone kind of instinctively recognized where the margins were. For the type of operation, we had a good safety record. In looking back, I think that the students might actually have benefited from this less regimented structure – kind of like free-range parenting. We were not trying for that, but that's the way it was, and the graduates from there certainly knew how to fly airplanes when they left.

One incident we had was tragic. There was a kind old gentleman who was a regular around the club, in fact, he was on the board of directors. He was a licenced pilot, but had long since lost his proficiency. We wouldn't let him fly solo, even though sometimes he'd try to convince us that he was fine to go on his own. Every so often he'd pay for one of us to take him up so he could handle the controls, do some sightseeing, and practice some touch and go landings.

One day he was there when one of our newest instructors was working dispatch. Not knowing the history of the old gentleman, this dispatcher allowed him to take an aircraft and go. He got airborne okay, but the tower soon lost contact with him. One of our instructors, Robert, was airborne at the time, and he chased down the aircraft and flew up next to it.

The old gentleman was at the controls, just staring straight ahead. Nothing Robert tried could get his attention. They flew basically in formation for quite a long time, with Robert having no way to intervene. Eventually, the old gentleman had allowed the aircraft to descend over an open expanse of water, and as it headed back toward the land it flew straight into a vertical cliff face at the shoreline. Witnessing that was a traumatic experience for Robert, and for his student.

All the evidence pointed to some kind of sudden debilitation, and that was accepted as the "cause". But from a safety and accident prevention perspective, that was not the "cause" at all. The chain of events started with our lack of an effective dispatch system. We were relying on everyone knowing that this old gentleman was not safe to fly solo, but we had no way to ensure that everyone knew.

That was how things were run, and that was the tragic result. I was supposed to be part of the management structure putting safety barriers in place, but I was not actually doing that job. To this day I carry that story with me when I'm analyzing an accident scenario. I'm motivated to look at how a safety system is actually working versus how everyone thinks it's working. In almost every accident scenario, one of the links in the chain of causation comes down to some version of "everyone knows" something, when in fact not everyone does.

Another event associated with my flying club days has stayed with me. I was at home on a Saturday when I got a call saying that one of our students who was training for his commercial license had departed with a couple of passengers to fly to Toronto, his hometown. That was a 1,200-mile trip, each way. Somehow, he had talked someone into authorizing the flight.

I knew that our local civilian weather forecast called for bad weather on the Sunday, and he was flying westbound, towards where our next-day's weather was coming from. I checked the aviation weather along his route of flight, and sure enough, his route would take him straight into a mix of hazardous winter weather conditions. I contacted the control tower at his next waypoint and requested that they order him to turn around, and that's what happened.

When I arrived for work on Monday morning, all the talk was about how this guy was furious with me, and how he had cursed me out after he had landed. I wanted to talk to him, so I phoned him to ask if he could come meet with me. He hung up on me. I have already explained that I was born with almost no temper, but that was something that lit a fuse in me.

I knew he was down in the dormitory, not far from our dispatch office. Even as I write this, I can feel my skin heating up. On that day, I was boiling over when I met him in the hallway of the dorm. I remember having his shirt, just below his neck, clinched in my left fist. I remember him being up against the wall next to the payphone as I explained how instead of cursing me out, he should be thanking me for saving his life, and the lives of his passengers. People tell me that all the while I was explaining this to him, his feet never touched the floor. I think I was afflicted with anger strength. Anyway, I made my point.

I wish this story had a happy ending, but it does not. When he had first arrived for his training, we had high hopes for this student. His father was an airline pilot. He was a first-solo student of mine. But throughout his training, this guy had an attitude that to me seemed incompatible with flying. He was overconfident, and anti-authority. In general, he just seemed to lack respect. The normal cautions and guardrails that evolve in other pilots had never emerged in him.

Not long after he graduated and went back home, we heard that he had been killed in a plane crash, along with some of his friends who were his passengers. He had rented an aircraft from the local flying club and tried to buzz his old high school. He was attempting some sort of aerobatic maneuver that was beyond his and the airplane's capability. They were all killed instantly when the airplane dove into the ground.

His family donated a trophy to the flying club in his name. For a number of years that trophy was presented to the student who was deemed to have worked the hardest during their training.

When I am doing an accident investigation, I have this story as a reference point. I know that aviation is not immune from having people whose temperament is incompatible with their tasking. In particular, piloting an aircraft is a mismatch for someone whose very disposition predisposes them to make unwise or irresponsible decisions. Recklessness in flying inevitably takes you down only one path, and that path does not lead to a do-over.

6

THE GREAT TRANSITION — OFF TO TRANSPORT CANADA

All my hard work and planning paid off. On 28 March 1978, I joined TC as a Civil Aviation Inspector (CAI) in the Atlantic Region, based in Moncton, New Brunswick. What a relief to have the stability of working for the government, and I didn't have to move away. At the time, my wife and I had two little girls, a three-year-old, and a three-month-old. It was great to finally have stable working hours and financial security.

The Atlantic Region was responsible for the four eastern most Canadian provinces. I was now one of two CAIs responsible for monitoring all of the region's flight training facilities, including the Moncton Flying Club. It was great fun to be able to interact with Don and Jim and the others in my new role. I wish there were some good stories to tell about that, but I can't think of any. I guess that's because MFC was pretty self-sufficient. They did most all of their own flight testing, and their operation didn't need any special attention from us "government" people, so I never really went there much as an inspector.

I was very confident going into my new job. I knew the flight training industry inside out. I really enjoyed getting checked out on TCs Beech Barons and Queen Air. We used those aircraft to transport ourselves around the region to do our work.

I loved that job, but after only eight months fate intervened again. Our region had a job opening for a training pilot in their flight operations section. There were some forty-five CAI pilots in our region, and each of them needed to be kept current. I was asked if I wanted that job, and I jumped at the chance. It was another natural fit for me, given my instructor background. I started at Flight Operations on 8 January 1979.

The move to Flight Ops was another of the many fortuitous steps that led to me becoming an accident investigator. At the time, the manager at Flight Ops was Dave Owen. I mentioned Dave earlier – he would later become region manager for CASB, and he would hire me into accident investigation. At Flight Ops, Dave and I really hit it off. Life was good. We had a good mix of aircraft, and as training pilot I had to be sharp on each of them. We had two Beech Barons, a Beech Queen Air, a Beech 90, a Beech 100, and a classic old DC-3. Later we got a brand-new Beech 200, which became my favourite aircraft.

It was great fun getting checked out to captain status on the DC-3. We used that aircraft to transport people and equipment around the region. My most memorable trip on that aircraft was on 2 September 1980 when I got to take my wife and our oldest daughter along on a passenger run from Moncton to St. John's, Newfoundland and return. My logbook shows the outbound flight took 3:05 and the return flight took 4:35. I remember the headwind on the way back across Cape Breton Island was so strong that we could look down and see transport trucks on the highway covering ground faster than we were. The old DC-3 was not built for speed.

Another memorable flight was when we took the DC-3 on an apple run. This was an annual happening where we took orders for apples from our fellow civil servants. Of course, we were not supposed to do that sort of thing with a government aircraft, so it was always kept hush-hush. We especially had to keep it from Doug, who was Dave's replacement as Flight Ops manager. Unlike Dave, Doug had no tolerance for such kind acts, especially if they involved the misuse of Her Majesty's aircraft.

I saw the goodness in it all – helping out the apple farmers, and my wonderful co-workers – so I was flying, with Nick (not his real name) as my co-pilot. Austin was in the back as our flight engineer, his actual job being guardian of the apples. We flew to Greenwood, in the heart of apple growing country, and loaded the passenger cabin with dozens of big paper bags full of fresh apples. We piled them on the seats and in the aisle. We were fully loaded.

Unfortunately, on our landing approach back into Moncton we hit some extra strong turbulence, throwing everything to the ceiling. All of the paper bags overturned and ripped open, and thousands of apples spilled onto the floor. If you know the DC-3 you know that it's a tail-wheel aircraft, so when it's on the ground the deck angle slopes steeply from front to back. The exit door is at the back.

When we stopped in front of our hangar, Austin came up to the cockpit to report that the apples were completely blocking the aisle. Worse than that, they had rolled down the slope and were piled high up against the exit door. Opening it would spill the apples all over the ramp. Doug would most certainly see that from his office window. What a mess we were in. Not only would our apple-run scheme be exposed, the apples would be damaged. I could envision photos appearing in the media with captions like "government pilots use government aircraft to make applesauce".

Fortunately, the engineers in the hangar came up with a plan. Someone went to Doug's office to keep him engaged. We stayed aboard the aircraft while they moved other aircraft out and towed us into the hangar. Someone went to get us some new bags, and they handed them in to us through the emergency exit. Austin, Nick and I re-bagged all those apples, and the hangar folks smuggled them out the back door to the waiting vehicles. It all ended well, and Doug never found out. We were left with yet another neat story to tell.

At the time of this writing that old DC-3 is still flying. It's registered in the United States as N1XP. An internet search will show you what it looks like now, and if you search for the Canadian registration C-FDOT you'll see what it looked like when I flew it. Interestingly, the only significant change is the paint scheme. On the inside, the cockpit, radio racks and cabin areas are configured exactly as they were back in the day, the only changes being the addition of some graphics work for displays.

Looking back, I could not have had better training for accident investigation than my four years as the regional training pilot. The flying part was amazing. I got to study the inner workings of various aircraft types. They sent me on some excellent courses, including to the world famous Eastern Provincial Airways to get checked out on a Boeing 737. I flew test flights with the engineers, and I flew missions in all kinds of unique circumstances and weather conditions. There are not many places in the world that present more challenges in flying than Canada's east coast.

Just as important, I learned how to handle the one-on-one exposure to the other forty-four CAIs. This was not a homogenous group. Most had come from the military. They had been either fighter jocks, or transport weenies (that's what the fighter jocks called any military pilot who never flew combat aircraft). I was still only 29 years old when I became training pilot, and I was the youngest in the group. To me, most everyone else was either middle-aged, or ancient.

To give you some context here, let me explain something about the civilian/military pilot dynamic. For my entire thirty-one years in government service, I worked with pilots from both military and civilian backgrounds. Each thought their background to be superior. The military pilots believed the military's discipline and structure gave them superior skills which they could impart to civil aviation. The civilian pilots believed they had much superior seasoning, accumulated through their many years of making a living in the real world.

Basically, many civilian pilots disliked the idea of military pilots being hired to oversee civil aviation. In many cases, the military people lacked an understanding of what it was like to progress through low-paying jobs while competing for revenue flights, frequently in unsafe conditions. Civil aviation was full of jobs where you either had to do that or you would be replaced. At a coffee break one time I remember the discussion ended with this question to a vocal military guy: "how do you think military pilots would like it if the government brought in civilian pilots to oversee their military flying?".

It was great seasoning for me to work with this diverse group. I learned how to stickhandle in the bureaucracy and deal with the management structure. I found we had a diverse mix of piloting skills. We had some excellent pilots with amazing backgrounds in aviation, both civil and military. I learned much more from them than they ever learned from me. We also had a few, particularly from the military side, who were so far past their prime we had to put dispatching restrictions on them to render them harmless. I was determined that on my watch we would avoid a tragedy like the one at the flying club where the old gentleman flew into the cliff face.

My new relationship with these pilots led to some real eye-openers. Some of the situations were so unexpected or unusual that they remain important reference points for my investigation career. I found out that unsafe operating environments and complacency can hide in the most unexpected places. These CAI's had a singular duty, which was to ensure safe flight operations in the industry, but they allowed exceptional weaknesses in their own operations.

Here's an example. When I got there, we had two King Air aircraft that were used exclusively as flight calibrators – a King Air 90, and a King Air 100. The calibration instrumentation in the back took up most of the area where the passenger seats would be. These two aircraft were used to calibrate the instrument landing systems at the various airports, so most of their flying was done at low level, shooting approaches to runways. On a calibration run they wouldn't land; instead they would fly to less than 100 feet above ground and then pull up abruptly in a climbing turn to go and do it all over again. There was lots of wing loading, all this down low where the turbulence is greatest.

One of the pilots who flew the King Airs, David Slayter, was a guy I had known for a long time. I got to know David when he was a student at the flying club. He went on to be one of our instructors, and we worked together for a couple of years before he joined TC. David is one of smartest, most honest, and most capable and conscientious people I have ever worked with.

David was concerned about how these aircraft were being operated. He had convinced his manager that something needed to be done about the lack of safety standards. When I got there, we started working together to put a program in place. A major safety issue was that they had no procedures for weight and balance control. They would load up with two pilots, two or three technicians, and all the luggage needed for a week away. Nobody seemed to know or care that they were operating the aircraft grossly overweight.

Surprisingly, David and I were rebuffed for pointing it out. Complacency was rampant. I couldn't believe the hypocrisy. Some CAIs who were turning a blind eye were the same guys who had delighted in chastising me about even the smallest indiscretion they discovered at the flying club. The overriding issue was this: grounding these calibration aircraft would negatively affect operations at all the region's airports, and that would result in serious economic repercussions.

The more we dug, the more safety issues we found. This was serious stuff. We found mandatory maintenance items that were not being completed. We even found writings from Beechcraft (the King Air manufacturer) indicating that these aircraft weren't suited to the role of low-level calibration aircraft.

I had been a CAI for less than a year, and training pilot for only a few weeks. I was in a weak position to demand changes. Thankfully, David was dogged. He took the lead in pressing the issue to the national head office. Disappointingly, nothing much happened there either.

Everything changed on 1 May 1979. Flying out of Montreal, a sister ship to our King Air 90 was in level flight at 1,700 feet when its right wing broke off. Both pilots were killed. The aircraft (registration C-FCAS) crashed into a field near Sherrington, Quebec. I didn't know the two pilots personally, but they were my fellow CAIs, and I felt terrible. The wing attachment failed because of the exact safety issues that David and I had uncovered.

I had feelings of guilt for not being able to get that aircraft grounded, along with the entire calibration fleet across the country. They should have been grounded because of what we had found. There was (and still is) no doubt in my mind that I personally could have done more. I should have been more vocal, even though I recognize that my extra voice wouldn't have made much of a difference.

Remember how I described my natural predisposition to be a "chicken". I had a "stand up and be counted" challenge, and I backed off, working mostly in the background. David, to his full credit, was brave enough to be in the limelight, and I basically let him carry that load alone.

In my defense, I did help rally the troops to support David, and motivated by that Montreal accident I continued to supply him with useful material that I was uncovering in my new position at Flight Ops. We were all concerned that the Montreal accident would not be investigated properly. In those days, accident investigation was done by Transport Canada. There would be an obvious conflict of interest – they would be investigating themselves.

Working with our national pilot association, David was instrumental in convincing political leaders to set up an inquiry into the whole mess. It was called the "Commission of Inquiry on Aviation Safety", more commonly called "The Dubin Inquiry" because it was led by Justice Charles Dubin. It was very high profile at the time. Its findings led to many changes in how aviation was regulated in Canada.

Ironically, that inquiry ties directly to my career. Influenced by our input about the shortcomings at TC, one of the Dubin Commission's key recommendations was the establishment of an independent accident investigation board, to be modelled on the National Transportation Safety Board (NTSB) in the United States. That recommendation was accepted by the government, and CASB was established in 1984. When CASB opened its regional office in Moncton, with Dave Owen as its first manager, I was his first hire. That's how I became an aircraft accident investigator. The work I had done with David Slater, and my close following of the investigation of the loss of C-FCAS, had tweaked my interest in accident investigation, and I had made that known to Dave Owen.

As I mentioned, the training pilot job exposed me to all manner of situations and circumstances. Imagine how unique it was for the youngest member of the group, with a civilian pilot background, to be in a one-on-one assessment scenario with each of them where it was my call whether they got a pass or fail. And as I mentioned before, there was no way they could hide any flaws – they all came out.

Here's just one example. When I was still at the flying club there was one inspector from TC who none of us could stand – I will call him Winston. He was one of the TC inspectors they used to do the final check rides on our students trying for their multi-engine and instrument ratings. I hated to see Winston come through the door. He was a nasty little man in his fifties, who came out of the military to show us civilians how things should be done. He had almost every trait I dislike. He was intense to a fault, dominating, quick tempered, combative, humourless, uncompromising, bullying, overconfident, argumentative – you name it.

Winston specialized in combing through the air regulations and guidance materials to find "gotcha" questions. He delighted in humiliating our student candidates. He double-dipped his enjoyment by reprimanding me and my instructors for not having the students prepared. It was incredibly difficult to get the students ready to deal with him.

I had Winston pegged as a phoney. People who act that way are inevitably masking something – most often it has to do with inability. I asked Don McClure to use his connections at TC to get Winston removed from his duties. Don tried, but it didn't work.

Then came the day at the flying club when Winston was doing a multi-engine check ride on one of our students. We got an unexpected call from the control tower. Our Piper Seneca was sitting on the runway with its landing gear retracted. I went out to have a look. The belly of the aircraft was all scraped from sliding down the runway. The propeller blades were all bent and twisted from hitting the runway while the engines were at full power. The engines were severely damaged – they had come to an instant stop. Thankfully, nobody was hurt.

It didn't take long to find out what had happened. They were doing a touch-and-go, and during the takeoff portion Winston panicked when he thought the landing flaps were still down (they were up, where they should have been). He reached over in an attempt to select the flaps up, but he selected the landing gear up instead. As soon as the weight of the aircraft started coming off the wheels, the landing gear retracted, and the aircraft settled onto the runway. Both engines and both props were ruined, and the aircraft was out of service for several weeks.

Most aircraft have a "squat switch" that keeps the landing gear retract mechanism from engaging when there is weight on the wheels. Old aircraft didn't have those. One time I heard someone ask an old timer about a particular aircraft he used to fly – they asked, "can you raise the gear on the ground?" "No", he replied, "but you can lower the aircraft".

Even after the accident, TC wouldn't relieve Winston of his check ride duties. When I moved to Flight Ops, I gained the upper hand on dealing with Winston. It wasn't long before he required some mandatory recurrent training on the Beech Baron. We took off on an overcast day where the ceilings were quite low. Right after takeoff, Winston selected the autopilot on, and he used it to climb above the cloud layer. When we got "on top" (above cloud) we did some standard exercises like stalls and steep turns, and then I asked ATC to clear us for an instrument approach.

Without Winston noticing, I pulled a circuit breaker to stop the autopilot from engaging. As we descended into the cloud, Winston tried the autopilot. When it wouldn't engage, he became fixated on trying to find the cause. He was really struggling to hand fly the aircraft in cloud, and he started to sweat – he was panicking. He lost situational awareness, and he got so far behind the aircraft (the aircraft was travelling faster than he could think) that we had to break off the approach and climb back above the cloud.

When we broke out above cloud Winston was exhausted – a beaten man. He didn't say much, and neither did I. Nothing much had to be said. We both knew what had happened. We did more troubleshooting, and together we found the circuit breaker I had popped (I never told him I had pulled it intentionally). We reset it, and we used the autopilot to fly another approach to a landing.

I allowed Winston the dignity of bypassing a debrief. In the background, and with the help of Dave Owen, we got Winston removed from his check ride duties at the flying club. We put hard restrictions on his flying at Flight Ops. Eventually he took a job flying a desk. I wish I could report that he magically changed his belligerent ways, but that never happened. He was still a nasty person when he retired, and probably long after. In my investigations, I use Winston to help place others on the spectrum of variances. Winston is at one end point.

As training pilot, I had a unique relationship with the senior managers who were pilots. With me, they had no way to hide any knowledge flaws or flying weaknesses. One guy I ended up flying with a lot was the top manager in our region – I will call him Travis Hunter (not his real name).

Mr. Hunter was new to our region. He was another pickup from the military, and the word was he was sent east to get some regional experience before assuming a senior position at head office. Much later on I found out that TC had actually banished him to the region because they found him to be less than capable as a manager, and they couldn't figure out what to do with him.

Travis had somehow managed to make his way through a pretty solid military career, including a stint with their elite aerobatic display team on the airshow circuit. I don't know how he survived that, because he was a terrible pilot. He must have been shielded by the others. His hands and feet skills were okay, but his situational awareness and judgment were near nonexistent. I couldn't get him checked out on any of our aircraft. There was no way I would let him fly solo in one of our Beech Barons, and he couldn't check out on our King Airs. It was kind of a delicate situation, because he honestly thought he was doing great.

Dave Owen and I talked it over and came up with a plan. Fortunately, Travis really took a liking to me, and he especially liked flying with me. Dave convinced him that he was my all-time favourite guy to fly with, and that I wanted to fly with him as much as possible. Our plan was that whenever Travis flew somewhere, I'd go with him. Travis loved to fly, and he had full control over when he could use our aircraft, so we flew together a lot.

This meant that we had lots of time together in the cockpit, and at meals and such. We would engage in long discussions about all manner of subjects. Travis had a quick wit. He could also be quite humorous in a story-telling kind of way, and we were quite close in how we could pick out humour in places where we were the only ones to see it. I enjoyed that, and so did he. But what Travis really enjoyed was using me as a sounding board, and a source for feedback. As the region's most senior manager, he didn't get much direct access to working level people like me.

It was during these feedback interchanges that Travis would hear things that surprised him. I never held back from delivering reality to him, but I never believed it would do much good because Travis always knew best. He would explain the intricate rationale behind his decisions and actions. It was these explanations that to me laid bare his flawed thinking.

If Travis sensed that I was not engaging, he would do his best to provoke me into an argument. Frequently, these exchanges would get animated; never angry, just heightened enthusiasm by each of us making our points. I never held back, but I could never win of course, because Travis judged who won. For the most part I was entertained by our exchanges, but sometimes they were just tiring.

Travis liked to talk about his interactions with the intelligentsia, and how he fit nicely into their ranks. He attributed this to his study of worldly topics. As best he could, he simplified these sophisticated topics down to my level – philosophy, world history, religion, international governance, interpersonal relations, and so on – all things that I might one day hope to grasp if I worked as hard at it as he did.

On our long flights over the wilderness, Travis explained how he applied his grand understanding to mundane things like flying these civilian airplanes and ruling over our unsophisticated region. Other than absorbing his wisdom, my job was to keep his superior judgment from navigating us into the nearest hillside or thunderstorm. He had an unmatched ability to locate and fly into unsafe circumstances.

I found it interesting to study how Travis operated. I discovered that his incompetence as a pilot was matched only by his ineptitude as a manager. He was well read, and well spoken, and had mastered the social niceties expected in his circles, but beneath the façade was a man of humble intellect and limited ability. Travis had no idea how things actually worked in the real world. He passed himself off as senior management material by posing as a cerebral thinker.

Travis left our region to return to TC's head office while I was still the training pilot. But in a strange twist of fate, we ended up reconnecting when each of us joined CASB. As I mentioned earlier, I joined CASB in Moncton through my connection with Dave Owen. When Travis returned to TC's head office they needed another place to ship him off to, so he was sent to the newly established CASB – he joined their head office, to be a senior manager there. There will be more about my dealings with Travis later.

Larry (on the left) after a Training Flight in the Beech King Air 200 – circa 1980

A tourist couple stopped in a small community in Cape Breton and were talking to one of the locals. They remarked on how different and basic everything was – that it seemed like such a simple way of life – so remote – so quiet and peaceful. "How many people live in this village", they asked? "Almost 100", was the reply.

The local lady asked, "so, where do you live"? "Philadelphia", they replied. "How many people live in Philadelphia", she asked? "More than a million", they answered. "I always find it amazing" said the lady, "why so many people choose to live so far away from everything".

7

AN UNUSUAL ACCIDENT, A SOLO INVESTIGATION, LESSONS LEARNED

First, the unusual accident. Before I started in accident investigation, I had left the training pilot job to take a turn at the downtown office – to diversify my knowledge base. We got a report that a single-engine aircraft had been damaged while trying to land after dark at a remote landing strip – what's known as an unprepared runway, with no runway lights. Landing after dark without runway lighting is illegal. We were told there were no injuries or anything, so the accident investigators weren't going to investigate it – there was nothing to be learned from a safety/accident prevention point of view.

In the enforcement section, where I was helping out at the time, we were interested. My co-worker, Howard, found out who the pilot was – he was someone Howard had been chasing around for a long time. There was kind of a cat and mouse game between the two, and Howard never won. This guy was not big on following the air regulations. His offences were mostly minor, but some of what he did bordered on dangerous. Howard wanted to rein him in before someone got hurt.

It had been hard for Howard to put together a solid and winnable case against this pilot. He was far from a criminal. In fact, this guy was an ordained minister – a man of the cloth, and he was well respected in his community. This was not someone who was easy to prosecute in court, but finally Howard had what he thought to be a rock-solid case against him. This guy had landed at least one hour after sunset, and without the required runway lighting. Case closed; he was guilty according to the law, and according to Howard.

As we drove down to the landing strip to check it out, Howard talked about how a man of the cloth could be such a lawbreaker. I told Howard about my uncle who was a minister. He and my aunt (my dad's sister) had been missionaries in Africa. They sent letters to us from there, which gave me bragging rights for my stamp collection. My uncle was a good and kind man, but he was not a perfect follower of everyday rules and regulations. One time I asked him how he could so comfortably ignore things like parking restrictions and speed limits and hunting licenses. He explained that those were all man's laws, not God's laws, and as a man of the cloth he was only obliged to follow God's laws.

49

When we arrived at the landing strip, we met the police officer on the case. He had completed his initial investigation, and he briefed us on his findings. This is what he told us. On the previous night, the pilot had landed more than an hour after sundown. The pilot regularly used this landing strip because it was closest to where he lived. He did most of his preaching in the evenings, so quite often he would arrive back at the landing strip after dark. His wife would monitor a radio scanner, so she'd know when to go to the landing strip to pick him up. She'd listen for his communications with air traffic control, and he would use code words to let her know his estimated landing time.

An airplane should always be landed into the wind, so they had a way for her to let him know which runway was facing into wind. She would check the windsock, then drive to the threshold of the appropriate runway and park the car so the headlights were pointing in the direction he should land. He would then make his approach to pass over the car and touch down in the area lit by the headlights. It was an ingenious system; not legal or especially safe, but it worked.

On the night of the mishap, the pilot changed things up. He knew that the landing strip wasn't level. It was slightly uphill one way, and downhill the other. On this night, when he saw where the car was parked, he knew his landing would be downhill. He figured that the wind was very light, so he decided it would be better (better for stopping) to land uphill, this would point him towards the car. When his wife saw he was landing directly toward her, she panicked. She turned off the headlights, shut off the engine, got the kids out, and herded them all into the woods. The pilot kept coming, but he no longer had sight of the car. The result was that he smashed his aircraft headlong into his own car, writing both of them off.

The police officer read from his notes in a monotone. As his briefing unfolded, I watched Howard struggling to remain stone-faced. This was funny stuff. Howard was all but bursting with glee. After years of frustration he was finally seeing some justice. There was instant justice – the destroyed car and airplane both belonged to this pilot – and there was justice to come – a fine, and a license suspension from this obvious breach of the regulations.

A few months later Howard and I were in court where Howard would testify for the prosecution. The judge went through the preliminary formalities, and just before our prosecutor called his first witness, into the courtroom came the pilot's wife, with all their children. I think there were five or six of them, all dressed up in a most pious fashion. The kids looked precious, and innocent, and very sad. It was an impressive showing.

Our first witness was an employee from the environment department who was there for a single purpose; to establish the time of official darkness at the landing strip on the night in question. Nothing could be easier to determine. Official darkness is thirty minutes after sunset, and the time of sunset at a specific location on any given date is consistent over millennia. The witness was asked to state the sunset time, which he did by referring to the sunset table in his reference book.

The prosecutor had no further questions. As the witness got up to leave, the defense attorney sprang into action. I remember his black lawyer's robe swirling as he turned to face the witness. It was amazing to watch. The entire trial was over in no more than a couple of minutes. The questioning went like this:

LAWYER   Sir, I see you used a reference book to find the sunset time.

WITNESS   Yes sir, I did.

LAWYER   Would you please tell the Court the title of that reference book.

WITNESS   (Not a direct quote, but something like this)
          The title is: "The United States Navy Table of Sunset Times".

LAWYER   Would you please tell the Court the date of publication of that book.

WITNESS   (Searching for the date – and reporting something like this)
          It was published in June of 1938. (Decades previous)

LAWYER   And can you confirm for the Court that what you are using is the latest version of that reference book.

WITNESS   (Looking a bit flustered)
          I am not sure if this is the latest version.

LAWYER   So, you have brought to this Court a reference book that is out of date? (Not leaving time for a response from the increasingly nervous witness)

LAWYER   Let's move on – can you tell me, what is the elevation of the landing strip in question?

WITNESS   (Looking even more flustered) I am not sure what the elevation is.

LAWYER   Can you tell me what the elevation is of the ground to the west of that landing strip – the ground that lies between the landing strip and the setting sun at the horizon?

WITNESS   (Showing some panic)
I don't know the elevation of that ground.

LAWYER   Would you agree with me that the elevation of the surrounding terrain can change the time when the sun actually disappears below the horizon?

WITNESS   (Elevated panic) Yes, I would agree with that.

LAWYER   (With his voice rising to the occasion) Sir – you have been asked to provide this Court with the exact time of sunset at that landing strip on that day. You have tried to use a reference book that is out of date. You have told the Court that ground elevations can change the sunset time, and yet you have admitted that you have no idea what the elevation of the airport is, or the elevation of the terrain that surrounds it! These are important and significant lapses by you! I submit to you that you have no idea what the exact sunset time was at that airstrip on that day! Would you agree with that?

WITNESS   (Completely beaten and resigned)
I would have to agree with that, yes.

JUDGE   With that, ladies and gentlemen, I declare this case closed. I find the defendant not guilty.

Down went the gavel, and that was that. The judge had been provided with his excuse to shut us down. The community would be satisfied. Poor Howard was frozen in his seat. Sunset time is one of the most consistent things in the universe, and we had lost our case because we had failed to establish it in the court. The pilot had landed a whole hour after sunset, and it was illegal after thirty minutes. Our expert could have explained that the tables in his book would never go out of date, and that the relatively minor ground elevation changes in that area were irrelevant in determining the time of official darkness. His task was too easy, so we failed to prepare him properly. He was eaten alive, and I felt sorry for him.

The path to becoming experienced is paved with lessons learned. For me, it's the negative-outcome experiences that seem to implant the deepest. This one left a profound and lifelong impression on me. Energized by my "avoid embarrassment" phobia, I'm driven to prevent any kind of scenario similar to the one with our sunset time witness.

Now for the solo investigation. Early in my career, after I first joined CASB, Dave Owen sent me out alone to do an ultralight aircraft incident. There were no fatalities, so this was not something we would normally investigate. But it was quick and easy to get to, within easy driving distance, and it happened right beside a road. Basically, Dave just wanted me to go out and get some experience handling everything alone.

Here are the circumstances. It happened on a Sunday morning. I drove to the site in our response truck. I didn't yet have my CASB jacket, so I wore my oldest sports jacket – anyway, it was obvious who I represented, and why I was there. The wreckage was in a field that ran perpendicular to a country road near a small village. On the opposite side of the road there was a church, and a few houses. There were cars lining the road – even more were in the church parking lot. As I got close, I saw a police car with flashing lights. There were lots of people standing along the roadside. Obviously, this was something unique for the small community, and there was plenty of local interest.

It was apparent that everyone had been waiting for me to arrive, and I was immediately in charge of everything. The police officer said he had another call, and he had to leave soon. He told me he had interviewed the pilot before an ambulance took him to the hospital. The pilot told him that he had checked out the field the day before, but this was his first time trying to land in it.

The pilot reported that he had touched down too fast, and that his ultralight was not equipped with brakes. He decided to try to slow down by dragging his feet on the ground, but when his feet touched the ground the force broke both his ankles. The ultralight coasted to a stop just before it got to a wooden fence. It wasn't damaged – what made this reportable (by regulation) as an accident was that the pilot sustained injuries. As you might imagine, over the years I've been able to use that story many times at my "let's take a pause" interventions (it's sad, of course, but if you tell it right it's quite entertaining).

Many things needed my attention. The aircraft was fully visible from the road. It would be up to me to figure out how to keep the site secured after the police officer left. I had to interview a couple of eyewitnesses. I did that right away, while their memories were fresh.

The pilot's sister was there, so I took some time to talk with her. She asked me questions like "was the pilot in trouble with the law", "would he lose his license", and "what will happen to the aircraft". There was no one else for her to ask these questions to, and I saw it as my duty to help her, even though technically it wasn't. She was comforted, which made me happy.

I did a media interview for television, and one for a newspaper. I completed all the standard investigation tasks, like checking over the aircraft and taking photos and measurements. I arranged to interview the pilot a couple of days later. After I got all the evidence I needed, I made sure the file was organized, and I got everything documented. Then I wrote a full report, and I shepherded it through the board.

The biggest lesson I learned from this one was that doing an accident investigation is not a one-person job. First of all, it's just too hard to keep everything organized logistically. And secondly, nobody – and most certainly not me – has all the skillsets needed to do a thorough analysis of all aspects an event. To be an effective investigator, you need to recognize when you need help, and you need to know where and how to get it.

Larry investigating an Ultralight accident – 1984

Labrador is a great place for funny stories. Here's one that was told to me by a couple of the RCMP guys I got to know up there.

One time they had a detachment commander in Goose Bay who nobody liked. They tried to make his life miserable, so he'd transfer out. One evening, a couple of them broke into his office and stole his boots – then they dipped them in a mudpuddle. Then they went back into his office, and they used a long broom handle to walk the boots across the ceiling. Then they cleaned the boots, and put them back.

The next morning when the commander saw the muddy footprints across his ceiling, he was livid. Knowing it was an inside job, he signed an official order declaring that whoever owned the boots was to be severely reprimanded, and immediately transferred. He sent notification of his intended action to head office.

It took less than a day to identify the owner of the boots, and less than a week for him to be transferred out.

8

BECOMING A FULL TIME INVESTIGATOR

Reconnecting with Dave Owen at the newly formed CASB Regional Office was a dream scenario for me. Having worked for Dave previously when I was the training pilot at TC, I knew this would be a perfect fit. Dave was such a wonderful guy to be around – honest, and fair, and very capable. CASB had its own facility – completely independent and remote from TC – we were on the other side of the city. When I first joined up, the office had only six employees. There were five investigators, and we had one support person. It was a fun place to go to work.

Dave and the others had transferred over from the accident investigation section at TC, so there was lots of expertise for me to tap into. We had a fully equipped workshop for examining wreckage, and an outdoor compound for wreckage storage. And the best part was that we had an agreement with TC to have access to their aircraft on a priority basis to fly ourselves around.

There was no better place for me to get seasoned as an accident investigator. In our region we had almost every kind of aviation imaginable; recreational flying, bush flying, business aircraft, regional carriers, national and international carriers, float operators, ski operations, commercial helicopter operations, you name it. We even had one of the world's busiest air corridors, the North Atlantic Tracks, running right across our region. That track system handles the massive air traffic flows between North America and Europe. We got plenty of work from incidents involving that traffic. And for even more variety, most of the flights between Europe and Cuba stopped at airports in our region to refuel (at that time, they weren't allowed into United States airspace). We had some interesting work whenever one of those would have an occurrence – dealing with operators from Cuba, and the old Soviet bloc.

As I mentioned, I worked in that Atlantic regional office for six years before I transferred to Head Office. I was exposed to all facets of accident investigation, in all manner of circumstances. I learned how to document, examine, interpret, and recover wreckage – and to preserve the evidence while doing that. I learned how to conduct effective interviews with surviving pilots and passengers, and with company managers, and with air traffic controllers, and with eyewitnesses, and with maintenance engineers, and with aircraft manufacturers, and with anyone else who might have valuable information. I learned how to write reports and steer them through the bureaucracy to get them released to the public.

On the logistics side, I learned how to work with police forces and coroners, handle media requests, set up and manage investigation teams, and how to ensure we had the right expertise for the circumstances. I learned how to stop people with a vested interest from swaying how things went. Doing all that got me ready for any level of investigation, including those with high-profile.

I'll give you a practical example of how I gained valuable experience during one of my investigation outings in Canada, and was able to use that experience 10 years later during another investigation in New Zealand.

On 14 May 1985 (while I was working in the Atlantic region), a Northrop F-20 Tigershark (a military fighter jet design) crashed in Goose Bay, Labrador, killing the pilot. This was a demonstration aircraft, designed, built and operated by the Northrop Corporation based in Hawthorne, California. An entire Northrop team had stopped over in Goose Bay on its way to the Paris Air Show to market this new generation fighter aircraft to potential military buyers.

Canadian Forces Base Goose Bay was a perfect place to stop over and conduct training flights for their upcoming aerobatic display. The airport had been built during World War 2 to support aircraft movements between North America and the United Kingdom, and it had all the facilities and ground support they needed.

If this had been a military operated aircraft, we wouldn't have been involved, but this one was civilian registered, so we had responsibility. When we got the notification, our regional office responded immediately. Dave Owen would be the IIC, and he choose me and one of our technical guys to be his support team. We loaded our gear into one of TC's King Airs, and we departed for Goose Bay.

Before we landed, we heard through ATC that another TC aircraft was inbound to Goose Bay, this one was coming from Ottawa. Head office had obviously decided this was high-profile enough for them to take charge – we knew they would bring a full go team. If you're wondering about a lack of coordination, you have to remember this happened in the time when communication wasn't as easy as it is now. The double response from CASB hadn't been coordinated, but they knew we were already on our way – they didn't turn us around because they wanted our local knowledge – we would be part of their team.

I remember feeling disappointed that Dave wouldn't be in charge. We had lots of confidence in ourselves, but I can tell you we had far less confidence in the people from head office. When CASB had started up only seven months previous, at head office they weren't able to attract the experienced investigators from TC. That was because they had initially decided to relocate their new head office to Montreal (that decision was later reversed). So, the new CASB head office was mostly staffed with inexperienced newbies (new to investigations) – many from the military.

Thankfully, the head office people brought with them some highly experienced and skilled investigators from CASB's Engineering Branch (that was our national laboratory facility – based in Ottawa but remote from head office). These people had transferred to CASB en masse from TC, and they were an invaluable technical resource available to all regions across the country.

Like the new guys from head office, I'd been with CASB for only seven months. But unlike them, I'd already been out in the field quite a few times doing real investigation work. I can tell you that I felt superior to them because of that. As I write this, I remember how I felt – it was like, "who do you think you are, coming here to take charge when you don't know as much as we do?" That's not a very constructive attitude, but that's the way I felt.

I'll get on with describing the experience I gained as a result of that investigation. The first bit involves my misplaced feeling of superiority. When I saw the final report that the head office guys eventually produced, I felt bad (dumb, actually) about feeling superior. This was a great lesson learned. Yes, we were ahead of them on the practical side of working with the wreckage and interacting with the airport folks. But in the end, they produced a final report, and recommendations, that were more complete and enlightening than what we (Dave and I) could have produced. They really came through in their detailed account of g-forces during the flight, and the pilot's inability to tolerate them.

They determined that during a particularly high g-force maneuver the pilot became incapacitated (he blacked out). He failed to recover in time to prevent the aircraft from striking the ground. They found that the pilot suffered from a medical condition called achalasia, which reduced his g tolerance. This was something that he had not disclosed when he went for his pilot medical. The head office guys came up with numerous other factors and findings that were impressive. Dave and I would likely have come up with these same findings, but head office had better resources to chase it all down, including their military backgrounds and contacts.

That was a lesson for me from the negative side – now for one from the positive side – here's where I was able to contribute. The Ottawa team set about doing the standard grid pattern survey and documentation of the wreckage. The impact had occurred on snow-covered flat ground that was about one mile from the runway. The aircraft had struck the ground right-side-up, in a wings-level and slightly nose down attitude, at a speed of over 260 knots. The wreckage was fragmented, and it was spread out over approximately 1,000 feet, laying on the snow surface.

I went to talk to some of the airport workers – these were people I had met on my previous visits to Goose Bay. I pumped them for any ideas they might have about how best to recover the wreckage. I learned that the ground under the snow was all sand – there was no solid structure to it. It was the middle of May, so the sun was strong, and the snow was melting fast. They told me that if the wreckage wasn't picked up the next day, that most of the pieces, heated by the sun, would melt down through the snow, and all the smaller ones would disappear into the sand.

They told me that using heavy vehicles on that snow wouldn't work because the snow wasn't solid enough to take their weight. They would break through, and the snow/sand combination would mire them in a soupy mixture – they would get stuck, and not be able to escape. I went to a local helicopter operator, and I asked them for advice. They said we should lay out sling nets on top of the snow, all along the wreckage trail. On top of each sling net, we should place a tarpaulin to keep small pieces from falling through. We should get enough manpower to pick up the wreckage pieces by hand, so they could be placed onto the tarpaulins/sling nets. Then, they would use one of their helicopters to lift everything out, one sling load at a time.

When we gathered for the evening progress meeting, the head office team briefed everyone on their plan. They planned to spend two to three days documenting the site. Then, they would bring in trucks to recover the wreckage. With my newfound knowledge (which I never mentioned was newfound) I convinced them their plan wouldn't work. I told them how it needed to be done – I recall mentioning my regional experience, and taking far more credit than I should have for being so insightful. I convinced them to get some aerial photography – that would help with their wreckage plotting – and I convinced them to use a helicopter for the wreckage recovery. They accepted everything, and I felt good about it all.

The next day everything went according to "my" plan – that is, until we tried to recover the big jet engine that had broken free in the crash. It was too heavy for the helicopter we were using – it didn't have the lifting capacity. It so happened that at that time the German Air Force had a fighter squadron in Goose Bay – they were there on a training mission. As part of their mission, they had brought over a rescue helicopter that was big enough, and powerful enough, to lift the engine. They agreed to sling the engine out for us.

The Germans didn't have a sling line strong enough to take the weight of the engine. I was the "local" guy within our CASB team, so I was tasked to go find something suitable. I probably looked confident as I drove away to go looking, but inside I was churning. I had no idea where to go, or what to get. As I drove along the service road parallel to the runway, I spotted the airport's maintenance garage – that's where they fixed their heavy equipment, such as their snowplows. I drove over there, and I went in.

I explained to the mechanics what my problem was. They told me they had a roll of steel cable that was strong enough to pull a snowplough. It would easily handle the weight of an engine. They agreed to cut off a length of that cable for me, and to put a hook on each end. What a great relief for me – that was the answer. Then they asked me what length I wanted.

Of course, I had no idea. I could visualize the helicopter flying away with the engine dangling below, but I couldn't relate that to the cable length I needed them to cut. Was it best to hook onto the engine in the middle? Or at one end? Was there anything on the engine to attach the hook to? All I could think about was how dumb I'd look if I got them to cut the cable too short, so I asked them to spool it out to the full length of their workshop – I asked them to cut it to that length, and that's what they did.

When I got back with the cable, we laid it out next to the engine. It was obviously way too long – probably 4 times longer than the length of the engine front to back. I could feel my stress rising. The Germans were polite, but they made it known to everyone that they couldn't carry the engine on that long of a line. Just before I was about to speak up to volunteer to take it back to have it cut to a more appropriate length, someone (someone with much more vision than me, I'm not sure who it was) spoke up to say it was actually the perfect length.

Whoever that person was directed that the cable be fed through the core of the engine from front to back. Then, they fed it out each end far enough to where the hook could be attached back to the cable at the engine's half-way point. The remaining length gave the perfect sling distance between the

61

helicopter and the engine. As it turned out, everyone just assumed that's what I had in mind when I had the cable cut to that length in the first place, so from the very start it was referred to as Larry's plan.

It didn't take long for the Germans to sling the engine out according to my plan. They reported back that the cable and the plan were both perfect in every way, and that they would have never thought about doing it that way, and they would report that plan back to their operations people in case they ever had to use it again. I was a mini hero, and our head office guys were impressed. But of course, I intentionally played it down. I told them that it was all in a day's work for us regional guys – child's play really.

You can appreciate how relieved I was to avoid looking dumb. I had set myself up heading out to get some kind of sling line without getting some input on exactly what I should get. I recognized that my limited investigation experience didn't warrant my swagger. I was humbled, and that was a good thing.

The good part was that I got schooled on how to get good ideas from others, like the airport maintenance guys, and the helicopter folks. Over the years I've come to realize that the biggest part of putting together a successful investigation is finding the best sources for information and ideas, and then melding everything together. Investigations need a team of investigators and experts. No individual has enough expertise to do it alone.

Now I'll tell you how my experience at this F20 investigation paid off 10 years later. On 9 June 1995 (I was now working at TSB's head office), Ansett New Zealand Flight 703 crashed while attempting to land in Palmerston North. There were 21 people on board. The impact killed one flight attendant and two passengers. Fifteen others were seriously injured, and one of those later died in hospital. It was a very high-profile event in New Zealand.

The aircraft was a de Havilland Dash 8, which was manufactured in Canada, so Canada was obliged to send an Accredited Representative, and that was me. Two specialists from de Havilland went with me; Jim Donnelly, their lead flight safety investigator, and Louis (big Louie) Sytsma, a pilot specialist. I had done quite a few investigations with Jim over the years, and we had a great working relationship. Big Louie turned out to be a great guy – sharp as can be, and with a great sense of humour.

Needless to say, we wanted to get to New Zealand as quickly as possible. We had to travel halfway around the world. When we finally got to Palmerston

North, we went immediately to the accident site where they were anxiously awaiting our arrival. With that, I endured the longest stretch of awake time in my entire life – a full 44 hours between bed sleeps.

I remember being so exhausted after that first day at the site that I never made it through their end-of-day wrap-up briefing. As I sat there listening, I got dizzy, and I literally passed out sitting in my chair. I slumped forward, and my head thumped down and hit the table – big Louie said it made a hollow sound. How embarrassing – I had to excuse myself and head to my room. But earlier that day, before I unceremoniously fell asleep on duty, I had used my experience from the F-20 Tigershark investigation to do some good work at the Palmerston North accident site.

The Dash 8 had crashed in bad weather while descending to the airport at Palmerston North. The instrument approach in use had a steep and relatively complicated step-down descent profile – it was over some very hilly terrain. When the pilots selected the landing gear down at the top of their descent, the right main gear got hung up, and it failed to extend.

In that circumstance, pilots would normally break off their approach. The standard procedure would be to fly to a holding area to get things straightened out. The landing gear can be extended using alternate procedures, but to do that takes time and focus to follow the checklist steps properly. In this case, for whatever reason, the captain decided to continue descending on the approach – he obviously expected that they could get the gear down in plenty of time for the landing.

Unfortunately, his plan didn't work out so well. The co-pilot got mixed up doing the checklist, and the captain got distracted trying to help him. In the cloud, and without visual reference outside, they allowed the aircraft to descend way below the required flight profile. As their descent profile took them ever closer to the hills below, the GPWS (ground proximity warning system) sounded. They started to pull up, but it was too late.

Fortunately, their pull up at the last second saved them from going nose-down into the terrain. Instead, they miraculously careened off the grass-covered surface of a gentle upslope. They briefly went back airborne, and they hopped over a gully before the right wing gouged into a nearby hillside and broke off. The fuselage ended up sliding along yet another gentle upslope before it finally came to rest.

These glancing blows with the gentle upslopes took significant energy out of the crash dynamic. As it absorbed the impacts, the aircraft had sustained significant damage, and it had shed parts all along the wreckage trail, but the g-force deceleration had remained within human tolerance. Most fortunately, the interior living space was not extensively crushed. That's why there were so many survivors – that, and the fact there was no fireball at the time of impact.

On that first day, when we arrived at the top of the hill looking down over the wreckage trail, we were met by members of the New Zealand investigation team, including the IIC, Ron Chippindale. The first thing they asked us for was our input about how to recover the wreckage. The slopes had a solid rock base that was covered with several inches of substrate built up by decades of sheep grazing. There was an incredible cover of lush green grass, kept short by the ever-present sheep. The recent rains had saturated everything down to the rock base, and even walking around was treacherous. Not only was the grass surface slippery, any step could cause the entire top layer to give way. It was actually more slippery than walking on slick ice, given the uneven localized slopes.

I had not met Mr. Chippindale before, but I knew of him by reputation. He was New Zealand's Chief Inspector of Air Accidents. He had lots of investigation experience, and he was well known for his leadership roles in various international flight safety committees and such. He had participated in some high-profile international investigations.

Ron was highly thought of at that time, but 16 years previous his reputation had taken a hit. In 1979, he had been the IIC for an infamous crash known as the Mount Erebus Disaster. That was an Antarctica sightseeing flight operated by Air New Zealand. The DC-10 crashed into the mountain in Antarctica, killing all 257 people on board. In his final report, Ron attributed the accident to pilot error, a go-to finding in those days. Back then, if you found nothing technically wrong with the aircraft, you would write a report to reflect that the defective pilots flew a perfectly good aircraft to its demise. In the Mount Erebus case, that finding was widely viewed as simplistic. There was a public outcry, and the New Zealand government was forced to set up a Royal Commission to have another look.

The commission came to an entirely different conclusion. Their broad-based investigation looked at the operator, Air New Zealand, and they discovered systemic deficiencies in how the sightseeing flights were being conducted. They found that Air New Zealand had supplied the pilots with incorrect navigation information; they concluded that is what had caused the pilots to fly into the mountain. None of that had been found by Ron and his investigation team.

The commission's findings were an eye-opener internationally. That whole drawn-out drama in New Zealand changed accident investigation. New procedures evolved internationally – procedures that required investigators to look for underlying and systemic issues and deficiencies. Modern accident investigation techniques were kind of kick-started because of that high-profile episode.

At the accident site, Ron and his team gave us a quick overview of what their wreckage recovery plan was. They wanted to get all the wreckage moved to a secure site in Palmerston North. The fuselage was mostly intact, and it was far too heavy to try to move in one piece. Their plan was to cut the fuselage into smaller pieces, and they would use a small tracked vehicle to move these smaller pieces to the road. The problem was that the tracked vehicle was struggling to even get around on its own in the slippery conditions. To move anything with it would be tricky, and dangerous. For the smaller wreckage pieces scattered over the slopes, they planned to hand carry each piece to flatter ground where the tracked vehicle could take over.

You can see where this is going, and how my experience in Goose Bay during the F20 accident 10 years previous led to a better plan. The two situations were very similar. We told them there was a better plan. We explained how everything needed to be slung out with helicopters, including the intact fuselage. They got access to a huge Russian helicopter – it happened to be in the area placing electrical towers – it had a tremendous lifting capacity.

We had them cut a hole through the cockpit windscreen and run a heavy strap through it. The strap needed to be long enough to go through the full length of the fuselage – and even longer – long enough to have its two ends meet up to where they could attach to a long sling line – the same idea as the cable we put through the F20 engine. Jim calculated the weight of the damaged fuselage, and he confirmed the fuselage stringers would be strong enough to hold up to carrying the load. They used a 200-foot long sling line, and the Russian helicopter plucked the fuselage off the side of that slope with no trouble at all. It was a wonderous sight to watch the fuselage fly away under that helicopter. Everyone cheered.

The Russians also recovered the other larger pieces, like the right wing. For the smaller pieces, we again used the Goose Bay method. We had them strategically place sling nets with tarpaulin liners, and the hand carrying of wreckage went smoothly. The nets were lifted out of there using a smaller helicopter. All that tells the story of how experience at one site can save a lot of time and effort at another site, and also preserve important evidence.

Ron Chippindale turned out to be a great guy. He had a kind of a gruff exterior, but he had a good sense of humour and a calm way about him. He commanded respect, and he took charge, but he let everyone give their input freely and without intimidation. I watched him carefully so I could absorb what he did that was particularly effective. I participated in some media briefings with him, including live television, and I found that experience particularly helpful – Ron was really good at that – very polished.

I'll share with you a quick story from New Zealand that I've told at many investigations – during "let's take a pause" times. Jim and big Louie and I were passengers in a government car that Ron was driving. To us, it was awkward to be driving on the wrong side of the road – they drive on the left side down there. From a side-street we came to a busy four-way intersection, and we stopped at a red light. After we had sat there for a while, I asked Ron if it was legal in New Zealand to turn left on a red light. He said it varied depending on the community, and he was not familiar with the local rules, so he was waiting.

Then came a gentle tap on Ron's window. Ron rolled it down, and there was the driver of the car behind us. He must have recognized Ron from his recent television appearances, because he called Ron by name. The gentleman says, "Mr. Chippindale, sir – this is one of those intersections where it's legal to turn left on a red light." Ron thanked him very much, and they exchanged pleasant good-day's, and the guy went back to his car. Soon, our light had turned green, and away we went. I looked behind us, and there were at least seven or eight cars that had been waiting behind us to get into that intersection.

That small event left a lasting impression on me about the good people of New Zealand. There was no horn blowing, there was no fist pumping, or any other unpleasantries. I'm sure they have some of that down there too, but it sure was refreshing to watch people in that circumstance interacting with such respect for each other. I remember wishing the whole world could be like that.

I lost touch with Ron after he retired in 1998. It was years later, in 2008, that I heard he had been killed in a road accident. He was out for a walk when a young man lost control of his car and struck him. Reckless driving was involved. How tragic it was that someone who had worked his whole life promoting safety should be taken that way. Ron was 74 years old and in good health. He had lots left to give.

My main investigation partner in the Atlantic Region was Roy, and we did many investigations together. For fun, Roy and I called ourselves the "Hallmark Team" (from the greeting card company) and we had that printed on the front of our tee-shirts. On the back we had their slogan, "When You Care Enough to Send the Very Best".

Here's an example of a story that I have used to see if everyone's okay during an investigation – to see if they can still laugh. Like most of these types of stories, much of the "funniness" is in the telling – but I'll do the best I can using just written words.

One time they sent a new guy from head office to our region to see how we did things. He introduced himself as Vernon O'Conner (not his real name) – he said he was a retired pilot and lieutenant-colonel from the military. We soon found out that Vernon was quite full of himself, along with being a twit. By good fortune (for the purpose of his visit), we got a call about an accident that we could take Vernon to – it was a simple one – a single-engine aircraft – only minor injuries. Roy and Vernon and I would go – it was a three-hour drive in our response truck. We were told the wreckage was in a farmer's field – it was too far back from the road to see, but it was within easy walking distance. At a set time, the farmer who owned the property would meet us – he would park his truck at the spot along the road where he could point us in the right direction.

It so happened that Vernon had once been stationed at the nearby military airport. He told us about the farmers around there – in his opinion they were quite unsophisticated and hard to deal with. Apparently, they had had the audacity to complain about fighter aircraft taking low-level runs at their cows, just for sport. We told Vernon that any time we had been down around there we always found the locals to be very helpful and friendly. Vernon said that if we had any trouble with the farmer, he knew how to straighten him out because he had experience. He told us (like we didn't know) that we had badges – big red ones with our picture on them – that gave us the right to access any property and seize anything we wanted to, and so on. We were all powerful. We told Vernon that we never felt a need to show our badges – that we had never had an issue.

We knew we had arrived at the site when we saw an elderly gentleman sitting on the tailgate of an old pickup truck. We parked behind it, and we all got out. I started getting our gear out, and Roy went over to introduce himself. Vernon stayed to watch me. We could see the farmer pointing across a barbed-wire fence and down over a ridge. Roy came over to fill us in. He said that the farmer told him we shouldn't cross that fence right now because it wasn't safe to be around the wreckage. The farmer's brother was on his way over in his cattle truck to make things safe.

Vernon never waited for any further explanation – he launched into action. He had predicted the farmer would give us trouble, and he was now going to show us how to deal with it. He marched over to the farmer and introduced himself as follows – "my name is Mr. O'Conner – I represent the Canadian Aviation Safety Board – and you must understand that this badge gives me the authority to go onto your property to examine aircraft wreckage that I know to be there – and in these matters it is I – not you – who has the expertise to decide what's safe and what's not safe". To which the farmer replied – "I don't think it's a good idea for you to go down there right now Mr. O'Conner". Vernon got all animated and waved his badge at the farmer and told him he was exercising his rights, and off he went. He pushed down the top strand of the barbed wire fence and flung one leg over, followed by the other one, and then he marched off down the ridge until he disappeared below our sight line.

It wasn't long before we saw the top of Vernon's head – and then progressively more of him moving toward us – he was slowly and carefully walking backwards up the slope – staring straight ahead and saying nothing. Soon enough we saw what he was concentrating on. There was a gigantic bull with a full set of horns, with its head lowered and waving back and forth, and it was traveling at the same pace up the slope as Vernon, looking exceptionally menacing and ready to charge. And as this tandem got close enough to us to provide full affect, the farmer yelled out – "show him your badge, Mr. O'Conner."

Larry and Big Louis at the wreckage site of Ansett

Larry and Roy – "The Hallmark Team" – circa 1999

9

WAS THIS THE RIGHT CALL?

When you're assigned to respond to an accident, you have to be ready to take charge. There will be many decisions to make. Some will be connected to what caused the airplane to crash, but others will be more like judgement calls to do with handling the overall dynamic. In this chapter, I've chosen an accident scenario to demonstrate just how heart wrenching some of these judgement calls can be.

I was the standby investigator on a Sunday morning when I got notified that a small aircraft had just crashed next to the runway at an airport in Newfoundland. The pilot was the only occupant, and he was dead. There was no post-crash fire. The body was still in the aircraft. The local police had the site cordoned off, and everything was secure. I told them to keep everything in place, and that we would be responding. We would be there in about 4 hours.

I quickly arranged for Roy to go with me. I called my contact at Transport Canada to get an aircraft ready. Roy and I were soon airborne, with an estimated flight time of just over two hours. Our destination airport had only one runway. We were about halfway there when I was reminded that the runway had been closed because the wreckage was too close to it. All aircraft movements were blocked. They were getting pressure from some commercial operators who wanted them to move the wreckage.

I had the authority, and I made the decision to keep the wreckage undisturbed until we got there to examine it. I gave myself special dispensation to land on the closed runway, and they bought into that. To this day I am not sure if I had a right to do that, but nobody ever challenged it. As we were landing, we could see the wreckage, and we saw that it was basically all in one spot. That told us that the aircraft had crashed while descending vertically – this pointed to an aerodynamic stall/spin. We taxied straight to the terminal building, where we were met by two police officers.

We got the standard brief-in. They gave us the chronology of what had gone on, and what they had learned from their initial interviews. The aircraft was an amphibious model, meaning it could land on either water or land. The pilot had flown to the airport to refuel, and the crash happened when he was taking off to fly back to his lakefront cottage. Witnesses said they heard the engine backfiring and sputtering after takeoff. The pilot tried to turn back, but he never made it through the turn. The witnesses described the aircraft entering a spin from a low altitude, exactly as the wreckage suggested.

The crash vehicles had gotten to the aircraft quickly. There was no fire. It was obvious to them the pilot was dead, so they parked their vehicles nearby and waited for the police to show up. The police secured the site, and put up their barrier tape. Then, they finished their standard documentation, taking photos and measurements. They collected the names of people with some connection to the event, and they did their standard interviews. The police had done a good job, which is typical.

They told me the local coroner was on his way. It was the coroner's job to determine the cause of death. In cases like this, coroners are able to quickly attribute the death to blunt force trauma from an airplane crash. The police told us the body was in pretty rough shape. They said that once I gave the go-ahead, the coroner would remove the body and take it to either a morgue, or to a funeral home. That would depend on whether or not I wanted an autopsy done.

In this case, there was one additional factor. The son of the dead pilot had shown up – he was in a nearby room. They said he was exceptionally distraught. They said that at one point he had come close to being out of control – that had happened when his emotions boiled over when they refused to let him go to the site to see his dad. They had calmed him down by telling him they didn't have the authority to allow him to go to the wreckage site – but they assured him that I was on my way, and I could make that call.

As I left to go view the site for myself, I purposefully walked past the room he was in. I took a glance in, and I saw that he was a young guy – maybe 20 years old. He was sitting bent over with his head in his hands, and he looked to be quietly sobbing. He never looked up. There was somebody with him, who I presumed to be a grief counsellor from the police, but he was basically alone in his grief. I felt incredibly sorry for him, and I thought about how close he and his dad must have been. I thought about how much grief there would be in the rest of the family, and how he would carry back to them the story of how he was treated here.

Roy and I went to check out the wreckage. Our investigation was routine. There was nothing complicated about it. The wreckage had all the classic characteristics of a stall/spin accident. The ground marks showed that the aircraft had almost no forward velocity when it struck the ground, it was all vertical. It was in a spin when it hit, as evidenced by how the tail was twisted. Everything was consistent with a low-altitude aerodynamic stall followed by a spin, exactly what the witnesses saw.

We took fuel samples from the aircraft's tanks and supply lines, and Roy asked for samples from the supply source. We did all the standard documenting, and we had a quick look at the aircraft's systems and flight controls. We found nothing out of the ordinary. As for the engine, the propeller condition told us it was not developing much power at impact. We would ship the engine and propeller to our workshop for teardown. That would reveal what had caused the engine issues.

The loss of engine power should not have resulted in a crash. The pilot was departing from a runway that was 10,000 feet long, and he would have used less than one-tenth of it to get airborne. When the engine started to act up, he could easily have landed straight ahead – back on the vast length of runway ahead of him. Instead, for whatever reason, he attempted to turn back.

Could the pilot's decision-making have been influenced by something more than poor judgement? We needed to find out if medical distress was a contributing factor. Therefore, we would need an autopsy. I looked to see if there were signs that his hands and feet had been on the controls at impact. There was nothing obvious. The autopsy would look for broken bones and injury patterns – that might tell us something.

I thought about the son who was insisting that he be allowed to come for a look. His dad was all in one piece, but he was in bad shape. His seat had deformed under him to where he was twisted in an unnatural way. He had facial lacerations, and blood had flowed from his nose and mouth. As frequently happens with a sudden death, his body had released bowel and bladder contents, and that was clearly evident.

Roy stayed at the site to finish up his technical look through the wreckage. I went with a police officer back to the terminal to meet the son. While we were driving there, I had a couple more minutes to decide what to tell him. I can tell you that I was conflicted – this was not easy. There was no technical reason to deny the young man his request – there was no policy or safety issue I could fall back on. It was purely my call. I had no time to get advice from anyone.

What would be right, ethically? I thought about what would be best for this young man in the long run. Either way I went, what effect would my decision have on him physiologically? What would his family want me to do? What would his dad want me to do? This was tough stuff.

Here's how I handled it. I followed the police officer into the room where this young man was. I could tell he had been waiting anxiously. The police officer introduced me, and I expressed my sympathy for his loss. Normally when you first meet a family member, they want to know about the cause the crash, and

73

maybe something about the investigation process. If they don't know what to ask, I take the lead and assure them they can have confidence in our investigation – we're going to do everything we can – that type of thing.

Not this time. In his grief, all this young man wanted was to go see his dad, and he asked me that straight away. I went into full professional mode – no emotion – all business. I told him that my investigators were still on the site. It would not be possible for him to enter the investigation zone – I was not prepared to allow that. It would cause a distraction to the people who needed to collect evidence there. This was a formal investigation, and I was not prepared to have it compromised. Once again, I offered my quick condolences. Then, I turned and walked out of the room, leaving the police to handle the emotional aftermath.

A small part of me wanted to turn and run back in and give him a hug and tell him I had changed my mind. I felt so incredibly bad for this young man. He was heartbroken from the loss of his dad, and now he was doubly heartbroken because he couldn't be with him. Maybe he thought he could help somehow, I don't know. Most certainly he thought it was his place to be there. I had prevented that, and both of us would have to live with the consequences. I waited until the police officer came out. We never spoke much. We just went to the car and drove back to the site.

The coroner arrived, and I gave him the go-ahead to remove the body. I informed him that we would need an autopsy. He said that he didn't need one for his purposes – he had declared the cause of death. Neither did the police require an autopsy. I told them that I needed to confirm there were no medical issues, and I needed testing for alcohol and drugs. The coroner said he would try to book a forensic pathologist. Roy had finished, and I gave permission to move the wreckage. They soon had that done using airport equipment. The airport was reopened.

The next morning Roy went to crate up the engine and arrange for its shipping. I went to interview a couple of eyewitnesses. Late in the morning I got a call from a pathologist who said he could do an autopsy later in the afternoon. He didn't sound too enthusiastic – I think he had been conscripted to this task – anyway, I could tell he didn't want to do it.

On bigger fatal accidents we would make sure we had a TC medical examiner available to coordinate the pathology. As a backup, we carried a sealed box in our go kit that we could give to a local pathologist. The box had a checklist of our specific requirements – things like what x-rays to take and what specific samples we needed to be tested. It had never been a problem to get a local pathologist to fulfil our needs.

This time was different. This pathologist told me that I could bring the box over, but if I wanted samples, I would have to get them myself. Needless to say, that was quite a shock. I contacted the police officer I had worked with. He said he would attend, but he wouldn't get our samples. I talked it over with Roy, and we concluded that for the integrity of the investigation we needed the samples. We decided that both of us would go to the autopsy, to support each other. Neither of us had attended an autopsy previously, and we could go through it together.

I will admit that curiosity spurred me on a bit. I had seen lots of accident sites, but this would be a new experience – something that could broaden my overall knowledge and make me more well-rounded. I can report that by the time it was over I had more than my fill of broadening. This is not something anyone should do simply out of curiosity. But duty called, and I hung in there. I toughed it out mostly because of my strong aversion to embarrassment. Leaving the autopsy room, or throwing up, would be embarrassing. We managed to get through our checklist, and we got our samples – that part was with more thanks to Roy than me.

The experience taught me much about the process and capabilities of clinical pathology, but nothing I experienced had any real application in my actual job. I vowed to never get roped into that duty again (I did – one more time, as you'll see later). To add further insult, the lab to which we sent the samples failed to appreciate our work. I got a nasty letter complaining that the samples we sent were not properly labeled, and that my incompetence had caused them no end of extra work.

The fact is, we hadn't labeled our samples at all. Roy and I missed that part of the instructions. The kit contained a few dozen condoms to put the samples in. It seems you're supposed to put each sample in one condom and tie it off. We did that. But then you're supposed put that first condom in a second one, and include a label saying what the sample was and where it was taken from. Who knew? We never saw the labels in the bag. Nobody had trained or briefed us. We just automatically assumed the lab would know what they were looking at. Anyway, they reported that all the samples were negative, so that closed off that part of the investigation.

We arranged to go to the pilot's lakefront cottage where he kept his aircraft. We made sure nobody would be there. He had a great setup where he could land on the lake wheels up, and then extend them and taxi up a sloped concrete ramp to a turntable. He used that to turn the aircraft around so he could taxi back into the lake for takeoff. Everything was spotless – no signs of oil leaks or anything. His aircraft logbooks showed all maintenance was up to date.

Everyone described him as very cautious and meticulous. He never pushed the weather; he was not a risktaker. He had been flying for years, and everyone thought he was the safest pilot you could imagine. It's not at all unusual to hear this kind of thing in a case like this. Here was a guy who by all accounts was a very fine gentleman. He flew because he loved it, and he tried to do it right. Nobody had any stories about close calls. Everyone saw him as a wonderful pilot.

Back at our shop we found a number of partially clogged fuel injectors in the engine. The misfiring and the engine's power loss would have come from that. This accident was from a classic cause. When the engine lost power, instinct told the pilot there was safe runway behind him. With that thought, he had attempted what's known as an "impossible turn" – a tight turn, at low altitude, with reduced power. Such a manoeuvre inevitably leads to an aerodynamic stall followed by a vertical spin to the surface. This accident was a classic example.

Here is another typical finding for this type of accident. This pilot's logbook showed he had not had any recurrent training for more than eight years. That's a killer. With regular training he would have been ready for this type of emergency – it would have been easy to handle. But without regular training, this pilot was safe only so long as nothing unusual happened, such as this engine issue. His neglect to get regular training had cost him his life.

From a personal experience perspective, I had two big takeaways from this investigation – the autopsy, and the encounter with the son. It's the circumstance with the son that I've thought most about over the years. I still question whether I made the right decision. I wonder what other people would have done – how others would have handled it. You don't have to be an accident investigator to deliberate about this. What would you have done?

My investigation work frequently involves trying to figure out why people make the choices they make. I've thought long and hard about what led me to keep that young man from seeing his father. As I was weighing things while trying to figure out what to do, I believed my choice could go either way.

I distinctly remember thinking that. But in reflection, I now recognize that I was pre-wired to make only one decision – the one I made. In fact, in looking back I recognize that I wasn't really deciding at all. What I was actually doing was gathering up the rationale to forgive myself for denying this young man his dearest wish in that tragic moment.

Logistically, it would have been easy for me to authorize the police to take him to see his dad. I wouldn't even have to be there. Either way, I would never see him again. I would never get any feedback as to how my decision affected him. But my makeup forced me to be concerned about his welfare, to protect him, in both the short and long term.

After I saw his dad in that cockpit, I distinctly recall these thoughts being in my brain. It would not be right to allow that cockpit scene be the last vision this young man had of his dad. If it was my dad, I wouldn't want that scene in my head for the rest of my life; neither would my dad want me to have it there. I wouldn't want my son to see me in that condition. Neither would this dead pilot want his son to see him in that condition. Right or wrong, those are the thoughts that sealed it for me.

After I knew what I was going to tell the young man, the rest was automatic. After telling him what I had decided, I'd be in no position to offer any meaningful comfort or support. There was no room for debate about my decision, and no channel to deliver the logic behind it. It had to be a clinical "no", and that's the way I delivered it. He would need someone with a cold heart to focus his anger at, and my gift to him was to let that person be me.

One of my granddaughters, who was maybe three years old at the time, told me she would like to write me a story. So, she launched into that, at her little table and chair, and I sat and watched it happen. I watched her write for a bit, and then think for a bit, and then write some more. She couldn't form actual letters or words, but eventually she had produced enough scribbles to present the final manuscript to me.

Naturally, I was most impressed with it, and I thanked her for her work. My question to her seemed appropriate – I asked her, "what does it say?" – She looked up at me with a quizzical look well beyond her years, and she answered, "I don't know – I can't read".

10

A PERSONAL TRAGEDY

In the previous chapter, I explained how I had made a decision to not allow a grieving son to visit the site where his father lay dead. I told about how I was predisposed to not allow him to be exposed to that circumstance. This story about a deep personal loss will shed light on my predispositions.

In 1976, Charlotte and I had settled in to our second new house as a married couple – it was a big step up from the first one. Entering that year, we were each 26 years old, and we had a two-year-old daughter to enjoy. In February, we found out that another child would arrive in November. I was still plugging away at the flying club – biding my time and waiting/hoping to join TC – but Charlotte had a good teaching job that paid the bills. All was well.

The new baby was due on 10 November – a Wednesday. I went to work that day – same as normal – my schedule was 6 a.m. to 3 p.m. Everything to that point had gone exceptionally well with the pregnancy. Charlotte had an appointment for a checkup. She could take herself, no problem. In those days there were no cell phones, so we couldn't stay in touch, but Charlotte was great at looking after herself. I was happy. A new baby would arrive any day, and I would get a couple of extra days off in a row – not too many days off though – it was a "no fly" "no pay" situation at the flying club.

When I got home, Charlotte was waiting for me – she had devastating news. After I had left that morning, when she got up things didn't feel right. Instead of constant movement in her belly, she felt the baby move only once – then nothing. Later, when she went for her scheduled checkup, her doctor said he couldn't find a pulse for the baby. He sent her to the hospital, where they confirmed that there was no pulse – the baby had died. They told her that the safest option was to wait for a natural delivery, and they sent her home. She had arrived home shortly before me. Thankfully, our two-year-old was staying with her grandparents.

What followed was the worst kind of misery. We had suddenly gone from great happiness and excitement and anticipation to the depths of despair. It was agonizing, passing the time together in grief, wondering what had gone wrong. We had to inform everyone – that was awful. We had the whole house set up for the new arrival – a room, a crib, baby clothes, diapers, toys, all the baby shower gifts – everything had to be factored in and be a part of how we would handle this loss.

And then we had Charlotte's condition to deal with. She was still pregnant – still waiting for mother nature to put her into labour, but there would be no baby to bring home. We went through five excruciating days before the labour pains came. We went to the hospital, and I waited in the waiting room with all the other expectant fathers. I never told any of them about our circumstance. I was happy for them.

We had decided we would not give the new baby a name – it would be called Baby Vance. And we decided we would not have a funeral. We brought a baby outfit for it to be clothed in, and it would go to the funeral home in that outfit. We made arrangements to have our baby buried at the head of the plot where its grandmother (Charlotte's mom) would one day be laid to rest.

Our little boy was delivered on Monday, 15 November 1976. We were asked if we wanted to see his body, but neither of us wanted to. That was not an image we wanted to carry with us – we would rather have memories of our anticipation of his arrival. Charlotte said she caught a glimpse of one of his legs, that's all. She said his skin looked normal. They told us that he had a full head of dark hair. He was fully developed, and he was a normal weight. They told us that he was breech – born feet first – and they said the umbilical cord was wrapped around his neck. The implication was that he had somehow strangled to death – or maybe the umbilical cord had gotten pinched – it was all beyond anyone's control, so it didn't much matter.

I decided I wanted to be there when our baby was buried – so he would not be there on his own. That would happen two days later, on Wednesday, 17 November. There would be no funeral, just a simple burial. My dad volunteered to go with me – just the two of us. We got to the cemetery about half an hour before the scheduled burial time. We parked where we could look across to see where the site had been readied.

At the appointed time we saw a funeral car arriving, and we walked over to the graveside. We saw where the hole had been dug at the head of the plot – the hole was covered with a small staging – there was a cloth covering the staging. We watched as two men from the funeral home walked towards us. One was carrying a tiny box. They walked to the little raised staging, and the one man placed the tiny box on top. Then he took a step back, and they both bowed their heads.

It was at that moment that I experienced the most intense emotion I have ever felt in my life – before or since. Nothing even comes close. I knew I was about to start crying – uncontrollably. I felt that kind of emotion that makes your face tense up, and your eyes squint – the kind that makes your head feel like it's about to explode. Then, all of a sudden, I found myself running – running as fast as I could. I remember that I wasn't running in a straight line – I was weaving left and right – I wasn't controlling that – I was just following where my leg muscles were taking me.

And then I was stopped – at no particular place – just stopped, and I was sobbing to where I could hardly breathe. In hindsight, this must have been the release of everything that I had been holding in over the previous week. To me, babies and children are the most precious things in life, and I had lost one, and it was too much to bear. Also, in hindsight, I recognize that it would have been incredibly embarrassing for me to have stood there at the graveside crying uncontrollably in front of my dad and the funeral home people.

After a bit, I felt the presence of someone, and I turned, and it was my dad. He didn't say anything, he just stood nearby – he was there with me. It took a while, but finally I got some control, and I started to walk back to the graveside – with my dad walking with me. We took up our previous positions. The funeral home guy finally spoke – he asked if we wanted to say anything, or if we wanted to be there alone for a while. I shook my head no. Then my dad spoke to thank the funeral home guys for their good work. I managed a thank you, and we turned and left them there, with the tiny box still on the staging. We walked back to the car, and we left. There was never a time when I appreciated my dad more than I did on that day.

To stay true to the theme of this book, I need to explain how this personal tragic experience has played out in my accident investigation career. It's very difficult to put that into context. My personal experience with the loss of Baby Vance had put me in a state of grieving that I judged to be at the limit of potential grief. Maybe I'm wrong – but I'm not sure there could be a place beyond where I was.

In my work, I've had plenty of exposure to people who were grieving the unexpected loss of someone close – including the loss of children, or multiple loved ones. I've interacted with people who I knew were in that place – the one where I had been. That young man who wanted to see his father in the wreckage – the one that I had stopped – he was in that place. There have been many others. Did it help in any way that I had been to that place myself? I'm not sure. One thing is for certain – when I encounter them, I have more understanding for where they are.

There's another element to the loss of Baby Vance that I think about sometimes in my work – specifically the work I do now that's connected to litigation – blame and liability. It wasn't long before Charlotte was pregnant again, and doing her regular checkup visits with the doctor. On one visit, the doctor left her alone in the examination room, and her medical file was there. She took the opportunity to have a look, and she saw something entirely shocking.

There was a note explaining a complicating factor with Charlotte being pregnant. Charlotte's blood is Rh negative. The note explained that she had already lost a baby due to Rh negative complications – a specific note said that after the birth of our first child she hadn't received the standard treatment – she should have received an injection of Rh immune globulin – a standard procedure needed to keep the next baby from harm. It was also obvious that she had not received proper blood screening during her second pregnancy. Baby Vance hadn't died from anything to do with the umbilical cord or the breech birth. He had died because of mistakes made by those we had trusted to look after things.

Charlotte didn't confront the doctor with her discovery. He hadn't been her doctor through all that. She brought the news home to me. Understandably, we were shocked. This was a classic case of negligence – a failure to use reasonable care – it led to the death of our baby. We had an option to go down a legal path, but that was not something we wanted to do. People had made mistakes, but we viewed them to be honest mistakes, made by people who cared about what they were doing – they were trying their best. We didn't see any point in raising a big stink about it. We decided to just let it drop.

In looking back at how we handled the negligence issue, I still agree with how we handled it back then. For us, it wouldn't have been right to file a lawsuit – to look like we were trying to profit off of our loss. And it didn't seem right to go about exposing good people to public scorn or embarrassment.

The thing that I was most disappointed in was that nobody in the medical system saw fit to tell us what had happened. If Charlotte hadn't snooped into her file, we would have remained in the dark about what had actually happened to cause the death of our baby. I guess it wouldn't have mattered much, but it's nice to know.

A couple of final thoughts about this. I do recognize that the loss of our son prior to his birth is different from a loss suffered in a tragic accident. Because I never got to know my son, I've not had to suffer the long-term grief that would be there if we had gotten to hold him, and nurture him, and raise him up, and make memories with him, and of him. I'm certain that my grief was just as deep, as I described, but for sure it wasn't as long-lasting.

Here's something else I'm certain about. We made the right decision to not view his body. I have always been able to visualize him in whatever way I want – we eliminated the chance that a flashback would ever interfere with that.

EXPERIENCE EMBARRASSMENT — GAIN EXPERIENCE

I will share with you my two most embarrassing experiences in accident investigation. Countless times over the years I've regaled my fellow investigators with these two stories. To me, they aren't the slightest bit funny, but they make for good accident site distractions when distractions are necessary. I also tell them to students at my investigator training courses, with the hope that they will avoid the embarrassments that I felt.

To make these two self-inflicted bungles even more memorable, each of them happened on foreign soil. This first one happened in Iceland in 1988. As you'll see later, the second one happened in Armenia in 2008 – they were 20 years apart.

WORLD-CLASS EMBARRASSMENT – CASE #1

Reykjavik, Iceland
CASA 212 Aviocar – Canadian Registration – C-GILU
2 August 1988 @ 17:42 Local Time

Roy and I went to Iceland to help investigate the crash of the above-mentioned CASA 212. That's a box-shaped high-wing aircraft, with two turboprop engines. In a passenger configuration, it has about 25 seats. This particular aircraft didn't have passenger seats like that. It had been extensively modified to do geophysical survey mapping. That's where they fly along and use magic technology to see below the earth's surface, looking for minerals and such.

The Canadian operator was ferrying the aircraft across the North Atlantic to France, where they had a contract. Two pilots and one technician were on board. They had left Ottawa, their home base, on 31 July 1988. They had planned fuel stops in Goose Bay, Narsarsuaq (Greenland) and Reykjavik.

Weather delays slowed them, and they finally departed Narsarsuaq for Reykjavik on 2 August 1988. Everything was good with the flight until something went terribly wrong as they were on their landing approach to Reykjavik's Runway 20. They lost control, and they crashed nose down about 900 feet short of the runway threshold. The violence of the crash killed all three occupants instantly. Then, there was a post-crash fire that destroyed most of the fuselage. It was a mess.

It so happened that around that time Roy and I had been going through a busy stretch of accident responses. We got word about the Iceland occurrence while we were flying home after looking into no less than three other occurrences over the previous four days – that's when Head Office relayed to us that we were needed in Iceland. The Icelandic authorities had asked Canada to lead the investigation. Head Office would send an IIC, and someone from the lab, and TC would send an observer, but they needed us to fill out the team (in other words, they wanted us to do the on-site investigation part). We landed, got some clean gear, and booked our airline travel to Iceland.

On a stopover, we met up with the team traveling from Head Office. We all arrived in Reykjavik on the same flight – on the day after the accident. We got briefed in, and we were told that weather hadn't been a factor during the approach. The pilots never made an emergency call. This was weird – the aircraft was close in on a stabilized approach when it suddenly went out of control and crashed. Obviously, something catastrophic had happened to the aircraft, and whatever it was, it had happened quickly. If it wasn't weather, the options would be an incapacitated pilot (unlikely, as there were two of them), or a mechanical failure, or a structural failure.

We knew of previous issues with the type of propeller governor that was on that aircraft. There had been instances in that model of aircraft where the propeller's blade angle suddenly changed to a reverse thrust pitch. When that happens, one engine is still trying to pull the aircraft forward – but the other one starts trying to push it backwards (propellers can be intentionally put in reverse thrust after landing – that helps to slow the aircraft down). If that asymmetric power condition happened in the air, the aircraft would be uncontrollable. With that knowledge, we had a lead hypothesis, but of course we would have to keep an open mind – we needed to look at everything.

They took us to view the wreckage. At that time of year in Iceland (early August) the daylight hours are long, so Roy and I changed into our worksite gear. We wanted to get as much done as possible on that first day. It wasn't long before everyone else left the wreckage site. Only three of us stayed; Roy and I, and a police officer for security. We were inside the airport's parameter fence, so security wasn't much of a problem.

The wreckage wasn't spread out. The fuselage had crumpled in length wise, indicating the impact angle had been quite steep. There had been an intense fire, but the rescue people had put it out before everything was completely consumed. We set about completing the initial documentation, getting our photos and measurements and the like.

They had already removed two of the bodies. The third body was still there, but they had not been able to locate it in the wreckage. After we had completed our basic documentation, Roy and I concentrated on finding and removing the third victim. We soon found remains, which were difficult to differentiate from the scorched surroundings. Their coroner's office sent a response vehicle and two attendants, and they took away what we removed.

The wreckage site was maybe 200 yards inside the airport's parameter fence. Just outside that fence was one of the main highways serving the city. The crash had made the local news, and our activities had drawn quite a crowd of onlookers. We weren't bothered by that, as nothing we were looking at was confidential – nothing much was even identifiable. In actual fact, we felt quite proud to display our work, and to show off the big CASB lettering on the back of our coveralls. It let everyone in Iceland know that Canadians had come to look after their own.

We tried to look at the propeller blades on each engine to see if we could determine what blade angle they were at when they hit. We couldn't make any determinations on the spot. That would have to wait until the next day when we would bring in some equipment to move things around for a better look. We figured that if everything went right, we could get all the wreckage recovered the next day.

Before we left to go back for the evening wrap-up meeting, I took some time to sketch out in my notes the position of the wreckage in relation to the runway centerline. The crash site was slightly right of the runway centerline. But there was something odd. The heading at impact was 90-degrees to the runway centerline. It looked like the pilots were trying to get back to the centerline, but why would they be closing on it at a 90-degree angle. How could that happen?

I remember feeling right at the top of my game; I was good at this. I had the "look at me" excitement from seeing the people outside the fence watching what I was doing. I think I even looked towards the sky and added some subtle arm and hand gestures, like I could visualize the track of the aircraft through the air. I was the expert doing this great thinking. I was into it, that's for sure.

It came to me that the only logical sequence would be this: on final approach the right propeller governor failed, and the prop went into reverse. The asymmetric thrust caused a sharp right turn and a steep descent. The pilots managed to start a left turn back towards the runway, but the prop came out of reverse and they overshot the turn. That's how they ended up going 90 degrees to the centerline. I sketched all this out, and took it with me to the evening meeting.

All the people you would expect to be there were at the meeting. Along with our entire team, there were representatives from the Icelandic aviation authority, the police, the airport, first responders, and so on – a pretty large group. When it came my turn to speak, I briefed on what we had done at the wreckage site, and what we had planned for the next day – all standard stuff. Then I gave them my thoughts about what must have led to the aircraft being where it was, with references to my sketch. I went to bed that night feeling pretty good about what we had accomplished.

The next day the same group got together for the morning briefing. They started with a briefing from the police – they reported on the results of a request through the media for witness information. It turns out that this accident had happened during the evening rush hour, and there were hundreds of eyewitnesses. They were in their cars – slowed by the standard evening traffic jam along the highway – hundreds of them saw everything that had happened. They saw the aircraft fly over them on approach, and then go out of control, and then crash.

They all reported seeing the same thing. The aircraft was on a normal looking glideslope to the runway – then it suddenly entered a steep right turn. It continued in its right turn, all the way through a full 270 degrees – then it entered a steep descent, and it struck the ground. That's how it got to be flying at 90 degrees to the centerline. My vision of there being a right-turn followed by a left-turn – the one I had briefed them on – was completely wrong – it was blown out of the water.

As I listened to the police officer's briefing, I had a feeling come over me that was truly frightening. It was some mixture of shock, anxiety, disbelief, despair, humility, and disappointment in myself. Very quickly, I formed a clear vision of how this professional disaster had happened to me. It was pure vanity. I knew better. I was experienced. I knew how imprudent it was to put forth a "feeling" about what I thought had happened. But despite all that, there I was, feeling foolish and exceptionally embarrassed. Somehow, I had succumbed to some ego-driven need to show this group how much better I was at this than everybody else, and especially my Head Office teammates.

When the police officer finished, I stood up and asked to speak next. I can remember my words sufficiently to paraphrase them here, as follows:

> At last evening's meeting, I briefed you on what my investigation in-
> stincts told me about the track line for the aircraft. Obviously, I was
> wrong about that, but far more importantly I was wrong in making

that guess. That's not how proper accident investigation is done. I was asked to come here because I have experience enough to know what to do. Instead of showing you how it's done right, I gave you a perfect example of how to do it wrong. The worst thing you can do as an investigator is to lead with your best guess. You shouldn't even have a best guess – or even develop a secret best guess in your head. That makes you vulnerable to looking only for evidence to support your guess. I've seen that happen to others, and I try my best to not let it happen to me. I already realize that I was motivated by trying to look good in front of you, to pump up my ego, and instead, I'm embarrassed because I look like such an amateur. I am very sorry for that. Thankfully, I'm certain that together we'll be able to figure out what happened to cause this accident. If you take away anything from this investigation, please remember how embarrassed I feel right now. Never allow yourself to get into a situation like this – it feels terrible. Roy and I will be working at the site today and we expect to have the wreckage ready to be recovered by tomorrow.

And with that, I sat down. There was a bit of silent time before the head Icelandic guy spoke up to say that he was very confident we would get to the truth. We all moved on with the rest of the meeting.

On the brighter side, I was pleased with myself for mustering up the courage to make that little speech. Maybe it was over the top, but for me it was cathartic. At this investigation, this entire issue just died away – nobody commented on it. Years later, I met one of the Icelandic guys who had been there – we met at an investigation seminar. He told me about how much of a favourable impression my confession speech had made on their team, and on him in particular. It made me feel good that he had remembered it. I can assure you I have not put myself in that predicament again.

Roy and I spent the rest of the day at the accident site documenting and separating the wreckage. That evening, they brought in some heavy equipment, and we moved the bigger pieces out. We packed up the engines and propellers for shipment back to our Lab for teardown. There was lots of smaller debris still left at the site, and the next morning we went there to clean it up and move it out. We were careful to find even the smallest pieces, not wanting to leave any Canadian debris on the Icelandic landscape. We could tell that our fastidiousness impressed them, and that made us feel good.

Just to close out this accident for you, at our Lab we found an incorrectly installed speeder spring in the right propeller governor. In the right circumstances, this would cause large fluctuations in the power output of the right engine, and basically make the airplane unflyable. We found other irregularities with the operation that were not directly related to the crash. Neither pilot had a valid instrument rating, and yet they filed an instrument flight plan. They were 3,000 pounds over the allowable gross weight when they departed Narsarsuaq. On approach to Reykjavik they used 25 degrees of flap when the maximum allowed by the flight manual was 10 degrees. This did not reflect well on Canadian standards for this type of operation – it was kind of embarrassing, actually.

I'll share a personal anecdote about being in Iceland. I never had an opportunity to get any of their local currency before I arrived there. From the start, the Icelandic authorities looked after all the logistics, and they provided all the transportation, and they covered the meals and accommodation costs. It ended up that I never had time to buy souvenirs. As per normal, I never went out to any bars or anything like that. On my way home, I realized that during my entire time in Iceland I never actually spent any money at all. Maybe I'm the only person who can say that they travelled to Iceland and stayed for 5 days without spending a single penny.

WORLD-CLASS EMBARRASSMENT – CASE #2

Yerevan, Armenia
Bombardier CRJ-100ER Regional Jet – Belarus Registration – EW-101PJ
14 February 2008 @ 04:19 Local Time

My embarrassment in Armenia in 2008 was even more acute than the one in Iceland. The aircraft that crashed was Canadian designed and built, so Canada sent an Accredited Representative (me) to help with the investigation. I had two experts from Bombardier with me as Technical Advisors.

This was a scheduled flight operated by a Belarus carrier, Belavia Belarusian Airlines. There were 3 crew and 18 passengers on board. Nobody was killed, but there were serious injuries and the aircraft was extensively damaged. Armenia, as a member of the Post-Soviet states, asked that the investigation be conducted by the Interstate Aviation Committee (IAC), based in Moscow.

I travelled from Canada to Yerevan with the main Bombardier representative, I will call him Johnny. He was relatively new to his job at Bombardier, and I had not worked with him before. I had asked around, and some people said that Johnny was a bit quirky and hard to control. They said you had to keep him reined in. Let me say here that I found Johnny to be very dedicated, knowledgeable and helpful. He was a bit quirky all right – kind of impulsive – you never knew what he was thinking or about to do – but I enjoyed his quirkiness. He was entertaining and funny, and a great guy to travel with. Somewhere during a stopover, I think in London, we were joined by a pilot specialist from Bombardier who I will call Leonard – a quiet guy, but also very knowledgeable.

Johnny knew me by reputation, which was a good thing. Jim Donnelly, and others at Bombardier, had told him stories about how I had worked on a bunch of high-profile investigations, and how we had all worked together many times over the years. On the way over to Armenia, I had lots of opportunity to implant in Johnny (in a very nice way) the rules he had to follow if he wanted to stay a part of my team. Given his reputation, I laid it on pretty thick.

There would be no room for freelancing. When our team had anything to say, I would say it. I needed his input, but not his voice. If he wanted to touch or move anything, he needed to get a nod from me first. All of his creative ideas, suggestions and impulses were to be held in check until they were vetted through me. During our entire time over there, I watched Johnny fight to keep himself in line – you could see it physically, in his expressions and twitches. He did a great job with that, for the most part.

When we arrived, we went straight to the wreckage site where we met up with a couple of officials from Armenia. One of them, who I will call Bared, spoke halting English, and he briefed us in. He told us that the IIC, whose name was Boris, was from Russia. Boris had left instructions that we could look at the wreckage, and do all the documentation we wanted, so long as we didn't disturb anything. That was fine – it was standard practice.

The wreckage was about two-thirds of the way down the runway from where it had started its takeoff run – it was off to the right side of the paved surface. The infield on either side of the runway had a covering of light patchy snow. The aircraft's tail had detached, but the rest of the aircraft was mostly in one piece. It had come to rest inverted, with its landing gears sticking straight up in the air. There had been a fire, and the fire had weakened the wing root structures allowing the wingtips to droop down. The right wingtip was actually touching the ground.

You could readily see the direction from which the aircraft had come. There were scrape marks where it had been sliding on its top (upside-down) for quite some distance. Looking back from the wreckage, the scrape marks went all the way across the runway, where they disappeared into the patchy snow on the other side. Bared told us that there were markings in the infield all the way back to where the aircraft had initially departed the left side of the runway, several thousand feet away. I remember thinking that it must have been a merry old ride (that's a down-east expression – it means "terrifying") for those poor passengers, especially when they ended up hanging upside-down from their seatbelts in the dark.

Bared briefed us on the history of the occurrence. The aircraft had arrived in Yerevan as scheduled at about two o'clock in the morning. The planned layover was two hours, and during that time it was refuelled. The departure was on time. Boris and his troops had found the first ground scar left by the aircraft. The scarring showed that on takeoff the left wingtip had made contact with the ground at the runway's left edge. That meant that for some reason the aircraft had banked very steeply to the left as it lifted off. The trail of marks down the infield showed that the aircraft never really went airborne, other than maybe for a few short hops. Obviously, at some point it had flipped inverted before sliding across the runway to a stop.

That evening, we went to the daily wrap-up meeting where we were introduced to Boris and the others. The room was full up. Boris had his own team of about five. The Armenians had three or four investigators of their own, including Bared. Then there were representatives from other agencies, such as the airport, the police, crash fire rescue, air traffic control, and the operator. All this was normal. Boris gave his opening briefing, and then all the others gave their input, including me.

Right away it was apparent that we would have language issues. Barad was the only one in the room who could translate for us, and his English was not that strong. It was awkward, but we managed.

They had a working hypothesis about what had happened, and Boris briefed us about that. I will spare you any intrigue and tell you that they were correct in what they came up with. The left wing stalled aerodynamically at liftoff because it was contaminated with a thin layer of frost that had built up while the aircraft was parked on the ramp. The frost formed due to the temperature difference between the ambient air (-3°C) and the very cold fuel (-21°C) that was pumped into the wing tanks during the refuelling. (This is a well-known phenomenon that was also a player in the crash of Arrow Air Flight 1285 in Gander, Newfoundland in 1985 – as part of that investigation I surveyed a number of similar refuellings in Gander.)

As this initial meeting progressed it didn't take long to figure out that Boris was not going to be easy to deal with. He had an agenda. It was his intention to expose the inadequacies of the certification system that allowed the CRJ-100 model to be certified in the first place. It was easy to read his body language when he expressed his contempt for the deficient "western" procedures – referring to the certification procedures in the United States, Canada and Europe.

His contention was that this model aircraft was hazardous because it was not equipped with wing leading edge devices to improve its aerodynamic performance at lower speeds. In his view, this left the aircraft much more susceptible to an aerodynamic stall if there happened to be even a minimal amount of contamination – the margin of safety was too narrow. In his view, in allowing this high-speed wing design, the "west" had sacrificed safety in the name of increased profit.

In one sense, Boris was correct. The wing design on the CRJ-100 left no margin for ice contamination. But what Boris was failing to recognize was the adoption of the "clean aircraft concept" that mandated the removal of any and all frozen contamination prior to takeoff. That is where the margin of safety was regained.

As the meeting progressed, Boris started to aggressively question Johnny about why Bombardier failed to put high-lift devices on this model. I gave Johnny the nod to go ahead and answer, and I was pleased with how he conducted himself. He was very patient while pointing out that Bombardier had followed all the standard protocols in the certification process, and met all the requirements, and that the aircraft had a good track record in service.

But Boris wouldn't let up on poor Johnny. Finally, I spoke up. I let Boris know in no uncertain terms that we were not there to take part in this type of interrogation. I told him that I was not there to protect Bombardier from legitimate investigation activities. I was committed to making sure Boris and his team could get to the bottom of what happened, and I would help him to find out if Bombardier had any shortcomings, but things had to be done according to normal international protocols, and what he was doing did not meet those standards. I told Boris that I had been at these types of meetings all over the world, and what he was doing would not be accepted at any of them.

I could only hope that that is what was getting through to Boris via Bared's translation services. I expect it was, because I could tell that Boris got pretty steamed. He spent some time mumbling with his cohorts, after which he dropped his pecking at Johnny and got on with the rest of the meeting, which was uneventful. After the meeting, Johnny expressed his gratitude for me standing up for his right to not get attacked.

At the morning meeting I made a request that we be allowed to walk the length of the ground markings. We wanted to get our own perspective on what they might reveal. Boris said there was nothing much to see. He said they had found burned wreckage pieces along the trail that indicated a fire had started shortly after the left wingtip struck, but they found nothing else of any significance. He said it would be an inconvenience for us to go there because they would have to close the runway. After I persisted, Boris gave in and granted us his permission. They would close the runway for a couple of hours.

An airport worker drove us to the spot where the first markings started. He left us there – me, and Johnny, and Leonard. We could see the wreckage away off in the distance, on the other side of the runway. Even after three days the marks were still quite visible. You could see them in the skiffs of snow, and in the grass covered ground.

We took photos of where the left wingtip had gouged the hard surface at the runway's edge. After we had walked for a bit Johnny spotted a small piece of burned material. We figured they must have missed it in their sweep of the trail. Johnny picked it up so we could deliver it to them when we got to the wreckage site. As we walked further along the trail, we came across more pieces with burn markings, and we picked those up too. By the time we got to the main wreckage, we each had several pieces we were carrying like little gifts we could present to them.

When Boris spotted us with the wreckage pieces, he went ballistic. We didn't need Barad to translate what he was saying. It immediately swept over me that we had committed the greatest possible sin at an accident site. We had completely destroyed the evidence trail Boris needed to trace back to the origin of the fire. Obviously, they knew all these pieces were there – they had left them there on purpose. They had yet to complete their plot plan and documentation work to see what came off first, and then in what succession. With our actions, we had eliminated their opportunity to do that. We couldn't even offer to take all the pieces back to where we found them, because we never kept track of that.

At the first sign of shock from Boris, all the above came to me instantly. I was overwhelmed with a combination of panic and guilt and shame, all at an intensity that I had never felt before. This was embarrassment on steroids – an international embarrassment – much worse than Reykjavik. All I kept thinking was how could I have been so stupid that I allowed this to happen. It was easily my lowest point as a professional investigator.

Lucky for us that Boris finished up raging at us quickly. He knew we couldn't understand him, and he probably felt we were too stupid to take it in anyway. He just walked away, wanting nothing more to do with us. We found a container to put the pieces in, and then the three of us huddled to figure out what we should do. We didn't have our own transportation, so we never really had more than one choice. We went to work finishing up our documentation of the wreckage. After a bit, Boris and some others left. The tension dissipated, and things returned to normal.

I remember sitting down to figure out what had gone wrong. It came to me that an overarching factor that allowed this clown show to evolve was that I went into this project thinking that investigators over there were less capable than we were. Over the years, I had gone to a number of investigations in far-flung places where that had been the case.

When Johnny came upon that first tiny piece of burned material and picked it up, it had occurred to me that he shouldn't have done that. It was impulsive of him, and if he had asked me first, I might have thought to tell him to leave it in place. I know I would not have picked it up myself, but the fact that Johnny did it seemed to make it okay. At the very least, by my nature I was not inclined to make a big deal out of it.

In not stopping Johnny, I was rationalizing that Boris and his team had simply missed that little burned piece during their inspection along the trail. It was either that, or they didn't go to the bother of recovering it. Certainly, it must not have been important to them, because if they were going to leave it there on purpose, standard practice would have had them mark it with a little flag or something. It never occurred to me that we would find other items like that, so we just walked on.

As we found the additional pieces, I got even more convinced that Boris and his team had simply done careless work. This stuff had been laying there for three days. If we were in charge, we would have never allowed it to be subjected to the elements for that long. Some of it was light enough to be carried away by a brisk wind. It could even disappear down into the longer grass as the snow melted (like the situation with the F20 material in Goose Bay).

Most certainly, it never occurred to me that they were still planning to document and inspect all these pieces as an investigation exercise – so they could chase down how and when the fire started. But that's what Boris was apparently telling us, in no uncertain terms, language barrier aside. At that point I had already been in the investigation business for 24 years, and that episode in Yerevan reinforced in me the most powerful lesson in accident investigation. Don't make assumptions, and don't disturb anything without permission. I take every opportunity to pass that experience along to other investigators, and I always use it during my investigation courses. I hope it scares every other investigator to their core.

Boris was unexpectedly nice to us at the evening meeting. Looking back, I think he had a plan to give us a little poke. He proposed that we go to Moscow to be there for the readout of the flight data recorders. That would be standard, and we had a right to be there when the recorders were examined anyway, but it was nice of him to invite us first. The flight was leaving the next morning, and none of us had the required visas for entering Russia. Boris said that was not a problem. He would give me a formal letter that would allow us to get our visas upon arrival.

We had lots of trouble at the Aeroflot departure gate in Yerevan. The agents wouldn't let us board without visas, even with Boris' letter. Boris intervened by phone, and he convinced some airport official to let us on board. I remember the official taking us on the run through back passageways to get to the airplane – they actually had the airplane buttoned up, so they had to reopen the door to get us on board. I was surprised to see they were using a newer model Boeing 737, and we had a good flight to Moscow – about 2.5 hours.

I was expecting that we would be met at the arrival area by someone from the Interstate Aviation Committee (IAC), or at least someone who would have our visas ready. Instead, we had to make our way to the customs control area and join the lineup to pass through a customs checkpoint. It took more than an hour to make our way to the front of the line. We had only one letter for the three of us, and we decided that we would not approach the checkpoint together. Johnny volunteered take the letter and go up first, but I thought better of that and went first myself, handing over my passport and the letter to the customs officer.

The lady glanced at the letter for no more than three seconds before crumpling it up and tossing it towards an overflowing trash can in the corner of her booth. She flicked quickly through my passport before barking in my direction, "visa?". I immediately pointed toward the trashcan where the letter from

Boris had zoomed. It was now hopelessly lost in the pile of similar looking crumpled throwaways. For a second time, she barked out, "visa?". All I could do was give the international signal for "hopelessly confused" – giving her the shrugged shoulders, arms out to the side, palms up, strained brow, with a gesture towards the trash corner.

She would have no more of this from me. She gave a signal, and within seconds I was under the marching orders of a uniformed officer with a menacing-looking military weapon at the ready. He gestured with the barrel of the weapon for me to move smartly towards the rear of the foyer where we had first joined the line.

After I took a step or two, I gestured towards Johnny and Leonard, who were giving it their all to indicate they were with me. The guy picked up on that, and he allowed them to join me in my quick march. We reached an area at the rear of the foyer, where there were a few chairs. He gave us hand gestures – like the ones you use to train a puppy – for sit, and stay. We were in a pickle.

As I thought about it, I couldn't help wondering whether Boris had something to do with this. Maybe his letter said we were imposters who deserved the gulag and nothing less. If it did, those words must have been in the subject line, because the customs officer never read the rest of it. I concluded that Boris was probably not directly responsible, but for sure he didn't do much to help. I considered that with this, he and I were now even.

As we sat there, it didn't take long for me to remember that while we were still on the aircraft, I had needed to go to the washroom. I decided to postpone that until after we landed. As it turned out, that was not a good decision. After about an hour sitting there, I really had to go bad. I could see a washroom only a short walk away, and maybe that made it worse.

The guard with the gun had not taken his eyes off of us. When I knew he was focused on me, I pointed toward myself, then walked two fingers across my hand, and pointed at the washroom. I gave him my best "I'm suffering here" look and started to get up. It actually startled me when he turned the weapon a bit in my direction and gave me a loud "nyet". I was quick to settle back into my seat.

A very uncomfortable three hours later there was a shift change for our guard. His replacement had a similar weapon, but a much better disposition. It wasn't long before I tried the same gesturing with him, and when I pointed at the washroom, he flipped his gun barrel in that direction, and I squirmed my way over there. Needless to say, I was most relieved. It wasn't long before Johnny and Leonard followed in succession.

With this new guard we felt more comfortable to talk among ourselves. Leonard's cell phone had a connection, and he phoned home to Bombardier. They told him that when we never checked in, they had called their Moscow field representative (who spoke Russian), and he was now at the airport tracking us down. Leonard then made direct contact with this guy. He told him where we were, and asked him to check at security.

He quickly found out that our visas had actually been issued, and they were being held on the domestic side of our customs checkpoint. But of course, we had not made it that far, having been turned back by the lady who threw our letter away. It wasn't long before the new guard marched us through the checkpoint without any further questioning, and we were free to go. Apparently, we had spent over four hours in detention because of some bureaucratic miscommunication. I'm not sure when we would have gotten out of there if Bombardier had not had their field representative based there.

The next morning, we went to the IAC Headquarters to sit in on the readout of the recorders. Their head of investigations, a man named Alexei, came to greet us. I had met Alexi a couple of times previously, during investigations and conferences. I think the fact that I knew him personally gave me some credibility with the other investigators.

Alexi took us to the briefing room where their experts had gathered. I'm not sure if everyone Alexi had assembled there was actually working this case – perhaps he was just putting on a show – but the people gathered there were an amazing group. Alexi introduced each of them, and he went through their history and credentials.

Everyone was a top specialist with doctorates in this and that. There was one older gentleman who had been the lead design test pilot on something like 80 different models – one guy was the chief designer of some of the most powerful jet engines ever developed – there was a designer of spacecraft – it went on and on. There was enough military insignia to light up the room, and a good number of those hats with the big round tops that are all the style over there. When I introduced myself, I skipped over the formal education part. They don't give out a certificate for completing grade 11.

No surprises came out of the Moscow meetings. They gave Bombardier more grief about their aircraft being so susceptible to ground icing, but their inputs were not overdone. As to the causes of the crash, they uncovered a miscalculation in the pilot's calculated takeoff speed, and weaknesses in how the pilots were instructed to do their ice checks prior to departure, but their primary focus was the takeoff with contamination, which caused the left wing to stall and hit the ground.

Johnny, Leonard and I had a couple of evenings in Moscow to take in the sights. We went to check out Red Square and the Kremlin, and we walked the streets around the center of the city. It was all most impressive, even in the cold of mid-February. Johnny bought an ushanka hat so he could mix in better with the Muscovites. It also increased his confidence to lead us to where we shouldn't be. We had lots of laughs, the most memorable being when, during a menu exchange at a classy restaurant, we burned a hole in the nice white tablecloth. We investigated how that happened, and concluded that those little yarn tassels that hang from menus can be easily ignited by a table candle.

I left Moscow with a much deeper appreciation for the expertise they have over there, and with a deep sense of humility after finding out that I could still make fundamental mistakes even after so many years in the business.

One time I was with my oldest daughter and her family visiting on the east coast – back where we came from – in southern New Brunswick. We took a car ride to travel a route to where my wife's parent's cottage had been, all those years ago. I was in the back, entertaining my two little granddaughters.

We were travelling along the old rural road I had travelled so many times, and I was reminiscing – pointing out all the things that I remembered. We came around a corner to yet another view, and I said, "Look at that – I remember that – and after all these years it looks exactly the same". To which the youngest inquired, "But wasn't everything back then just black and white?"

12

A REMOTE LOCATION – SAME INVESTIGATION TECHNIQUES

I'll tell you about one of my most unique and interesting investigations. This one involved another CASA 212 Aviocar, the same type as the one in Reykjavik. This accident happened on 2 September 2011 just off the coast of Robinson Crusoe Island, Chile. The aircraft was being operated by the Chilean Air Force. Basically, the pilots lost control while they were trying to land at the island's airport in very gusty wind conditions. The aircraft dove into the ocean, killing all 21 occupants – most of the passengers were civilians.

Robinson Crusoe Island is one of three islands that make up the Juan Fernandez Islands in the South Pacific Ocean. About 850 people live there. It's 416 miles west of the Chilean coastline, making it one of the most remote inhabited places in the world.

This investigation is a great example of how the mysteries of a complex accident scenario can be solved using tried and true investigation techniques, even if you don't have a Flight Data Recorder (FDR) or Cockpit Voice Recorder (CVR). This aircraft crashed literally in the middle of nowhere. We had no recorded radar tracking data, or any other recorded performance information. Neither did we have any recorded communications. Despite these limitations, the conclusions we reached were widely accepted, and the investigation was deemed to be highly successful.

With this investigation, I'll take the opportunity to demonstrate how accident investigation is done. This book wouldn't present a full reflection of my investigation career unless I included some detail about how evidence is found. Therefore, I'll lay this one out in enough detail to show all the sources of information that are available, and how everything must be knit together to make a solid case. I'll do my best to present the information in non-technical terms, so I don't lose the non-aviation folks. Personally, I think it makes for very entertaining reading, but this has been my life's work, so maybe I'm biased.

First, I have to explain how I got involved in this investigation. After I retired from the TSB in January 2009, I joined Accident Investigation & Research (AIR), which was based here in Ottawa. AIR had been founded in 1984 by my good friend Terry Heaslip. Terry, along with his team of Robin (Robbie) McLeod and Steve Roberts had developed a relationship with CASA (the manufacturer of the accident aircraft) by providing them with independent accident investigation services. At the time that this accident happened, CASA had become part of the Airbus Consortium, but I'll continue to call them CASA.

Just for context, Terry and I are no longer part of AIR. We do the same kind of work, but our partnership now operates as HVS Aviation, and includes Elaine Summers – Elaine is an aircraft maintenance engineer and a highly experienced investigator – she joined us after retiring from the TSB. (By the way, HVS = Heaslip/Vance/Summers)

Normally, if a military aircraft crashes, the military conducts their own investigations. But in this case, with the civilian deaths, and in a move to maintain public confidence, Chile's President designated a civilian judge to oversee the entire investigation response. The judge set up two independent investigation teams, the standard one to be led by their Air Force Investigation Board, and the other to be led by CASA. In November 2011, two months after the crash, CASA contracted AIR to assist with their investigation, and Terry and I travelled to Santiago on 7 December 2011. We worked on this investigation there for eight days.

CASA had already brought in some very competent people. They had their own experts – people who knew the aircraft inside out. Then they brought in experts from the propeller manufacturer (Dowty Rotor from the UK), and from the engine manufacturer (Honeywell from the USA). It's obvious what these specialist experts were there for – I needn't go through that – but I can report that they did excellent work, as they always do in these circumstances.

Terry and I were tasked to carry out a full analysis of the aircraft's movements leading up to the sea surface contact. Specifically, they asked us to do a complete wreckage analysis, and to work that backwards into a reconstruction of the flight path. We were to answer these two questions. One, what was the aircraft's speed and attitude when it struck the water? And two, was it a mechanical failure that caused this, or did the pilots simply lose control? We were to write our own independent report, and include analyses, findings and conclusions.

This tasking was right in our wheelhouse. Both Terry and I had plenty of experience doing this exact kind of work. Terry started investigating in 1964, and he is a world-renowned accident reconstructionist. He had done many water-impact accidents. Unlike me, Terry took the time to formalize his education – he actually got some certificates. Among them are: Master of Applied Science – Professional Engineer – Degree in Metallurgical Engineering – Diploma in Aeronautical Engineering – Degree in Materials Science – etc., etc.

He doesn't flaunt his certificates; he just hangs them in his office where they can be easily seen – I do the same with my calendar and my clock.

I also felt comfortable taking this on. I had worked on a few water-impact accidents, the most high-profile one being the crash of Swissair 111 in 1998. I was with that investigation from beginning to end, helping to extract and analyse the evidence available from the wreckage pieces.

As indicated above, this crash in Chile was a high-profile event. Eighteen months previous, a major earthquake and tsunami had caused severe damage on Robinson Crusoe Island. The accident flight had been arranged jointly by a non-government organization (NGO), and National Chilean Television to take this group there. They were to film a segment about the progress of the reconstruction. Two particularly high-profile individuals were among the dead – one was Chile's leading TV personality – and the other was the broth-er-in-law of Chile's Defense Minister. For the Chilean Air Force, this flight was a humanitarian gesture to help with relief fundraising efforts.

The military investigators briefed us on what they knew. The aircraft was up to date with its maintenance, with no outstanding defects reported. The flight planned time to the island was 2 hours 40 minutes, but unexpectedly strong head-winds had pushed that to 2 hours, 57 minutes. Their fuel load gave them 3 hours, 35 minutes of total flight time, so we knew they hadn't simply run out of fuel.

The circumstance of this flight put the pilots in a unique situation. The dis-tance they had to travel, and the fuel load they carried, meant that they had no alternate airport. Once they got to Robinson Crusoe Island, they didn't have enough fuel to go anywhere else. They had no choice but to land. In their operating procedures, they deemed that to be acceptable.

On the day of the accident flight, they had delayed their departure waiting for a cold front to pass through the island. In the wake of the front, they would have good ceilings and visibility, but they would have very strong and gusty winds. The two pilots were properly qualified, but they lacked experience. The captain had only one previous flight to the island, and the co-pilot had never been there.

We heard (indirectly) that because this was a Friday flight, and one that wouldn't get back until late, it was turned down by the more senior crews. It slipped down the pecking order until it finally got to these junior pilots. It would be quite a challenge for them. And to make it even more challenging, for whatever reason the captain allowed the co-pilot to fly the aircraft from the captain's seat. We found that out by watching a recovered video tape shot from the passenger cabin by one of the passengers.

On 14 December, I went to Robinson Crusoe Island with some other members of the investigation team. Our small group included the judge who was overseeing the investigation. The Chilean Military flew us out there in a Canadian made de Havilland Twin Otter, a perfect aircraft for the job. I felt proud to be flying in this fine Canadian product. I felt even prouder when I found out it was the oldest Twin Otter in the world that was still in active service.

On the way out there, I remember reflecting on how incredibly interesting all this was. I thought about how far I had come from having that flying scholarship accidently fall into my lap so many years previous. My descriptions that follow are based on seeing the Robinson Crusoe Airport, and the surrounding area, firsthand.

The three islands in the Juan Fernandez archipelago were formed from volcanic eruptions. They're covered with steep and jagged mountains that can reach 3,000 feet high. At the water's edge, there are near vertical sea cliffs – the ones on the approach end of the runway they were trying to land on weren't quite vertical, but they were some 300 feet high. In every way, this is rugged territory.

The lone village, which I didn't get to visit, is on the opposite end of the island from the airport. Transportation from the airport to the village is by boat, and that takes more than an hour. Alternatively, you can walk, which they said takes five or six hours. Lots of people must walk, as evidenced by the well-worn path leading off into the hills.

The landing strip is very basic. On the plus side, it's straight, and relatively flat. It's sealed with low-grade asphalt. But it's only 3,304 feet long, and a mere 59 feet wide (for context, a typical runway at a more developed airport would be at least 6,000 feet long, and 200 feet wide). There are no electronic approach aids – all landings and takeoffs are done visually. I saw only one lonely windsock for pilots to check for wind direction and speed. The airport is completely unattended – there is no control tower. The airport chart warns about the steep cliffs at each end, and about the possibility of animals being on the runway.

The runway is oriented 14/32 – which means that by using runway 14 you are pointing southeast, and by using runway 32 you are pointing northwest. No matter which direction you choose for landing, it's like landing on an aircraft carrier – an aircraft carrier with a 300-foot-high deck. Your landing approach is over the sea, and then you pass over the cliff face, and then you arrive immediately at the button of the runway. Then, you have an extra incentive to get stopped, because if you don't, you soon come to the 300-foot drop at the other end.

On both sides of the runway there are hills sloping up, not nearly as dramatically as the seaside cliffs, but still enough to make you feel like you're in a kind of valley. All these geographical features create lots of trouble if you're trying to land in windy conditions, especially crosswinds.

On the day of the accident, there was one individual at the airport waiting for the flight. To watch for it, he went out on the ramp in front of the small support building that served as a terminal. That structure was on the west side of the runway, at about the runway's halfway point. This witness watched the aircraft arriving, and he described the aircraft's track based on his perspective standing on the ramp, facing the runway.

The witness said he saw the aircraft approaching from away off to his left, on the opposite side of the runway (arriving from the northeast). It was descending, and it turned to line up with runway 14. But he said it didn't seem to be trying to land on runway 14 – it was just doing a flyover – no doubt checking the windsock, and looking for animals. The wind was very strong and gusty, and the witness said it was coming from behind him (from the west), blowing almost straight across the runway at 90 degrees (this was a very strong and gusty crosswind). If anything, it seemed to be favouring a landing on runway 32 – that would give them a slight headwind component (or at least not a tailwind component).

It seems that's what the pilots figured out from looking at the windsock. He watched them fly the full length of runway 14 (passing by from his left to his right), and then turn to their right through about 45 degrees. That was the start of a teardrop maneuver, where they would reverse course and get lined up with runway 32. To do a teardrop, you track away from the centerline at a 45-degree angle – in this case they turned right – then you judge when you're laterally far enough from the centerline to make a turn (in this case to the left) all the way around to where you would be perfectly lined up on the centerline for your approach (in this case for runway 32).

The witness said that shortly after they turned right to start that teardrop, they disappeared below the cliffs. To disappear from the view of the witness, they had to be flying their teardrop at less than 300 feet above the water (that's very low – it's not normal). But we know they made it all the way through the teardrop because they reappeared to the witness when they were close in on the approach to runway 32.

The witness said they were too far to the right of centerline – they weren't properly lined up with runway 32, so they couldn't land (obviously, they had misjudged the timing during their attempted teardrop). He watched as they did another low-level flyover – this time from his right to his left. For this entire flyover of runway 32 they remained well off to the right of the centerline (this meant they were on the opposite side of the runway from where he was standing).

After they flew the full length of the runway, when they reached the end, they started a climbing left turn. This would be what they would do if they intended to fly a circuit pattern to try again to land on runway 32 – they would fly a standard left-hand circuit pattern.

Bear with me while I introduce some circuit pattern terminology for non-aviation people – terms that will be very helpful for describing what happened to this aircraft (it crashed while attempting to complete this circuit pattern). We will start with their climbing left turn after their flyover of runway 32:

CROSSWIND LEG:

- This is where you turn and fly at 90 degrees to the runway for a little while
- That gives you some lateral distance away from the runway

DOWNWIND LEG:

- When you get far enough away laterally, you turn left to fly downwind, parallel to the runway
- The downwind leg is normally flown at 1,000 feet above the elevation of the runway – this particular runway is 433 feet above sea level – this puts the circuit height at 1,500 feet (rounded off)
- On this downwind leg, you fly the full length of the runway – actually, you extend a bit past the end of the runway
- The trick here is to visually watch the runway, which would be off to your left
- You have to track far enough past the button of the runway to allow yourself enough distance to line up for a standard final approach

BASE LEG:

- At just the right spot on downwind, you make a left turn to once again fly perpendicular to the runway

- This base leg is where you make up the lateral distance you flew on the crosswind leg

- It's standard to start your descent from circuit height at about the same time you start your turn onto base leg

FINAL APPROACH:

- While on base leg, as you're closing in on the extended runway center-line, you start a left turn at just the right spot where you'll finish the turn lined up with the runway on final approach

- If you've judged your distances and turn spots correctly, you end up on a perfect glideslope to the button – with no dramatic adjustments necessary

Flying a circuit as described above is routine for every pilot. From the very start of their training, pilots learn to judge the right distances and turn spots and descent rates. In training, you go around the circuit so many times that the rhythm and timing of it get implanted into your head. The fundamentals of a circuit are the same for every aircraft type, but you have to adjust to account for your aircraft's speed and manoeuverability (you also have to account for the wind direction and speed – spoiler alert – extreme wind and turbulence played an important role in what happened in this event).

The witness on the ramp watched the accident aircraft do its left turn onto the crosswind leg and fly a normal distance away. He then saw the left turn onto downwind. He knew by how far the aircraft had flown on the crosswind leg that the downwind leg would be flown over the channel between Robinson Crusoe Island and nearby Santa Clara Island, a tiny island just off the coast.

He said that the aircraft didn't get too far along on its downwind leg before it disappeared from his view, hidden by the hills to the west of the airport. The hills would not have blocked his view if the aircraft had flown downwind at the standard 1,500 feet. To find out how low they must have been flying on their downwind leg, we had our Twin Otter pilots fly the same circuit. To be blocked from view on downwind, the accident aircraft must have been flying at less than 650 feet above sea level. The witness said that after the accident aircraft disappeared behind the hills, he never spotted it again.

We knew where the wreckage was found on the sea bottom, so that gave us the exact location where the aircraft had crashed into the water. With that, we confirmed they had completed their full downwind leg, and they had started their turn onto base leg. It was at some point during their turn from downwind onto their base leg that they lost control, and the aircraft plunged into the ocean.

When Terry and I arrived in Santiago, it had been more than three months since the accident. The military had recovered important pieces of the wreckage from the sea bottom, and they had them laid out on the floor of a hangar, kind of like a reconstruction. This layout had its limitations, because it wasn't three-dimensional (there was no frame to hang pieces on according to their height). Nevertheless, the layout gave us a visual depiction of the overall damage caused by the impact with the water.

Our first request was to have them reposition the pieces of each wing, and both of the engines. In their layout, they had placed all the stuff from the right wing where the left one should be, and vice versa. Then we set about looking for witness marks. These are marks (such as scratches, dents, abrasions, etc.) that are left behind on individual wreckage pieces – marks made during the impact when the pieces contact each other, or make contact with whatever else they might have struck during the impact.

Without getting into great detail, I'll present (in bullet form) some of the key evidence that we got from examining the wreckage – this is typical of what's available if you know how to look for it.

- From the wreckage in the hangar, and from examining underwater videos of the unrecovered wreckage, we confirmed that the aircraft had not experienced an in-flight breakup – we had pieces from all extremities of the aircraft in close proximity on the sea bottom – all flight control surfaces were accounted for – nothing had fallen off prior to impact.

- As happens during a high-energy impact, the fuel gauge indicator needles had slapped against their respective gauge faces. The "slap marks" that were created (as viewed through our field microscope) confirmed that the aircraft had not run out of fuel (the pilots had lots of fuel left to fly at least a few more circuits – they didn't have to land right away).

106

- The rotating parts within the engines left marks that proved both engines were developing at least medium (and more likely high) power when the aircraft entered the water.

- Damage to the propeller blades, and damage marks on the internal propeller gearing, confirmed that both propellers were rotating at normal speeds, with normal blade angles, at the time of impact. There was no chance that a runaway propeller was involved (such as what had happened in Iceland). The "slap marks" on the propeller RPM gauges also showed both propellers were within the normal range.

- The outer part of the left wing was smashed into tiny pieces. We found one small section of the left wing's leading edge that had been completely flattened. The left wingtip had been ripped off when it entered the water. We were able to conclude that the left wingtip was the first part of the aircraft to hit the water.

- Damage along the leading edge of the right wing confirmed that it had slammed into the water symmetrically. The right wing was broken into much larger sections. This told us that the right wing struck with far less energy than the left wing.

- The nose of the aircraft was destroyed at water impact – nothing was left of it. But the substantial support structure pieces that the nose broke away from were available, and they showed that before being broken to bits the nose structure had rotated 30 degrees to the right.

- The heavy ramp at the back of the aircraft had travelled forward into the fuselage.

- Interestingly, the skin from the top of the fuselage had been "rippled" as it was being ripped off by friction with the water surface. There was no such "rippling" in the bottom fuselage skin. This told us that when the aircraft entered the water it had already gone past 90 degrees of bank – in other words, the aircraft had gone inverted.

- Fractures and deformations on the vertical parts of the tail confirmed that when the tail entered the water the aircraft had gone completely inverted. But even though it was inverted, the aircraft still had lots of forward speed – enough to rip all these tail pieces off.

The investigator in me would like to go on with dozens more examples of the witness marks we found in this wreckage, but I recognize it might be overkill and you might zone out. Just so you know, Terry and I studied countless numbers of these marks, seeing what each of them could tell us. When you study them in that detail, they reveal an overall damage pattern that allows you to reverse engineer the crash dynamic sequence. When doing any wreckage analysis, you can literally start at the initial surface impact point (in this case the water) and back the aircraft up inch by inch to see its flight attitude just prior to impact. With that you can work on the sequence of events that would bring it to that pre-crash state.

Here is a summary of what our wreckage analysis uncovered. There were no pre-impact failures associated with the aircraft. When it struck the water, the pilots had totally lost control. The aircraft had rolled well past 90 degrees to the left while still airborne. It was still rolling hard to the left when the left wing entered the water, causing the aircraft to go completely inverted. There was a relatively high forward speed (over the water surface) at the time of impact, some of which was provided by the strong tailwind on base leg.

CASA worked with Madrid Polytechnic University to do extensive wind tunnel testing and flow modeling to assess the influence of the strong winds blowing around and over the mountainous terrain. They showed how there would be severe instability between the islands, including powerful down gusts. No doubt these conditions contributed to the loss of control. Perhaps these down gusts were enough to simply throw the aircraft out of control.

Personally, I believe there was another element in play – an illusion. If you're flying at a low altitude, and make a turn so that you introduce a strong tailwind, you have a situation where you're suddenly travelling much faster over the surface. If you're distracted, your brain interprets that increased groundspeed as a dramatic increase in airspeed – but of course there's only a dramatic increase in groundspeed – not airspeed.

In the case of our pilots, I think that when they turned onto base leg, they were looking outside to get visual contact with the runway. They didn't want the wind to push them to the right of the centerline like it did the last time when they flew the teardrop. I think they forgot to monitor their airspeed indicator, and they allowed their airspeed to get too slow, and at least part of their upset that turned them inverted was an aerodynamic stall – that combined with the extreme turbulence.

Regardless, we proved to everyone's satisfaction that the aircraft went out of control for purely operational reasons, and this accident was not due to some mechanical failure or other type of external intervention. And we did all this without having flight data recorders or any other type of electronic monitoring or tracking.

Unlike on other investigations, we had no mandate to look into the operational issues – in this case with the Chilean Military. In other investigations we look at things like crew selection and pairing, and their training and experience. Unofficially, we talked about why they would send two inexperienced pilots on such a treacherous mission. We questioned why these pilots chose to fly their procedures at such low altitudes – there was no apparent reason for that. Maybe the accident pilots thought it would be best to come at the "carrier landing" in level flight, rather than using a normal glideslope down to the button. That would be non-standard, for sure. What happened certainly had something to do with their training, or lack thereof, with the Chilian military – but it wasn't our mandate to look into that.

As a side note, with others from AIR I had the pleasure to instruct at two investigator training courses for Airbus Military (CASA). Both were held in Madrid, one of my favourite cities in the world. One training session was held prior to this accident, and the other one after. Investigations like this one in Chile are ideal for teaching how to extract information from wreckage, and how to integrate it into the overall picture.

Larry on Robinson Crusoe Island – 2011

Larry with the Chilean Military Twin Otter Aircraft
at Robinson Crusoe Island – 2011

The Chilean Military Twin Otter parked on the ramp at Robinson Crusoe Island – 2011

One day we had our three youngest grandkids over for a day of play. The oldest of the three had perfected a trick that she showed me – she took a deep breath, and then blew it hard against her closed lips and puffed out cheeks, and held it to where her face and neck turned a scary shade of deep red. It was actually quite impressive – I hadn't seen that shade of red before – I thought she might pass out.

When her younger cousin arrived, she went to show him. "Watch this", she said – "I can turn red". Then she went all out – her head was glowing red by the end of it. "Wow!!!" said her little cousin – "can you try green?".

13

CONSULTANT WORK – PROVING THE NTSB WRONG

As I mentioned before, I had an easy transition into consulting – that's because I joined AIR. They already had a solid client base and a worldwide reputation for quality work. But as time passed, and AIR's founders got older, we decided to shut AIR's offices and work from home. As I mentioned previously, three of us are still going strong, operating under the marketing name HVS Aviation (HVSaviation.com). The partners are Terry Heaslip, Larry Vance, and Elaine Summers.

There is work for us because of litigation, and here's how our work comes about. The victims of a crash (or their next-of-kin) hire law firms who sue for compensation – these are the plaintiffs. The lawyers litigate against everyone they can think of, such as the airline, the aircraft's manufacturer, the engine manufacturer, the avionics manufacturer, the airport authority, and anyone else they can think of – they cast a wide net.

The lawyers who are suing on behalf of the plaintiffs hire experts, and so do all the parties who are being litigated against (these are the defendants). At HVS (as with AIR before it), we rarely do plaintiff work – we stick to working for the defense lawyers. Frequently, we end up working for the same lawyers over and over again. The big players (as defendants) tend to always use the same law firms, and AIR's relationship with some of these law firms goes back more than three decades.

In my experience, the lawyers we have worked for as defendants want only straight up factual evidence and analysis. It can be different on the plaintiff's side. I know there are ethical lawyers who do very good plaintiff work, but I've seen others who specialize in creative (sometimes ingenious) interpretations of the accident circumstances. They make up clever stories that they hope will scare a defendant into a quick and lucrative settlement, or if that fails to work, to convince a jury to award a huge settlement. We get great pleasure in exposing their unethical work.

Working in this litigation world is not for the faint of heart. It can be very stressful. You have to be at the top of your game. As a consultant, you charge by the hour, in 15-minute intervals. You are expected to produce quality work for each 15 minutes. The liability exposures can be very high. Even a small aviation case can see exposures in the millions of dollars. The larger ones typically get into the high hundreds of millions.

Our lawyers are not looking for us to take their side. In fact, it can be quite the opposite. What they want is an accurate account of what happened. They need our help to assess their liability – to see where their vulnerabilities are – to figure out whether they should pay a settlement, or alternatively to go to the expense of trial preparation. One of our roles is to help them develop their negotiating position with the other parties.

In our consulting work, our modus operandi is to overwhelm all the other experts with solid and irrefutable evidence. We back that up with easily under-stood demonstratives – court-ready graphics that become the "go-to" references for the judge/jury. At the risk of sounding un-humble, we are very good at what we do.

Some of you have thought of this question – I'll write it out here on your behalf. You have investigated accidents as an IIC for the safety board, and now you investigate accidents as a consultant. Is there a difference in how you in-vestigate? If this was a question from a media interviewer I would say, "that's a very good question" – that's a go-to response to a media person. Here's the answer to your question – the investigation work is exactly the same, but the job is very different.

Let me explain. For each type of work, the process of organizing, assessing, and documenting the evidence is identical. The investigation work for both requires the same skillset. But as I said, the overall job is very different. As a consultant, I'm not on call to respond to an active crash site. Consultants typically don't get the case until well after the accident – that's when the litigation starts to happen.

As an IIC for the safety board, I had to run the show – be a project manager, look after all the logistics, look after the wreckage examination and documen-tation, and the team members, and the media, and the families – everything. In that way, the two jobs are totally different. In my work as a consultant, I can concentrate solely on looking at the evidence.

One thing I can tell you is that in many cases, the investigation work we do as consultants goes deeper, and is more revealing, than what we used to do in our government investigations. There are a number of reasons for this, which will be revealed in some of the writings to follow.

But for now, let me give you a key one. Safety board investigations are done for the purpose of identifying safety deficiencies – then they make appropri-ate recommendations to deal with the deficiencies – all that is done to try to prevent a similar occurrence from happening again. To find the deficiencies, obviously they must dig to find out what happened, but they have no mandate to discover every detail – to leave no stone unturned.

114

During a safety investigation, when they get to where they see there's no more potential to uncover another safety issue, they become leery about spending any additional resources, and they tend to wind things down. In the United States, they spell it out – the NTSB is mandated to write a "probable cause". All safety agencies are similar. Their reports and conclusions focus on the deficiencies they found – they write to support their safety recommendations. They are strictly forbidden from getting into blame and liability.

On the other hand, in the litigation world it's all about blame and liability. Investigations are done to whatever depth is necessary to be able to prove your point over someone else's. It's a dog eat dog world. Investigation specialists, most of whom have significant experience behind them, keep digging for any detail that might give them an advantage over their adversaries. And in the high-stakes world of litigation, budgets aren't normally an issue.

I'll give you a good example of how my thorough investigation for a client uncovered important evidence that wasn't discovered by an NTSB investigation. You're going to see here a wide gap between what we found (working as consultants) and what the official NTSB investigation came up with. I am not saying here that all of the NTSB's work is faulty – far from it – they are very competent overall. But in my work as a consultant, I've had lots of opportunities to review their work, and I've seen many cases where they failed to get to the bottom of what happened.

First, I have to explain that lawyer/client non-disclosure commitments prevent me from identifying this particular accident. Therefore, I can't include identifiers like the date, time, location, aircraft type, etc. But I can tell you that this accident happened in the United States – there were fatalities (less than 10) – and its profile attracted national (and international) media attention. The NTSB conducted an extensive investigation, and they wrote a detailed report, and it was widely accepted.

The aircraft was a modern design, and fully equipped with top-of-the-line technology. There was one pilot on board – he was also the owner of the aircraft. There were no mechanical or technical malfunctions involved in this crash – the aircraft performed as designed. The crash occurred because the aircraft got contaminated with ice while flying in cloud on final approach for a landing. The pilot had neglected to activate the aircraft's ice protection systems – that was a huge mistake.

He made a second huge mistake. He used the autopilot to fly the approach. This is a very bad idea in icing conditions. As we saw previously with the Cessna Caravan I testified about, ice contamination changes everything about the aerodynamics of an aircraft. You have to hand fly an aircraft like this one in icing conditions, because the autopilot doesn't know when its control inputs start to become excessive. The autopilot simply uses whatever control inputs it needs to keep tracking on the approach.

The pilot basically sat and did nothing while the aircraft slowed precipitously. Eventually, the airspeed got so low that the autopilot reached its limit of authority, and it automatically disengaged. As it turned out, the autopilot had been holding extreme control forces, and when those were suddenly let go, the aircraft went out of control. The upset was so severe that the pilot was unable to regain control before the aircraft hit the ground.

A lawsuit was filed by the families of those killed. Two parties were named as defendants – the pilot's estate, and the aircraft's manufacturer. We (Terry and I) were hired as experts for the law firm representing the manufacturer (they were regular clients of ours). The lawsuit claimed there was negligence by the manufacturer based on things like faulty design, and lack of warning about flying in icing conditions – all the regular stuff that comes from plaintiff's lawyers. The exposure was in the multiple millions of dollars.

Everyone acknowledged that compensation had to be paid. That was the easy part. How much the payout would be would either be agreed to among the parties, or it would be decided in court. The difficult part was the fighting between the two defendants about what percentage each would pay. Our task was to look at all the evidence and give our client an account of what happened, and to offer advice as to who was most at fault – the pilot or the manufacturer.

I'll skip all the parts of our investigation that aren't relevant to the point I'm trying to make here – about the deficient NTSB investigation. To fly this type of aircraft, the pilot required a Type Rating, meaning that he had to undergo a full training program with an FAA approved instructor. He had to get a recommendation from that instructor, and then he had to pass a check ride with an FAA Designated Pilot Examiner.

The NTSB accident report stated that he had completed his training to a satisfactory level. His instructor stated that it had taken some time to get him there, but this guy eventually achieved a good standard. The instructor said that during this pilot's training, they had encountered actual airframe icing – he said that all aspects of flight in icing conditions had been covered off. The Pilot Examiner stated that the pilot's check ride had gone well, and that he had no concern about this pilot's competency. The NTSB took their word for all this, and they wrote their report that way.

The aircraft had a modern flight data recorder (FDR) with lots of parameters. The NTSB studied the parameters for the accident flight, and for the previous flight, and they described them in their report. What the NTSB didn't do was go back to study all the training flights, and the check ride flight, all of which were available to them on the FDR. I asked for all that raw FDR data, and I had each flight converted to an animation that I could watch on my computer screen – that way, it's almost like sitting in the cockpit.

I spent weeks going through all the training flights, and then the check ride, in great detail. What I found was astonishing. Having been an instructor for many years, and a flight test examiner for many more, I had never seen anything quite like this. The accident pilot was not even close to being competent on that aircraft. Specific to the accident sequence that happened during an instrument approach, I found that in training he had flown a total of 57 instrument approaches. Incredibly, only two of the 57 were stable enough to get a pass on a check ride – on each of the others, he had exceeded the allowable tolerances (he had flown outside the allowable parameters for airspeed, altitude, glideslope accuracy, etc.)

Remarkably, as I documented the approaches from the start of his training to its finish, I saw no improvement in his flying ability. In a training environment, where repetition and consistency are key objectives, I found no consistency in the way his approaches were flown. No two approaches were alike – that made it all but impossible to discern what approach pattern they were trying to follow. They were certainly not following the pattern recommended by the manufacturer. This pilot never reached a standard where it was appropriate for his instructor to sign off on a recommendation for a check ride.

Here's what I think happened. As this pilot struggled through his training, the training pilot made a call to the guy who would do the check ride. They cooked up a way to give him the best chance of passing. For the final few training flights, they flew pretty much the exact same route and sequence that would later be used on the check ride. That's kind of like having the final exam before test day. That's not right – quite frankly, it's cheating.

Unbelievably, that's not the worst of what I found. The animation for the check ride showed that he should have failed. He completely messed up one of the required approaches – he flew away beyond the tolerances. That should have ended the check ride – this was a hard fail – go get some more training – but instead, I watched on the animation as they landed and took a short break. Then they taxied out, and the examiner let this pilot try that same approach over again. This time, it was barely within tolerances. On the check ride report, that approach sequence was assessed as a pass. Wow – on a check ride, there's no such thing as a do-over.

Another thing I looked at in the training was their actual use of the aircraft's ice protection systems. What the instructor told the NTSB about their training was untrue. In their report, the NTSB accepted his assertion that they had flown quite a bit in actual icing conditions, and they had to use the ice protection systems frequently. What a load of bunk. The animations showed that during all the dozens of training flights the anti-ice system was turned on only twice – once for a total of 18 seconds (not even one full cycle – obviously this was to show how the switch worked) – and a second time for 7 minutes, 34 seconds – in an environmental condition where the air temperature was actually above freezing – there would be no airframe icing.

Incredibly, I saw many flights where the ice protection was left off, even though the outside temperature required it to be on if they were in visible moisture. I had no way to tell from the animations if they were in cloud (visible moisture) during those times, but in his statement the instructor had said they were in cloud for much of the time during the training.

It's not difficult to see where what I found is directly relatable to the actual accident sequence. The aircraft crashed because the pilot flew into icing conditions without using the ice protection. Then he let the autopilot fly into an unstable approach condition. Unlike what was implied in the NTSB report, this was not an isolated case of bad judgement on his part – the one case of bad judgement of a fully trained and qualified pilot. This accident was entirely predictable. He flew the accident approach exactly as could have been predicted. He flew it the same way he flew during his training. He was allowed to go off on his own, and the first time the right conditions lined up, he wasn't ready. For a competent pilot, the accident approach in the icing conditions would have been routine – this guy was not prepared to handle it.

If the NTSB had done a thorough investigation, they would have discovered that the FAA's type check system had failed miserably in this case. This guy should never have been a captain on that aircraft. The NTSB could have recommended there be an audit of the training and flight check system, and they could have called for the FAA to step up its monitoring. They missed all that entirely.

118

The lawyers who hired us used my findings to convince the other side that the aircraft's manufacturer had nothing to do with this crash. It was all on the pilot. Our side was let out of the lawsuit before it ever went to court, and with zero liability. Sometime later, I heard that as a goodwill gesture our side agreed to put a token amount into the overall settlement, throwing in something less than a million dollars – just to help out the families. My lawyers were happy to do that, because many more millions were saved.

As I said earlier, this is just one example (unfortunately, kind of a typical example) of what I find when I dig deep into the causes of accidents. At HVS, we always do our own independent investigations. That's what we're paid to do. But part of that is reviewing the safety board report. Far too often, we find them wanting – incomplete, and inaccurate.

Before I end with this issue, there's another element to it that I've struggled with. It has to do with my ethical obligation to point out safety deficiencies when I find them. A quick summary of the issue is this – in doing my work on this case I found a deficiency that wasn't found in the NTSB's investigation – the FAA approved training was deficient, and in need of greater monitoring. In theory, I should have reported that deficiency to the NTSB – but I can tell you that I didn't.

The reasons that I didn't are complicated. It basically comes down to the fact that in my opinion it wouldn't have done any good for me to do that. My input would have gone into a circular stream of bureaucracy, and ended up nowhere. I think that when you have finished reading this book, you'll have a better understanding of why I say this.

Our son has some colour blindness. His condition was discovered while he was in daycare when his teacher asked him why he was colouring his horse purple. His answer confirmed her suspicion – "because horses are green, like my cat".

A condition like his can lead to some funny stories. His first after-school job was at a local hardware store, as extra help during the Christmas season. It never occurred to him to tell them about his colour blindness. They put him in charge of the Christmas lights. When that didn't go so well, they transferred him to the paint department. It was always fun talking to him about work.

14

A CANADIAN INVESTIGATION – NOT THE BEST

Now I'll tell you about a Canadian investigation that I was part of back in 2005, when I was still with the government. The investigation had great potential to make passenger flying safer around the world, but we blew that chance, and I'll show you how. It was the nasty taste left by this investigation that convinced me to start my countdown clock to retirement from the safety board.

On 2 August 2005, Air France 358 was a scheduled passenger flight from Paris to Toronto. The Airbus A340, a huge four-engine airliner, carried 297 passengers and 12 crew. As they were approaching the runway to land in Toronto, they encountered the effects of a thunderstorm, with heavy rain and shifting winds. They touched down too far down the runway. They couldn't get stopped before they went off the far end, and they skidded down into a ravine.

The travel over the rough terrain didn't beat the passenger cabin up too much. There were only a few injuries from the jostling around. There was damage to the outside of the aircraft that caused a fuel leak under the left wing, and when they came to a stop the cabin crew saw a small fire out there. Smoke was starting to enter the cabin. They immediately ordered an evacuation, and they managed to get everyone off the aircraft in less than two minutes – a textbook evacuation by any measure. After everyone had evacuated, the fire spread rapidly until it engulfed the entire fuselage.

It was very dramatic. All this was happening during the afternoon rush hour (it happened at 4:02 p.m.), right next to one of the busiest highways in North America. Within minutes, the burning aircraft and billowing smoke was being shown live on television around the world. I remember getting home from work and watching it myself. Nobody watching it on television knew whether anyone had gotten off. It was frightening to see. Even before I got a call from work, I started to get my things together, anticipating that I'd be part of the response team.

Later that evening I got the call to join the team, and in that call, I got the news that there were no fatalities. I don't want to sound insensitive to other people's misfortunes, but when you're in the investigation business these are the calls you love to get. It was an unfortunate accident, yes, but nobody was killed. This one would be fun – no gloom and doom, lots of easy-to-get evidence, lots of witnesses, a live flight crew to talk to, flight data recorders, a great team to work with, lots of high profile so no budget issues – everything you could wish for.

To my delight, I got tucked into the organization structure with two management levels above me, meaning I didn't have to help run the whole show – this was a very comfortable assignment. My job was under the operations group chair, who was under the IIC. The Ops Group would look at everything to do with how the pilots and the other crew members performed, and we would examine the support they got from the company's flight operations people. Our mandate was to figure out what happened, look for safety deficiencies and make recommendations to stop another accident like this.

Right from the beginning this one looked like an operational accident – in other words, we didn't expect to find anything wrong with the aircraft (such as a brake failure, or thrust reverser failure). But of course, you can't assume anything, so the technical investigators checked everything, and they found nothing out of the ordinary.

On the operational side we put together a detailed sequence of events that took the aircraft all the way from Paris to the ravine – starting with the flight planning. Before takeoff, their weather package for Toronto included the possibility of thunderstorms, so our pilots (they are both first rate individuals, so I feel comfortable calling them our pilots) added some extra fuel in case of delays (enough for an extra 23 minutes of holding time). Adding extra fuel is a normal precaution, anticipating they might have to hold to let a thundershower pass through.

This was an 8-hour flight, and it was entirely uneventful until things started to get interesting in the final hour or so. At the half-way point over the ocean, our captain gave control to our co-pilot so he could log the landing (and the captain got to log the takeoff) – that's how it works for these long-haul pilots – they get lots of flying hours, but not many takeoffs and landings – they have to make sure they log enough of each to stay current. As they got closer, our pilots were told that Toronto was experiencing on and off thunderstorms, and landings were delayed.

Some inbound flights had already diverted, but others were getting into Toronto – they were the ones that had enough fuel to wait for ATC sequencing. Our pilots were told to slow down, which they did, and soon enough they were given radar vectors to put them in the traffic flow – the lineup for landing. They could hear by monitoring ATC that all the aircraft lined up ahead of them were getting in. Other aircraft were in line behind them.

By the time they reached 8.7 nautical miles from the threshold of runway 24 left, they had their aircraft stabilized and in its proper landing configuration – with the landing gear down, and the flaps extended. Everything was set. The aircraft immediately ahead of them landed, and it reported that the breaking action was poor (because of the amount of water on the runway).

As they got closer to the runway threshold, the conditions got worse. They started going in and out of low clouds, heavy rain and turbulence. Sometimes they could see the runway, and sometimes not. On their weather radar, they could see heavy precipitation encroaching on the runway – that shows up as bright red on their radar screen. Out the windscreen, they could see lightning on both sides of the runway, and they could see even more lighting at the far end. They could see on their navigation display that the wind was shifting, changing from a headwind to a strong crosswind from the right.

They kept the autopilot on all the way down the approach, until our co-pilot selected it off at 323 feet above ground so he could hand-fly for the touchdown – it is standard procedure to hand-fly the landing. When he took over from the autopilot, he sensed that the airspeed was decreasing, and that the aircraft was sinking too fast, so he added engine thrust. Just as he added power, the wind suddenly changed from a 90-degree crosswind to where there was a tailwind component. Spoiler alert – this sudden wind change was what caused them to go off the end of the runway.

With the extra power, and the tailwind, the aircraft started to deviate above the glideslope. Just at that time the full force of the thunder cell struck. The pilots described it this way – it was like flying into Niagara Falls – they had never seen rain so intense – it was near impossible to see through the windscreen – lighting strikes were everywhere – the sky lit up, and it was almost blinding – they could not keep consistent visual contact with the runway.

The co-pilot struggled to keep control and line up with the centerline. He leveled off at about 25 feet above the runway, and the aircraft's wings were rolling in the extreme turbulence. He fought it, and they reduced the engine thrust to idle as the aircraft lowered to the surface. But with the tailwind, they had already used up some 3,800 feet of the runway before they touched down. That left them only 5,200 feet to get stopped, and that wasn't enough on the rain-slicked surface. The groundspeed was still at 80 knots when they came to the end of the runway, and off they went, down into the ravine.

Before I start describing what in my opinion went wrong with this overall investigation project, it wouldn't be fair if I failed to point out that the investigation part itself was very well done. The accident was high-profile, and specialists came from all over to be a part of it. Our TSB investigators ran the show, and everyone performed at a high level – something we could all be proud of. We all measured, and documented, and photographed, and calculated, and researched, and analyzed, and we figured out all the speeds and power settings and distances and trajectories and passenger escape routes – all to world-class standards. Our work produced a report that is exceptionally detailed and easy to follow, and it provides a full accounting of what happened.

But in my opinion, in the end, we completely failed to fulfill our mandate, which was to identify any and all safety deficiencies, and to make recommendations to eliminate or reduce them.

Some of us who were assigned to Air France 358 had worked the Swissair 111 investigation, the one where there was an in-flight fire. We had released the Swissair 111 report only two years previous, having been immersed in aircraft flammability issues for more than four years. Through our efforts, the TSB became internationally recognized for leading the push for higher flammability standards and better fire suppression in aircraft.

Here, with Air France 358, we had an aircraft that was completely engulfed in flames in a very short time. Everything in the fuselage that had to meet flammability standards had been totally consumed – the cargo containers, the seats, the carpeting, the decorative trim, the insulation, etc. etc. – everything that was supposed to have some resistance to burning actually burned up in no time at all. Now the TSB had a tremendous opportunity to follow up our ground-breaking work regarding aircraft flammability – we had a totally different type of aircraft – an Airbus vs. Boeing. It was a no-brainer – a thorough investigation of this flammability issue should have been automatic.

But do you think we did that? Not a chance. When I saw the group structure, I saw there was no fire group. When I questioned why, I was told we wouldn't be looking into the fire – there was no need. I almost fell over – what??? No fire group??? How could that be!!! Would we not be looking at how each of these materials performed, and whether they met their fire-resistance standards, and if not, why not? Would we not be looking to assess the flammability issues in the context of passenger egress times? Would we not be looking into the issues to do with toxic fumes? I was told by the IIC that this was "not going to turn into another Swissair 111". This one was not going to drag on for five years, or cost multiple millions. This one would be done efficiently – on time, and on budget (I took all that to mean we would work with military efficiency, given the background of the IIC).

I encourage you to look up the TSB's Air France 358 report on the internet. You'll find everything they said about the fire on a single page – page 52 – and that space includes a photo of the aircraft burning. How sad. Nobody in our management structure intervened, even after I suggested they should. In my view, this was a complete abandonment of our mandate, but I'll move on now because I still get worked up about that all these years later, and it's costing me energy.

But there's an even more egregious failing of this investigation – the TSB failed to support a meaningful recommendation to prevent this type of accident from happening again. I'll explain how that happened. First, let's review a bit of theory about improvements to safety in aviation, and how they come about.

Investigations are done to improve safety, but you have to understand that the safety boards have no authority to dictate changes in operating procedures – they can only make recommendations. If you find a safety deficiency, and you make a recommendation, you can only hope that the operators will take action on their own, or hope that the regulatory authority will make a new rule to force action by the operators.

It's been my experience that when a safety action is taken within the industry as a result of an accident, it actually happens outside the direct influence of a Safety Board recommendation. A significant motivator for industry players is this – they see a safety deficiency that might be in play in their own operation – they assess that it could cause them a financial liability – they do a cost/benefit analysis – they determine that they can't live with the potential liability – then they make a change. They realize very quickly that they can't afford to be a part of a "repeat" accident – their liability payouts would be through the roof, and their "reputation" costs could be fatal.

Actually, it's more or less the same for regulators. They're very careful to avoid being overly burdensome on the industry. They tend to move more aggressively only if they conclude the political fallout from another similar accident would be unbearable. They move when it scares them to think about the wrath of the grieving families, and the media and the politicians.

On Air France 358, the big-picture mandate of the operations group was to come up with a recommendation that would prevent this type of "landing in a thunderstorm" accident from happening again. Our task was to explain exactly what happened, and if the evidence supported it, to convince all industry operators that their pilots were just as vulnerable to what happened as our Air France 358 pilots were – or better yet, convince regulators that all pilots are equally vulnerable – that they should introduce new regulatory restrictions. We had to show that this was not just "pilot error" by our pilots – that there were systemic issues in play that would put all industry pilots at equal risk of having this same accident.

Here's how we set out to put our facts together. We started with these two obvious observations. First, the accident happened because the pilots attempted to land when there was a huge and dangerous thunderstorm right next to the runway. Second, the pilots were not able to adequately control the aircraft in the severe conditions that the thunderstorm produced.

To get a handle on whether this was indeed simply "pilot error" or not, we studied the aircraft's arrival into Toronto. We needed to compare what actually happened with what was supposed to happen. We wanted to know – did our pilots do something completely unexpected, or were they simply following company norms and procedures?

We constructed a simple table, with the left column titled "Pilot Action" and the right column titled "Expected Pilot Action". It wasn't very complicated, and I've reproduced it on the right.

If you want to think like an investigator as you go down the rows of this table, ask yourself – where did this accident start to happen? – or better yet – where should this accident have been stopped? Which row represents the place where the pilots should have done something different so that this accident would not have happened?

You can see that my ops group concluded that all the way down the approach our pilots were doing exactly what they were expected to do; that is, all the way until the final row where we left it open for debate. When they got destabilized over the threshold, should they have aborted the landing (initiated a go-around), or should they have continued down to the runway like they did?

Let's review the first four rows. In row one, nobody should disagree that leaving Paris was an "expected pilot action". Pilots fly to airports every day when the forecast includes occasional thunderstorms. There were hundreds of other aircraft trying to land in Toronto that day, and they all had that same forecast.

In row two, they decided to have a go at Toronto, even though they knew there would be weather delays. They had taken on some extra fuel, so they had time to wait and take a look at the conditions when it was their turn. If they didn't like what they saw, they could go to their alternate. I think most people would agree that Air France would have expected them to make that decision, and so would most other operators. The only pilots not doing that were the ones that didn't have enough fuel.

	PILOT ACTION	EXPECTED PILOT ACTION
1	Left for Toronto with forecast of thundershowers	Left for Toronto with forecast of thundershowers
2	Decided to attempt an approach to Toronto in variable thunderstorm conditions	Decided to attempt an approach to Toronto in variable thunderstorm conditions
3	Flew a stabilized approach – anticipated a challenging crosswind landing on a wet runway	Flew a stabilized approach – anticipated a challenging crosswind landing on a wet runway
4	Continued on with their approach to the threshold despite the thunderstorm activity near the runway	Continued on with their approach to the threshold despite the thunderstorm activity near the runway
5	Continued with the landing when the approach became destabilized over the runway threshold	Abort the landing? or Continue with the landing when the approach became destabilized over the runway threshold

In row three, they got themselves established on a stabilized approach, and were set up for a crosswind landing on a wet runway. Pilots train for this. It's not at all unusual. Again, look at all the other aircraft that had landed in front of them, and all the ones lined up behind them. All of the pilots in that line were doing what their company managers expected them to do, and so were our guys, so for our pilots this gets an "expected pilot action".

In row four, our pilots were closing in on the runway. They had everything set up to land, and they continued their approach to the threshold even though there was thunderstorm activity near the runway. I bet you're thinking it's not so easy to give this one an "expected pilot action". We had lots of debate about this one in our ops group. We looked at all the Air France manuals, and all the Airbus manuals, and all the regulations – we looked at their training – we found nothing in all that material that would trigger them to abandon their stabilized approach. So, they carried on, just like all the other pilots ahead of them had already done, and all the ones behind them were about to do.

In row five, the aircraft became destabilized as it crossed the runway threshold, but our pilots continued with the landing anyway. I can tell you that within our team we had major differing views about this. The IIC believed our pilots blew it – they messed up. He was adamant that this destabilization should have triggered an immediate go-around. In his view, our pilots got so fixated on landing that they ignored the cues that dictated a missed approach. There was support for this view in the Air France manual, which stated very clearly that any approach that became destabilized was not to be continued.

Other investigators, led by me, urged that we not be so quick to pass judgement. In my view, there were extenuating circumstances. The first was that their approach never became destabilized until they suddenly got that tailwind when they were only 50 feet above the ground. At that point this huge aircraft was in an exceptionally low-energy state. Air France had no procedures for low-energy go-arounds in the A340 – low-energy go-arounds are dangerous, especially in large transport category aircraft, and they never trained their pilots for that. If we were going to say our pilots should have tried that, we would have to accept they would be trying it for the first time. In accident investigation, we see lots of accidents where pilots have gotten themselves into sticky situations and then crash while trying some made-up maneuver for the first time.

But there was an even bigger reason why our pilots would not have tried a missed approach. Earlier I described how the pilots described the conditions, but here's what we found out from experts studying the recorded lightning strike information. When the aircraft was 400 feet above ground, there was a group of five cloud-to-ground lightning strikes just abeam the touchdown zone. As the aircraft crossed the threshold, within a one-second period there were nine cloud-to-cloud lightning strikes off the far end of the runway. They said these numbers represent a conservative estimate of lightning strikes that would have been visible to our pilots, as some of the cloud-to-ground strikes don't get recorded.

The captain never came close to calling for a go-around, even when he realized they were in trouble with the landing. He said that the lightning was so intense it was like nothing he had ever witnessed. He said he felt like if he opened the throttles and tried to climb out, they would have crashed and everyone in the aircraft would be killed. In his mind, getting on the ground was far safer than trying to pass through all that lightning, with the associated turbulence and intense rain and windshear and microbursts.

There's no way to know what would have happened if our pilots had tried a missed approach. Perhaps they would have climbed away safely, but perhaps not. Imagine the outcry if everyone had died because the pilots attempted a go-around. Our pilots would be accused of mindless risk-taking when all they had to do was stay on the ground and accept some aircraft damage.

With all the above as background, here's some safety investigation thinking for you. It's easy to follow, and as a bonus, it's lots of fun. This is how to come up with a recommendation that would prevent this type of accident from happening again.

The table above gives us the five primary decision points for our pilots. We saw how at each of the decision points, our pilots made the decision we expected – they made the same decision that any other pilots would have made – to keep going with the approach. Here's what that means – this accident happened even though our pilots were doing exactly what we expected them to do.

And you know what that means – this accident wasn't a pilot problem – this accident was an expectations problem. To stop this type of accident from happening again, it wouldn't help to change the pilots, we must change the expectation. Here's what the new expectation needs to be – if you're lining up for an approach, and there's a thunderstorm in the vicinity of your runway, you are expected to abandon any thoughts of giving it a try – break off and wait it out until the thunderstorm is gone.

In aviation, expectations only change when you slap on a new rule – that's how it works in reality. Our ops group argued for a recommendation that would have regulators adopt an approach ban – the ban would stop pilots from conducting an approach if there's any thunderstorm activity within 5 miles of the runway. Our TSB board members wouldn't accept that recommendation, because they deemed it to be too "prescriptive" (they didn't want to give a specific number), so we backed off and asked for wording that called only for a distance-based restriction – to let the regulators choose their own number. We never got that wording either, but in the end, they put wording (and a watered-down recommendation) in the final report that at least got our issue on the table.

In the preamble to the recommendation there are some good words (I recall drafting them myself) such as:

> "… there is a need for clear standards for the avoidance of convective weather during approach and landing. This will reduce the ambiguity involved in decision making in the face of a rapidly changing weather phenomenon, and the likelihood that factors such as operational pressures, stress, or fatigue will adversely affect a crew's decision to conduct an approach."

The recommendation the board came up with was this (they directed it to regulators worldwide):

"... establish clear standards limiting approaches and landings in convective weather ..."

That was a pretty weak recommendation – with no minimum distance requirement – but with the preamble stuff it was better than nothing. If this recommendation were to be fully adopted, it would take the decision-making about whether to try the approach out of the hands of the pilots. I'm sad to report that even this watered-down recommendation never had any impact. Nothing has changed to this day. There are two reasons why that happened. First, the industry fights against restrictive rules, and second, the board undercut their own recommendation by issuing a second one, which I'll cover below.

But first, let me explain why the operators dislike rules like this. Surprise – it's all about money. It's best for them if their pilots are left to decide whether the conditions are safe or not. Operators know that pilots are mission orientated – pilots take great pride in getting the job done. I'm not saying they're risk-takers, but they are wired to put their piloting skills up against most challenges that come their way. Here's a question that pilot's think about, at least subliminally – "What will I say when I'm called in to answer for why I was the only one who didn't make it into the airport?" Pilots are sensitive to the fact that it costs multiple thousands of dollars to divert a passenger aircraft – there's a huge money cost, and there's a passenger relations cost.

Just in case you're wondering, control towers and airport authorities cannot stop aircraft from landing near thunderstorms. When there's lightning close by, they issue a red alert – they stop all activity on the ramp – that protects the ramp workers, but they don't stop aircraft from landing or taking off.

Before I reveal how the TSB undercut its own recommendation, let me set it up with a bit more about what we tried to accomplish in our ops group. We wanted to eliminate the risk from pilots trying to land with thunderstorms close by. We wanted to have a rule put in place that would give pilots no choice in the matter. Pilots could no longer be enticed into taking a risk, and they would no longer be held accountable for a costly diversion. If accepted, our recommendation would eliminate this type of accident – no approach allowed = no pilot decision making = no potential threat to safety = case closed.

Guess what the very next recommendation was in the TSB's report? Here it is, for all the operators and regulators around the world to see:

> "… civil aviation authorities mandate training for air transport pilots to better enable them to make landing decisions in deteriorating weather."

What better way to undercut your own recommendation about operating near thunderstorms – the recommendation that would have eliminated pilot decision making – than to ask for better decision-making training to be mandated? How could anybody not recognize that this second recommendation was a death knell for the first?

I put up a good fight, but to no avail. I argued that you couldn't have those two recommendations in the same report. I tried to explain that they were basically giving the industry two choices. Industry could either accept the first recommendation, which would come at a cost and change how they operated, or they could accept the second, which wouldn't change anything and would cost them nothing. The industry made the obvious choice, and the regulators took no action, and nothing came of our ops group idea.

How unfortunate. The TSB had a chance to make a huge difference, and they blew it. The Canadian TSB has a world-wide reputation, and they could have used that to front an aggressive campaign to stop these types of accidents for good. They had all the ammunition they needed – statistics galore to prove the status quo was killing people in large numbers. As I lived through this, I came to recognize that the TSB I knew in the days of Swissair 111 had changed. They had become blind to the big picture – they were unwilling to up their game – they were not fulfilling their mandate.

For dramatic effect, let me give you some examples of the accidents and serious incidents that would not have happened if our proposed approach ban had been put into effect – each of these occurrences happened subsequent to Air France 358.

> 23 August 2005 – TANS Peru Airline – a Boeing 737 that crashed while landing with heavy thunderstorms very near the runway – 40 fatalities out of 98 people on board.

> 16 September 2007 – One-Two-Go by Orient Thai Airlines – an MD-82 that crashed while landing in Phuket, Thailand in heavy rain and wind – the pilots initiated a last second go-around, but the aircraft was unable to climb, and it impacted the runway and

broke apart and burst into flames – 88 fatalities out of 130 people on board – (remember this – some investigators on Air France 358 criticized our pilots for not trying a go-around at the last second).

16 August 2010 – Aires Columbia Airline – a Boeing 737 landing at San Andres Island Airport, Columbia with heavy thunderstorms and rain at the airport – there were only 2 fatalities out of 127 people on board, but that was only through good luck.

14 September 2010 – Sichuan Airlines – an Airbus A319 landing in Wuxi, China – no fatalities or injuries – pilots were advised that the terminal area was covered by a thunderstorm and there was strong lightning happening – during their attempted approach the aircraft entered an aerodynamic stall – they came exceptionally close to flying into the ground.

4 April 2011 – Georgian Airways operating as a United Nations flight – a Bombardier CRJ landing at Kinshasa, Congo – they were attempting to land in a thunderstorm – initiated a go-around at low level – encountered an extreme downdraft microburst (another example of what can happen during a missed approach near a thunderstorm) – 32 fatalities out of 33 on board.

20 April 2012 – Bhoja Air – a Boeing 737 attempting to land in Islamabad, Pakistan during heavy rain and a thunderstorm – all 127 people on board killed.

6 December 2016 – Virgin Australia – a Boeing 737 landing in Darwin, Australia – landing in the vicinity of thunderstorm activity with a rain shower visible at the far end of the runway – no fatalities or injuries – in the five minutes before landing there had been several recorded lightning strikes within five nautical miles of the airport – shortly before landing the visibility suddenly reduced in heavy rain – the right main landing gear left the paved surface soon after touchdown – interestingly, the operator's crew operations manual stated that landings should not be attempted when an approaching thunderstorm is closer than five nautical miles (this is why our recommendation said that the decision should not be left to the pilots – in this case they ignored their own manual).

8 May 2019 – Biman Bangladesh Airlines – a Bombardier Dash-8-Q400 attempting to land when a thunderstorm was present, and the weather was very poor – skidded off the runway – the aircraft broke into three sections – a complete hull loss – no fatalities – 18 passengers and crew were injured.

5 February 2020 – Pegasus Airlines – a Boeing 737 landing in Istanbul, Turkey – attempting to land in heavy rain and strong tail-winds – a thunderstorm was passing through at the time – it skidded off the end of the wet runway at some 80 knots, went down an embankment and broke into three pieces before catching fire – three fatalities and 179 people taken to hospital (lots of similarities to Air France 358).

Again, these are just examples to show the extent of the risk that's still out there. In my opinion, there has been no change to the level of risk in the industry – the risk is exactly the same now as it was for Air France 358, and it will stay that way until some kind of approach ban is put in place. What a shame – it's so predictable – these types of accidents will continue to happen.

I have an interesting follow-up that fits here. About a year after the TSB's Air France 358 report was published, I was invited to speak at the annual meeting of a well-known pilot's safety group – the topic being Air France 358. These people were the cream of the crop. There were about 30 of them – all experienced airline pilots who also had an interest in safety investigations. Each of them had taken formal accident investigation training, and many had participated in actual investigations as representatives of their airline or union. You couldn't assemble another group that would be more inclined to make safety-related changes.

I started by giving them a quick briefing on the accident scenario – too close to a thunderstorm – landed long – nobody killed – etc. They were familiar with all that anyway, so I asked them to help me with an experiment. I was using PowerPoint, and I put up this question:

"If you were flying that aircraft – would that accident have happened to you?"

I told them I'd give them a bit of time to think about it, and the room went silent. I'm sure they were wondering if I was going to ask some of them to give their answer out loud, but I didn't do that. Knowing that they all knew each other, and many had flown together, I gave them another task:

> "Look around and try to figure out which of these pilots, if they had been flying that aircraft, would have had that same accident?"

I asked them to make a list, and I told them I wouldn't ask them to share it – it would be their secret list. Again, I left time for silence while everyone was trying to figure out what everyone else was thinking.

I didn't call on anyone – instead, I gave them yet another task. I set it up this way: let's say we could use magic to go back to the time before the Air France accident happened – and the two Air France 358 pilots who had that accident were part of this group, and they were in this room with us – here is my question:

> "Is there anyone here who thinks they would be able to pick those two pilots out from this crowd as being the ones most likely to have that accident?"

I gave them lots of time to think, but I kept introducing more thoughts and questions: would those two Air France pilots have somehow stood out as different from all of you – would you be able to see something about them that would make them susceptible to an accident like this – more susceptible than all the rest of us – would you be able to pick out the deficiencies that could make them susceptible?

Rather than ask any of them to speak, I told them that I already knew what their answers to my questions would be. I told them that I would reveal their answers, and I asked them to speak up if I got an answer wrong – I can tell you that nobody spoke up through this whole exercise – and I can also tell you that I had their full attention.

I said to the group – regarding my first question – "If you were flying that aircraft – would that accident have happened to you?" – I say that every one of you answered NO – this accident would not have happened to you. Am I wrong? – their silence and body language told me I was correct.

I said to the group – when you saw that question you immediately came up with thoughts like these: you've been in those situations before – many times – and you never crashed. You have your own way of making decisions, and your type of decision-making would keep you from getting into that situation – and if you did get into that situation, you have the piloting skills to get yourself out. And some of you had other ideas about why you are not vulnerable, but they would all be along these lines of thinking.

I said to the group – regarding my task – "Look around (in this room) and try to figure out which of these pilots, if they had been flying that aircraft, would have had that same accident?" I say that not one of you put a single name on your list. You never identified even one individual who you think would have had that same accident. Nobody stood out from the others. There's nothing obvious about any of them that sticks out for you – you have no reason to think that one of them would be vulnerable.

I said to the group – regarding my final task where I asked them to imagine the two Air France pilots being in the room with us – pre-accident – "Is there anyone here who thinks they would be able to pick those two pilots out from this crowd as being the ones most likely to have that accident?" I said – your answer to that is easy – there is no way that you would isolate on either one of those two guys – qualified pilots with Air France – they fly all over the world, in all kinds of conditions – places where thunderstorms are a constant threat – they are highly trained and highly experienced – there would be nothing about them that would single them out in a room with all of us as the most vulnerable to this type of accident.

It was then that I told the group I was about to share my answer to the first question, the one about whether this accident would have happened to me – I said – my answer is YES – I know for sure that this accident would have happened to me – and I know why this accident would have happened to me – and I know something else – in the exact same circumstances that led to the two Air France pilots having this accident, every single one of you would have crashed that aircraft also – you would have ended up in the same ravine they did, or someplace worse.

This is how I explained why I was so sure that each of them would have crashed that aircraft if they had been exposed to the exact same circumstances. I told them that I had talked to these two Air France pilots quite a few times, first in Canada and later in France. I got to know their backgrounds, and I studied their training and procedures. I learned about their personal characteristics and decision-making and their judgment. I got to know what they were thinking during the approach, and why they were thinking that way. Because we had live pilots to talk to, I knew everything about what was happening at every second during their approach. I knew the exact circumstances that led to this crash.

I told the 30 pilots in the room that in my opinion, the two Air France pilots were every bit as competent, and just as professional, and just as careful, and just as skilled, and just as well trained and equipped as any of them were. To add some credibility, I brought up the fact that for quite a few of them I had been their instructor at one time, or had given them check rides, so I had first-hand knowledge to base my opinion on.

I told them that they were wrong to think that this accident couldn't happen to them. They could only think that if they didn't know the exact circumstances of the accident – they needed to study the report again – if any of them had interest I would go through the accident with them second-by-second to show them the errors in their thinking.

Here we were, a full year after the accident, and not a single one of them felt vulnerable to that same type of accident. They were an accurate representation of airline pilots everywhere. If we were to expand that out, we would not find a single pilot anywhere who could stand up and explain why that accident would have happened to them. They would all be able to explain the opposite – to detail all their safeguards and tricks that would have saved them. The pre-accident Air France pilots could have joined that long line of explainers, telling us how such an accident could never happen to them.

As for my experiment with this group of 30, I summed up the result this way. The TSB's investigation and report didn't change anything. Everybody was aware of it, but it never caused anybody to feel more vulnerable to this type of accident, or to change their ways. It would not have been possible to predict that the two Air France pilots were vulnerable, but obviously they were. They must have had some deficiency that was not possible to detect. If they had only been as capable as any member of this group of 30, this accident would never have happened.

This brings up a very valid question. What's the purpose of doing all that investigation work if in the end there will be no changes? What's the point, if all you can come up with is a recommendation to give more training to pilots who are convinced that they have no vulnerability anyway? The fact is that every one of them is just as vulnerable as the two accident pilots, and the only way to make them safer is to force a safety improvement on them through a regulation – give them no choice – enforce an approach ban when thunderstorms are nearby.

In my experience, the biggest drawback to making systemic safety improvements is that people can't bring themselves to believe that the same accident could happen to them. That includes investigators working on aircraft accidents. That's what went wrong with the TSB's Air France 358 investigation. Right from the beginning there was a belief by our IIC that this accident would not have happened to him. He was convinced that this accident happened because our pilots were deficient – our pilots had poor judgment and made mistakes they would not have made if they had better training – like the superior training provided in the military. All that, of course, is crap.

For this group of 30, who were there because of their interest in investigating, I used this as a teaching opportunity. I told them about a natural instinct they'll have to overcome if they want to be an effective investigator. Here's how I described the instinct. Your brain instinctively prevents you from being able to trade places with someone who has had an accident. You know the instinct, it's the same one you get when you see a car wreck. Your instinct gives you your first thought – this event happened because somebody did something wrong – somebody was careless, or reckless – somebody made a stupid choice – and that makes them stupid, and you're not stupid, so that accident wouldn't have happened to you. It's quite amazing how these thoughts come to you immediately, even though you have no idea what happened.

This instinct is especially powerful when a pilot gets killed, and another pilot is the investigator. For some of them, it is very difficult to come at that with an open mind. Many can't fathom the possibility that the same thing would have happened to them – to do that you would have to accept that you would be dead – and your brain won't let you go there. Your brain tells you that the dead pilots are dead because they had some kind of latent weakness – some hidden deficiency – there was something wrong with them – and to find out why they are dead you have to find their flaws.

If they died because of some systemic issue beyond their control, that means you would also have died had you been faced with the same circumstance. I've seen it happen – where investigators shy away from looking hard for systemic deficiencies. If you get focused on finding flaws with the pilots, it will keep you from developing recommendations that would actually protect against what happened. Our industry has seen this historically, where the focus was always on finding the pilot's flaws – for decades, most accidents were categorized as "pilot error".

In the name of aviation safety, here is a final thought related to Air France 358. Thankfully, in our industry's safety evolution, it's no longer possible to predict what will cause the next major accident. All the old obvious causes are now protected against. But there is still one major cause that we've not acted against – the Air France 358 scenario. And mark my words, Air France 358 (or worse) will happen again. And when it does, we'll all be able to say that the TSB and others had a chance to prevent it, but they failed to act.

Visitors to Canada's east coast often tell stories about their encounters with the locals. This one is typical – it happened many years ago, long before modern electronic navigation. A couple from the United States wanted to experience real-life lobster fishing. They convinced a local fisherman to let them go along.

They started out early in the morning – it was so foggy they couldn't see from one end of the boat to the other. They chugged along in this fog soup for close to an hour – then they heard the engine go to idle. They watched the fisherman use a long pole to retrieve a trap with several lobsters in it. They were amazed. They asked him, "how did you know that trap was there"? He seemed surprised by the question. His answer – "because I put it there".

15

TEACHING — LEARNING — TRAVELLING — ADVENTURE

On 3 December 2016, I left Ottawa enroute to Ulan Bator, Mongolia. I was on my way to conduct an accident investigation workshop for the International Civil Aviation Organization (ICAO), specifically, for their Asia and Pacific Office (APAC). After retiring from the TSB, I had done quite a few of these kinds of workshops, but this would be my first one for ICAO.

I can tell you that this entire exercise almost never happened. When I said I'd do it, I considered myself to be kind of a volunteer. I'd get paid, but nowhere near what my normal rate was for casework, or even for my other training gigs. I was doing this one as part of my "giving back" effort, and also because it would take me to a unique place – I looked at it as kind of an adventure.

ICAO is a United Nations Specialized Agency. I soon found out that to do anything for the UN you have to go through the same paperwork process they use to hire a new Secretary General. I kid you not – this was like bureaucracy on steroids. Nothing was easy. They have multiple forms for everything, and acronyms even they can't figure out.

Somehow, my stubbornness got me through all that, and off I went – through Toronto, and then Beijing. I landed in Ulan Bator (Ulaanbaatar) at 11 p.m. their time on 4 December. Even though I've travelled quite a bit, when I arrive in a place like Mongolia, I still anticipate that it will feel really different. But that's not what typically happens. At the terminal in Ulan Bator, everything looked and felt the same as it always does when you arrive at a terminal build-ing – same doors and floors and walls and chairs and lighting and signage and washrooms and barriers and lineups and customs kiosks and baggage carousels and taxi stands. I always find it a bit of a letdown – to travel halfway around the world to a faraway land only to find everything looks so familiar.

They had sent a car for me, and we headed for the hotel in the pitch dark and bitter cold. We drove only a couple of minutes before we came to a halt. Now this was unique – a herd of wild horses was blocking the road. And there we sat – we were the first car in a line of maybe 10 or 20 – nobody honking horns or making any other attempt to get the horses to move. The horses had the right of way, and we would get through on their schedule. After quite some time the driver saw an opening, and we slowly weaved through the herd and left them behind. That was better – welcome to Mongolia.

In the morning I met up with my ICAO contact, a guy named Wayne, who was the main organizer of this event. Wayne was a retired Transport Canada inspector, who was now ICAO's head of safety in that part of the world. He was great to work with – a fellow Canadian – he knew all the main players, and he knew his way around Ulan Bator.

For this one, I had 62 candidates with diverse backgrounds. Many of them worked for government investigation agencies, but quite a few were from airlines. There were pilots, engineers, managers, airline safety officers, inspectors, and directors of this-and-that – a wonderful and diverse group. There were 50 from Mongolia, and the rest were from Malaysia (1), Philippines (2), Laos (2), Cambodia (2), South Korea (3), and North Korea (2).

With that number of people, it was difficult to get a good read on their language skills, but it seemed like I was getting through most of the time. It was interesting to watch the interactions. Some of these countries don't always get along, but I never saw any tension in the room, or when they were milling around. I even saw the North and South Koreans speaking and laughing together at times, which was neat. It seemed that during my instruction, everyone laughed when they should have laughed, and got really quiet and focused when I led them to that.

A quick word here about the North Koreans. I was asked ahead of time if I had any objection to them being there. Obviously, I had no objection because I approved them showing up. I had no state secrets to reveal, and from what I could find out I was not violating any Canadian restrictions. ICAO chose Mongolia for the training because it's one of the few countries that allows North Koreans to enter.

There were actually three North Koreans altogether. The two who were on the course were the Chief of their Accident and Incident Investigation Division, and one of his investigators. The third was not connected to aviation, but he came to the lectures anyway. It seemed he was there to make sure all went according to their government's expectations. We all stayed at the same hotel, so each day the four of us shared a ride back and forth to the training facility.

After I loosened them up a bit, to me they seemed to be just like most people – ordinary guys who liked to share a laugh and swap stories. I never tried to bring up politics or anything like that – it wouldn't have been appropriate. Of all the people there, these North Korean guys were as keen as any to get the most out of the training. They were very hungry to get information, and to get exposed to the latest thinking and techniques in accident investigation. On the last day, I gave them a flash drive with as much investigation related stuff as it would hold – investigation manuals and checklists and the like – none of it secret in any way, but not readily accessible to them in their country. They were most grateful, and I was happy to give them these tools that would help them make their aviation sector safer.

I have developed a whole repertoire of training modules that I can choose from, according to what best suits the audience. I refresh these modules constantly, adding new material and references to the latest accidents. Some of my modules got their start away back when I was with the TSB. For many of my years there, my "other related duty" was as a training specialist. I worked with another investigator to run workshops that gave our investigators a chance to share experiences and expertise. We also invited guest lecturers, and allowed outside safety people to attend, such as from airlines. These workshops were a great place to develop relationships between people who would inevitably meet up later, at accident sites.

In Ulan Bator I was the only instructor, and I had the entire group for three days. I had to choose my subjects carefully, given the time constraints and language barriers. I won't get too far down into the weeds, but I will share with you how I engaged them, and then led them through each of the chosen subjects. Here's an example of the type of material I teach – this would come in the opening hour or so – right after I say how nice it is to be there and do the introductions. I will direct this to you just as if you were in that class in Mongolia – except in these written words I can't recreate the "atmosphere" I like to create – I make it a lot livelier in the classroom.

> One day we will meet again at an actual accident site. I will be the IIC, and you will be on my investigation team. During this training, I have three days to prepare you to be ready. This will be a high-profile accident, and the whole world will be watching us. We will have only one objective at this investigation – we must ensure when our investigation concludes, the whole world declares that our investigation was a success. We will do everything possible to make that happen.
>
> By taking this training, you are confirming that you are willing and ready to go on an actual investigation. That means that when

you get the call, you drop everything else and get ready to travel. Being on call for an airplane accident is not like being a firefighter or paramedic. They are called away to something local – you can end up going halfway around the world – and you could be there for a week, or a month, or even longer.

Is your family ready for that? Does your family know that might happen to you? Have you talked to your kids about it? When you're gone, how will they get to school? Who will look after your house, and your pets? How will your bills get paid? Do you have a plan for all of that? I have been doing this for a long time, and I can tell you that it is not the right time to start thinking about these things when the bell rings. If you are going to be on my team, I expect you to have a plan.

(For credibility, I work in some examples of where I've been called away to remote places for extended periods, and where I've met people just like them – these students – and how I saw that some were prepared, and some were not. The pressures from home can make someone far less effective in the field, if they haven't covered things off.)

Let's make a list of who will be watching and assessing our investigation – who has to be satisfied if our investigation is to be judged successful. Here we go with the short version:

Government agencies, airlines, manufacturers, ICAO, pilot's unions, ATC, media, next-of-kin and loved ones, the general public, the insurance companies, lawyers and consultants, and litigation courts.

If we can keep all those people satisfied that we are doing a good job, we should get a passing grade. How do we keep them satisfied?

To have credibility, our investigation must be seen to be independent and open. We have to show that we are not under the influence of any company, or agency, or anybody with a biased interest in the outcome. The IIC must keep everyone (especially the families, the media, and the public) informed about the progress of the investigation. We must show that we are being thorough, and have no constraints on the evidence we can look at.

Our aim is to write a report that is based on verified factual information, and to make findings that are based only on those facts. Then we have to come up with recommendations that are fully supported by the findings – recommendations that will lead to meaningful changes that will prevent this type of accident from happening again.

As we go through the next three days, we will cover all the steps in detail about how we gather evidence, but here are the basics. We go to all the places where there is a potential for evidence to be, such as: the accident site, the aircraft's departure point, the maintenance facility, the operator's head office, the dispatch facility, the air traffic control centre, and the pilot training facility. We gather up all the records, and interview anyone who might have information.

We have to be ready to handle all kinds of environmental conditions, from extreme heat to extreme cold. We have to be ready for hazards that are not familiar to us – snakes, bugs, bears, biohazards, pathogens, toxic material, tangled wreckage, steep slopes, jungles, deserts, wilderness, high altitudes, isolated areas and unusual transportation. We are going to talk about all that.

In Mongolia, during the first day we covered how investigation teams are structured. I let them know about how many investigation groups might be required, depending on the complexity of the investigation. For example, on the operations side they might see the following groups: operations group lead, aircraft performance, human factors, flight recorders, weather, ATC, airports, witness, cabin safety and emergency response.

On the technical side, the groups might be set up like this: technical group lead, site manager, site safety officer, site survey, systems, structures, powerplants, crashworthiness, maintenance and records, and photo/video.

People on the team could end up in any one of these groups. I let them know why it is important for everyone on the team to be familiar with what each group is responsible for. Each group has a checklist so there is no overlap in effort, but it is important that they all share any information that might help another group. I explained how that is done, both informally and at the scheduled investigation meetings. In Mongolia, we had a detailed look at each group and its responsibilities – that's all stuff I'm sure you would find exceptionally interesting, but it would take up too much space to cover it here.

When I teach the mundane stuff, I try to bring it alive with examples and anecdotes from my own investigations, to show them how the knowledge

I'm giving them is important – how it will prepare them for an accident site, and keep them out of trouble. I highlight the times I made mistakes and was embarrassed. I explained to them how they could avoid making those same mistakes, if they payed attention to what I was telling them.

For these people from around Asia, I wanted to reinforce the international interdependence within the accident investigation community – the need to share safety findings based on quality investigations. To do that I showed them the parallel nature of two different investigations – one in Canada, and the other in Taiwan. Both were what we call "CFIT" accidents – Controlled Flight Into Terrain – where a perfectly serviceable aircraft is inadvertently flown into the ground.

The two accidents were as follows: in Canada – First Air Flight 6560, 20 August 2011, a Boeing 737 that crashed in Resolute Bay, Nunavut with 12 fatalities – in Taiwan – TransAsia Airways Flight GE 222, 23 July 2014, an ATR72 that crashed at Magong Airport with 48 fatalities.

To be clear, I was not an investigator on either of these crashes, but I had a connection to each. For the Canadian one, I did some review work for a client. For the Taiwanese one, I was asked by the Aviation Safety Council of Taiwan to speak about it at their 2016 Safety Information Exchange Seminar in Taipei.

These two investigations were very well done, so it was a good use of time to review them in detail for the class. I led them through the investigation processes that produced quality findings and good recommendations. I showed them how similar the findings were, and how the recommendations basically called for the same fixes.

But then I turned to what my real message was for them for this training segment. Long before either of these accidents happened, much was already known about the dangers of CFIT. There had been dozens of previous investigations that had produced good advice and recommendations for prevention.

My question for them was this – why did these two accidents happen even though good recommendations for prevention had been in place for many years? We talked specifically about how the recommendations from the 2011 accident in Canada failed to prevent the 2014 accident in Taiwan. The circumstances of the two accidents were not that different, and yet three years later the Taiwan investigation made very similar recommendations all over again. And then I showed them more CFIT accidents that happened after the accident in Taiwan. These new CFIT accidents show the Taiwanese recommendations never worked either.

Here was my point. Accident investigation agencies say they are in the accident prevention business, but so frequently they do a lousy job at it. Even when they make good recommendations, they most often don't push them hard enough or long enough to ensure safety barriers are put in place. They don't have the authority to mandate action, but they should make a lot of noise, in public, until action is taken. To me, if they are not willing to promote their recommendation aggressively, they shouldn't have made it in the first place.

We covered several other subjects, one example being witness interviewing – an important skill in accident investigation. The training is always a challenge when language barriers are in play, but I try to make it as interactive as possible, and we manage to have some fun with it. We look at the specifics of interviewing the different categories of witnesses – eyewitnesses, aircraft crew witnesses, passenger witnesses, management witnesses – there's lots to go through.

Perhaps the most important training I gave them was on accident site safety, and personal safety. When I was still at the TSB, I developed a full training program on this, and I've kept it updated. Crash sites can be very dangerous places for people who are not properly trained and equipped.

We covered how to protect against accident site hazards including weather hazards, physical hazards, chemical hazards, carbon fiber hazards, biological hazards, and psychological hazards.

We talked about the symptoms of heat stroke, and frost bite, and hypothermia. We covered chemical hazards, such as jet fuel, hydraulic fluid, brake fluid, greases, lubricants and sealants. We talked about the hazards from damaged or burnt carbon fiber – a very serious concern. We covered how to protect yourself from all these hazards.

We covered biological hazards, including blood borne pathogens. I explained the different pathogens that you must assume are present at an accident site where there are fatalities. There will be the bodies of deceased persons, and – liquid, semiliquid and dried blood – other bodily fluids – dispersed fecal matter (contents of the human bowel) – fragmented and otherwise unrecognizable bone, tissue, and internal organs. All these human remains are hazardous for accident investigators.

I explained the different pathogens that you must assume are there, and the symptoms they produce, including meningitis, HIV, and the different forms of hepatitis. We covered the universal precautions that are necessary to protect everyone from those. We reviewed all the immunizations that are available, and which ones are required before you can work on a site. We covered how to use personal protective equipment, and we practiced putting it on and taking it off safely.

We covered how to set up a proper boundary to isolate the accident site, and how to establish proper entry and exit procedures. As I talked about how to put the various protections in place, I showed them accident site photos from around the world where people were not taking proper precautions. When you show them dramatic real-life photos, it helps to persuade people to take their own safety seriously, along with the safety of others they might be responsible for. By the way, when I say dramatic photos, I don't mean gory ones – I don't use those because they're not needed. The photos I show are of people working in hazardous conditions who are not using proper protection.

I told them about how I got caught doing something stupid at a site in Brazil, and how they should always ask the locals for a safety briefing about local hazards. In Brazil, I was working at a site next to a banana plantation, and this was my first-time seeing bananas being grown. During a break, I wandered into the plantation to have a closer look.

I took four photos using my cell phone. The first one was from a distance, showing the banana plants, and the fact that each plant has only one bunch of bananas. The second photo was closer, showing the banana cluster on the plant, wrapped loosely with newspaper and covered with a plastic sheet. I took the third photo looking up from the bottom of the wrapping (the bottom was open), so I could show the little green bananas, and how nicely they were sheltered inside there. For the fourth photo, I stuck my arm as far up into the "tent" as I could reach – I wanted to get a close-up of the bananas, and I did.

When I showed my photos to the people from Brazil, they were shocked. One of them downloaded a photo on his phone to show me. It was of a Brazilian Wandering Spider, also known as a Banana Spider. It's one of the most venomous spiders on earth. He said that these spiders hide in the bananas during the day and go out to kill things at night. If you disturb them, like I did, they will attack. I guess my comrades thought I knew about that hazard. I had a close call, and it was a lesson learned by me. I always share that story in my training.

I ended the Mongolia training with my full module about the threats from psychological trauma, and the protections that are necessary. Most people never experience working in an environment where there are human remains and scattered personal effects. It can be very stressful and traumatic, and even

146

depressing. I asked for a show of hands, and most of these people had not been to a site like that. I told them that it is important to think about this issue ahead of time.

Again, I will direct this to you just as if you were in that class in Mongolia, but I will give you a shortened version.

My experience is that for almost everybody, you will not know how you are going to react to that environment until you actually experience it. One thing is for sure – you should decide for yourself if you think you are prepared and able to work at a traumatic accident site. There should never be pressure on anybody to do that kind of work.

Some people already know ahead of time that they are not able to deal with dead bodies or human remains. They just know that for them an accident site would be frightening or overwhelming, and the thought of having to work there causes them a lot of distress. If you are one of those people, make sure you let it be known that your duties with your Go Team must not require you to go to the wreckage site. I have worked with many very good investigators who do excellent investigation work, but they never go to the site – they wait until the wreckage has been recovered, or they work with other types of evidence.

Many other people feel that they would be able to work at a traumatic accident site, and in my experience, when they think that way, it turns out that they were correct. They find a way to put a mental barrier between the accident site as a tragic and sad place where people died, and a workplace that needs to be examined to find out what went wrong.

One thing that I want to make perfectly clear – someone is not "stronger" if they can work on a site – and nobody is "weaker" if they choose not to. It doesn't make you a better investigator if you work on the site, or less effective if you choose not to. My consulting partner Terry Heaslip, who is one of the best investigators in the world, can't even listen when people talk about bodies at accident sites. It almost makes him physically sick. But Terry is exceptionally good at analyzing wreckage, and data, and figuring out what happened.

If the site has not been cleared of all human remains before you get there, it is almost inevitable that you will encounter dead bodies, or body pieces. They will be mixed in with wreckage pieces.

147

Sometimes they are burned beyond recognition, and they can be hard to identify as parts of people. You are not responsible for recovering any bodies or body parts – that is the responsibility of the coroner or the police.

Some of you, like me, will be more affected by what you smell than what you see. Odors at an accident site can be very powerful and sickening.

You are not responsible for recovering any personal effects. You should be very careful to not touch any personal effects, including money, jewelry, wallets or purses, cell phones, and laptops. If you find any items like that, you should tell the site supervisor and have those recovered by the coroner or police.

In my experience, everyone who works on an accident, whether you go to the actual crash site or not, is affected in some way by the tragedy. It is perfectly normal and expected that you will feel some affects, but it is also normal if you feel no affects at all. It is normal to feel nervous, or to have a hard time sleeping, or to find yourself going over the details of the situation in your mind. These thoughts or experiences will decrease fairly quickly, and you should soon be back to your normal life.

We need to talk about PTSD – post-traumatic stress disorder. PTSD causes symptoms that you cannot control without getting help. What does this look like? You would suspect PTSD when things you experience at an accident site become overwhelming – and they cause you a lot of distress – and that distress lasts for a long time.

PTSD causes symptoms such as: re-experiencing the traumatic situation – having vivid nightmares – having flashbacks about what you have seen – having traumatic thoughts that seem to come suddenly and unexpectedly.

PTSD can make you feel very nervous or on edge all the time. Many people with PTSD get startled very easily. They can have a hard time concentrating, and feel disconnected from their body or thoughts. Some people who have PTSD have a hard time feeling emotions.

One thing you have to know is that when you go to an aircraft accident you will have experienced a very stressful and traumatic situation. There is no right way to feel, and there is no right way to deal with how you're feeling. Some people find that it is helpful to share their thoughts with others on the investigation team. Some people find that talking to someone trained as a counselor is helpful. On some investigations, the IIC will arrange to have de-briefings that you can attend. Debriefings can be good for sharing experiences, and for getting support.

Many people find that it is not necessary to do anything more than just do their normal activities. I have even heard some investigators say that paying too much attention to PTSD is harmful. I don't believe that. But I do believe that some people are better off not being involved in structured de-briefings.

One thing is for sure – if you have symptoms of stress that are abnormal for you – or that worry you – make sure that you let people know and get medical help right away. It is also important to watch for symptoms of unusual stress in others, and if you see that, to tell someone in the investigation team.

Whatever the case, when the field investigation is finished, and whether you are feeling any symptoms or not, you must recognize that you have been through a stressful situation, and it's both normal and important to allow yourself some time to recover.

At the end of the final day of training, I gave everyone a certificate saying they attended. I also gave each of them a card stating that they had been trained on site safety and biohazards.

Before I finish with my Mongolian adventure, I'll tell you a story about what happened to me during a stopover in Beijing on my way home. Having never been to China before, I decided to stay a couple of extra days there to see the sights. I pre-arranged to hire a guide, a car and driver, and to have them take me on a personal tour to the normal places you hear about, such as the Great Wall, the Forbidden City, the Summer Palace, the Temple of Heaven, and Tiananmen Square. I highly recommend this way to see things over there, especially if your time is tight. It's not as expensive as it sounds, and I had a wonderful experience.

Now for the "other" adventure. At the hotel in Beijing, I couldn't find my phone charger (I found it later, after I got home). Thinking I had left it in Ulan Bator, I set out from the hotel to walk to the massive Joy City Shopping Mall where there was an Apple Store. I checked it all out on Google Maps – it was only a 15-minute walk down a single street – nothing to it.

As I walked along, I was joined by a charming young couple who asked if they could walk with me. They explained they were trying to improve their English language skills, and they asked if I would mind if we just talked as we walked – I could help them with their pronunciation. They seemed like very friendly young people, so I was delighted to be able to help.

They asked where I was going, and I explained that I needed to buy a new charger at the Apple Store. They said there was a fantastic Apple Store in the mall, but that the mall was enormous (which it turned out to be), and if I wanted they could help me find it, and they would get me to a salesperson so I wouldn't be there all night. I took them up on that, and it worked out splendidly. I got the exact charger I needed in no time at all, even though the store was incredibly crowded. I would never have achieved that without their help.

As we were leaving the store, I asked them if I could buy them a drink to thank them for their kindness. They took me up on that, and said they knew of a special place that was not too far away. With that, I followed them through the mall and out an exit and up a street and around a corner and through an alley and within less than two minutes I was completely lost. This did not feel right.

We kept chatting all the while, in a most friendly way. They pointed out things they wanted to know the English words for, like flowers, and fenceposts, I helped them with the proper pronunciations. Eventually we came to a small entryway into a hole-in-the-wall kind of coffeeshop, and in we went. They gave us a table at the back, and we ordered some drinks – me a coke zero, and them something stronger. The waiter brought us some peanuts and other nibbles that we didn't order, and the young man asked if he could order some fruit, to which I agreed.

We talked for quite a while. The young lady showed me some very nice trinkets with beautiful engravings – she said she engraved them herself at a nearby studio. Eventually I found out why they had chosen this special place. I was presented with a bill for over 1,000 Chinese Yuan, close to $200 Canadian – for drinks and munchies worth at the most about $15. The waiter demanded my credit card. I mentioned to my guests that the bill seemed a bit high, and they just shrugged. I had already figured out that I was in trouble – now I knew the plot. They were all in it together – they had brought me there to rip me off.

There was no way I was going to willingly give up my credit card, so I dug into my pocket to see how much cash I had. Fortunately, I had been to an ATM to get 1,000 Yuan for my touring. I had just spent some 150 of that for my new charger, so I had about 850 Yuan left. I told them that for some reason my credit card wasn't working in China – it had been cut off by VISA – I had just tried again to use it at the Apple Store and it wouldn't work (all that was a fib). They bought into that, and when I offered the waiter the 850 Yuan, fortunately he took it.

I wasn't sure what would happen next. Everything between me and my criminal friends was still very good natured. I asked them to walk me back to where they had found me – I had no idea which way to go – and they said they would. On the way, we happened (just by coincidence) to pass by the studio where the young lady worked, and we went in. I was offered some amazing deals on trinkets, and I said I would like to buy dozens of them, except I had no way to pay for them. But I would love to come back the next day.

We left, and we walked and chatted very cordially for the next while until I finally recognized that we had come to the street that led to my hotel. My charming criminal friends got me pointed in the right direction, and I thanked them very much for their hospitality, and they bid their adieu. I figured we were all winners – they got a good lesson in English – and a share of my Yuan stash, and I got a pretty cheap life lesson that could easily have cost me a lot more – and another interesting story to tell.

Old Charlie wouldn't do accidents in Cape Breton. One day I got him to tell me the story about what had happened to keep him away from there. I have a confession to make. There have been times (as needed during an investigation) when I've stolen this story for myself, putting me in the place of Charlie. For the sake of accuracy in this book, I'll tell it faithfully here, as it was told to me.

Many years earlier, Charlie was sent to an accident in the Cape Breton Highlands. Nobody was killed, and the police had already escorted an ambulance to retrieve the three survivors. The wreckage was on rural land controlled by old man McClintock and his clan. They were loners, and they had a reputation for violence against those they considered intruders. Nobody ever ventured close to their boundaries.

The police weren't about to head back there with Charlie – he was on his own. When Charlie asked them for suggestions, they told him to look for a volunteer down at the local watering hole. Someone there would know how to get there, but it would be unlikely he could find anyone willing to take him.

By promising a case of beer, Charlie found someone, a young man named Billy. Later, Charlie found out everyone called him Crazy Billy, and for good reason. Billy said the roads were rough, but he had the truck for the job. A most notable feature of Billy's truck was the gun rack across the back window of the cab, holding two hunting rifles.

On the way to the McClintock property Billy asked Charlie all about investigating accidents, and Charlie regaled him with stories. Billy was quite excited to be helping with such important business. Billy told Charlie that he had never been onto the McClintock property, and he didn't know anyone else who had been there either. He said that when any of the McClintock's came to town, everyone gave them lots of room.

Charlie said that they drove up a long driveway with woods on one side and a fenced-in pasture on the other. In the pasture there were a number of beef cattle, and a couple of horses. They could see an

152

older man sitting on the porch of a house, but Billy stopped his truck some distance back saying he didn't want to get too close.

Charlie walked up to the house, not knowing what to expect. Surprisingly, he found the old man sitting quietly – he had tears in his eyes. Charlie told him he was there about the accident, and that he had good news about the occupants of the aircraft – everyone had survived. Charlie said the old man had no interest in that, so he asked the old man to point him in the direction of the wreckage. McClintock pointed across the pasture, but he told Charlie that he had no right to be there. He said that the wreckage was now his. But he said he would be willing to let Charlie look at it – on one condition.

With more tears in his eyes, the old man pointed to one of the horses in the pasture. He explained that it had been his favourite horse for almost 30 years. Now it was suffering, and he couldn't find a vet willing to come to his place to put it down, and he just couldn't do it himself. Neither could his sons – they couldn't even come out of the house they were so sad. Old man McClintock said he would give Charlie a rifle, and if he would shoot that old horse, he could go look at the wreckage, and even have it removed from there if he wanted to.

Charlie agreed right away. He told McClintock that he wouldn't need his rifle – he said that he had his own. Charlie said that on his way back to the truck it came to him that he had an opportunity to build up his reputation in those parts. When he got to the truck, Billy was all excited, and he asked Charlie what had happened. Charlie told Billy a modified version.

Charlie told Billy that McClintock had ordered him to leave, but he told Billy that he wasn't the slightest bit scared of old man McClintock, or any of his sons either. He told Billy that he had informed McClintock that he was going to look at the wreckage, and he warned McClintock that he and his sons had better stay out of the way. Then Charlie went on – just to show them that I mean business, watch this – see that horse over there – McClintock told me that that's his favourite horse – just to show him who's boss, I'm going to shoot that horse.

153

Billy was abuzz with excitement. Charlie asked Billy to get him one of the rifles, and to make sure it was loaded. Billy passed him the rifle, and Charlie moved away from the truck, aimed at the poor old horse, and pulled the trigger – BANG!!! Down went the old horse. Then Charlie heard BANG – BANG – BANG – and he heard Billy yell "I got three of their best cows, that'll show them!!!".

Charlie yelled at Billy to get in the truck and start driving as fast as he could – back to town. He gave Billy money enough for two cases of beer, and had Billy drop him off at the police station. The police gave Charlie an immediate escort to the bridge off the island, and Charlie never went back there again. The cause of the plane crash went unsolved.

Charlie never worried about his safety, so long as he stayed on the mainland – the police assured him the McClintock's would never leave the island. And they told Charlie not to worry about Billy either. Everyone knew Billy was crazy, and the McClintock's would never kill a crazy person because they knew what happens if you do that – their spirit comes back to haunt you.

16

LEARNING BY DOING – AND DOING – AND DOING

There's one segment of my career that I'll spend some more time on here, because it's where I learned the most about accident investigation. It was during the six years I worked as a regional investigator with CASB – from 1984 to 1990. What a perfect job that was for me. My wife and I each had good paying jobs, we had three children to raise, and we were still living in our home territory. And the bonus for me was that I was going to work every day at a small regional office with just seven or eight people in total, with Dave Owen as my boss.

It was an incredibly good setup. Three of us at the office were pilots, and we had full access to the same Transport Canada aircraft on which I had been the training pilot – perfect. We had a couple of technical investigators (Roy and old Charlie) and a couple of super support staff, and we all got along great together. We worked as a team.

Roy had joined CASB a few months after me, so we learned investigation work together. He had a strong background as a maintenance engineer, both in fixed wing and helicopters. No one could put anything over on Roy when it came to maintenance. He could turn a wrench with the best of them. And with my background on the pilot side, we were quite a team. Roy taught me the biggest difference between him, a mechanic, and me, a pilot – he washed his hands before he went to the washroom, and I washed mine after.

On investigations, Roy excelled at keeping our team's social interactions in good standing. I'd be in bed by 9 p.m. Roy would be out visiting the local establishments. He had an objective of course – to see if he might overhear some revealing evidence about the accident we were working on. The later he stayed out, the harder he worked the next day. He was quite a character – and in those ways he was the exact opposite of me.

One accident Roy and I investigated happened on 24 March 1986, in a remote part of Labrador some 40 miles north of Goose Bay. The crash happened at 9:55 in the morning, and we were notified at about 11 o'clock. We were airborne by 2 p.m. We were told it was a single-engine Otter (DHC-3) aircraft, and that the pilot and three passengers had been killed – one passenger had survived.

The deceased pilot was the president of the company that owned the aircraft. I had met him a few times, but I didn't know him well. He had left early

155

that morning to retrieve a party of four hunters from the wilderness near Snegamook Lake. It was still full winter conditions in Labrador, so the lakes and rivers were completely frozen over and snow-covered, and the aircraft was equipped with retractable skis.

During the return flight with the hunters, the pilot called his operations base to say that on takeoff from Snegamook Lake the engine had started to run very rough, but it had smoothed out some after he reduced the power for cruise. He called later to say the engine was getting worse, but he still had enough power to maintain altitude, and he would follow the Crooked River in case he had to land. Soon after that, he called to say that he was now getting an odour of smoke in the cockpit, and that he was going to land on the river. It was during this attempted landing that he crashed.

The company sent another aircraft with a mechanic to check out the engine, and to get the passengers. When that aircraft arrived at the site, they saw that the Otter had crashed and burned. They couldn't land because of whiteout conditions. Three helicopters were immediately dispatched from Goose Bay – one chartered by the company, one chartered by the RCMP, and one operated by the Canadian Military. They rescued the surviving passenger, and they left everything else undisturbed for us.

Roy and I arrived in Goose Bay too late to do anything that night. We found hangar space for our Beech Baron, and we arranged for a helicopter to take us to the accident site early the next morning. The RCMP would be there with us, and they would recover the remains. It was bitterly cold when we arrived in Goose Bay, and it turned even colder overnight. In the morning there were blue skies, but the wind was blowing making the windchill extreme.

It was in these weather conditions that we arrived at the accident site. The wreckage was in the middle of a wide section of the river – it was the size and shape of a small lake. There were no clouds, but in wind gusts the drifting snow made it feel like we were in a blizzard. Three RCMP officers had arrived ahead of us, and they had a fire going and a small shelter tent set up. Their campsite was about 50 steps from the wreckage – the wreckage seemed to be mostly all in one spot.

After we checked in with the RCMP officers, Roy and I got our cameras ready (35 mm film cameras) and made our way across the snow to check out the wreckage. What we saw was a mess. Unlike most aircraft which carry their

156

fuel in the wings, the single-engine Otter has belly tanks underneath the fusel-age. These belly tanks had ruptured upon impact, and the fuel had caught fire. The cabin area was completely incinerated. The intensity of the fire had melted the snow, and then the ice beneath the snow. The entire cabin area, including everything that was in it, was completely charred, and most of it had sunk into the water. When the fire went out, the water re-froze, so now everything was trapped beneath (embedded in) the solid ice.

The fire had stayed isolated to the cabin area. It had not destroyed the engine and propeller, or the wings and tail. Based on the heading of the wreckage, Roy and I walked back along what we presumed to be the direction of travel before impact. Amazingly, we found a large gouge mark in the snow – the gouge mark corresponded to damage we saw on the outer left wing – and we found the lens cover for the left-wing's navigation light in that gouge mark. We also found another spot where the aircraft had struck the snow surface, and then had bounced back airborne before striking again and coming to rest. Somehow, the drifting snow had not filled in those witness marks.

From all that evidence, we were able to estimate the bank angle when the wingtip hit, and to conclude that when the aircraft first struck, it had been in a steep left bank, and at a high sink rate – classic indications that the pilot had lost control in whiteout conditions. A whiteout conclusion was supported by the statements of those who were in the recovery aircraft – the aircraft that had arrived shortly after the crash – the one that couldn't land due to whiteout conditions.

With that, we made our way back to the RCMP's little campsite. The fire was bigger now, and there was some warmth coming off of it. But to get the full effect of the heat you had to stand on the downwind side – that put you in the choking smoke. It was worth it though, just to get some of the ice off of your balaclava. For those who are not familiar, a balaclava is a full head cover-ing most often made from knit wool. They have small openings for your eyes and mouth, and you can still breathe through your nose – the air passes right through the material. Balaclavas are sought out by bank robbers to hide their identity. I never used mine that way – I'm not sure about Roy.

In the Labrador cold, balaclavas are both a blessing and a curse. They keep frostbite to a minimum, but they also absorb the humidity from your breathing so that ice builds up. The ice makes them stiff and heavy, and that causes them to shift so that the holes don't line up. The humidity freezes on your eyelashes, and your eyelids freeze shut. That was a frequent happening during our time on Crooked River. It's very unpleasant to have to use a bare hand to melt the ice to allow your eyelids to open.

157

We had to figure out a way to get the wreckage documented. The engine had to be recovered so we could figure out what went wrong with it. Roy hatched a plan to detach the engine, and he would get a helicopter to sling it out. We needed to document the cockpit instruments and controls, or at least find out if that was even possible. Then there was the matter of the human remains. That was an issue for the RCMP, but in this case they couldn't do their work without disturbing our evidence. We would have to work together.

There was one badly burned body that was recognizable by shape, but even it was well stuck in the solid ice. The rest of the remains were unrecognizable because of the intense fire. Mixed into all of this were hundreds of charred and frozen ptarmigans – these were the small game birds that the hunters had harvested. We found fabric that told us their haul was being transported in potato sacks, stacked in the cabin. The sacks had split open during the impact.

There was only one way to proceed – we had to chop into the ice, and then try to figure out what each piece was as we freed it up. We used screwdrivers and a small axe to dig down into the ice. It was exceptionally unpleasant work. Each blow with the axe sent up a spray of ice mixed with everything else. The spray would fly into our eyes and mouth, and it would get frozen to our balaclavas. When you got too cold, or when you had an eye freeze shut, you had to walk over to the fire for relief. More than once I saw someone step close enough to the fire's embers that it made their boots smoke.

Eventually we got things sorted, and the RCMP sent for a helicopter and a coroner to get the human remains. They arrived with body bags, and they started to load those bags with what we had recovered. The one body that was mostly intact was misshapen to where it wouldn't fit into a bag, and the coroner used our axe to cut a leg off.

After they left, we got the engine unhooked, and a helicopter came and slung that out. Roy and I did our best to document the continuity of the flight controls, and to get the positions of the engine controls, and to get photos of everything – all the standard investigation actions. Then we packed up our stuff and sent for our helicopter.

A couple of weeks later, back at our workshop in Moncton, Roy led a small team in tearing down the engine. It didn't take long to discover a fatigue-initiated crack in one of the cylinder heads of the 9-cylinder radial engine. That's what had caused the rough running, and the power loss and the smell of smoke. It was a relatively easy job to write the report on this occurrence.

I learned a valuable lesson about making wrong assumptions when I was sent to investigate a crash in Nova Scotia. It was a single-engine aircraft on floats, and it had flipped upside-down while trying to land next to an island just off the southwest coast. I was told that the overturned aircraft had been secured by a line to the shore, and all that was showing above the water was the bottom of the floats. It was not a big deal, so I went by myself in our response vehicle.

It was a long drive, and by the time I got to the wharf where I was supposed to meet the local police, nobody was there to greet me. Everyone had already gone by boat to the site. Not far away on the wharf, I saw two older fellows sitting on chairs in front of a boat. I walked over to see if they could help me. I introduced myself as being from CASB – they could see that anyway from what I was wearing, and from the impressive big marked up truck I had arrived in.

They said I must be there about the aircraft accident, and I said I was, and they said everyone was talking about it. I told them I had to get to the site, and I asked them if they knew where it was, and they said they did – that it was out by (I can't remember the name of the island). I pointed to the boat behind them and asked if they could take me to the site, and they agreed.

It took them some time to get the boat started, but finally we headed out through the harbour and around a neck of land and into open water. After a while we spotted a small island where we could see a couple of other boats and some obvious activity – this would be the accident site. When we got closer, I asked the guys if they had time to wait there for me, and they said that personally they had lots of time, but they felt they had better get the boat back. So, I asked if they could come back later to pick me up and they said they would like to but maybe the owner of the boat wouldn't like that. I asked them who owned the boat, and they said they had no idea.

It came over me that we were using a stolen boat to meet up with the local police. Maybe the police would know these guys, and also know who owned the boat – this could go bad. I asked them to swing in as close as possible to a low rock outcropping and I would jump off the boat over to it. I asked them not to stop, and to go straight back and put the boat back where they found it. I thanked them kindly for their help. When my feet hit the rocks I never looked back. I heard the boat accelerating away, and I was pleased my arrival was drawing the attention of the police so they wouldn't be noticing the boat so much.

Nothing about my investigation of the overturned floatplane was remarkable, so I'll skip that here. When I arrived back at the wharf with the police, I was pleased to see our stolen boat back where I first saw it. In thinking about what had happened, it appears that the two older gentlemen might have thought that because I was a government official conducting urgent business, I had the right to commandeer that boat. It could be that they looked at it as their civic duty to help get me where I was needed. Since that incident, I've been much more careful in wielding my powers. Thankfully, I never heard anything more about the boat incident.

Dave Owen and I did several investigations together. I really enjoyed working with Dave. He was my boss, but he also was a good friend, and he taught me a lot. He was a giving person, and a true professional who took his job very seriously. He supported us at every turn, and we really appreciated that. Among the rest of us in our little office, we enjoyed foiling Dave's numerous attempts to impose the bureaucracy mandated by head office. Rebelling against head office was our primary way to team-build.

One accident Dave and I worked on together involved a Piper PA-31 Navajo that crashed into the steep seaside slope of Table Mountain, about 10 miles northwest of Channel-Port aux Basques, Newfoundland, killing all three on board. The Navajo was equipped to conduct aeromagnetic survey operations. It had a boom protruding from its tail, and inside it had electronic equipment to capture the ocean-bottom features it passed over while flying at 1,000 feet above the water. For precise navigation, the aircraft was equipped with the same type of Loran C that we talked about earlier on the Twin Otter – the one where my former student and the others were killed near Goose Bay.

On the morning of the accident, the Navajo pilot and one of his two technicians inputted the waypoints into the Loran C for the tracks they were to fly that day. Their objective was to survey an east/west block of ocean bottom just off the south coast of Newfoundland. Their flight legs, back and forth in the east/west direction, were to be flown two miles apart, and they were to fly 10 legs. Every leg except the 10th one would be completely over the ocean. With the aircraft's electronic technology, they were able to program the Loran C to control the autopilot, so everything would be flown with precision.

First thing in the morning on the day after the crash, Dave and I flew to Stephenville, the closest airport. From there we boarded a military CH-113

Labrador search and rescue helicopter, and we went to the accident location. Before we landed on the plateau at the top of the cliff, we asked to have a look at the crash site from the air. The pilot hovered the Labrador abeam the impact point below the ridge, giving us a good perspective.

It was obvious that the aircraft had been in normal cruise flight when it flew headlong into the cliff face. It had been all but obliterated. The outline of what was left replicated the size of the aircraft. Everything had been burned in a flash fire. We got the altitude of the impact from the helicopter's altimeter – 1,000 feet above sea level.

We saw two people who were down at the impact site, and they had a small shelter set up. They turned out to be RCMP members who were there to do their standard documentation and recover the human remains. When we landed on the ridge, our altitude read 1,160 feet, meaning the aircraft had hit 160 feet below the top. That's how far we would have to climb down, and then back up.

Our plan was to have the CH-113 stay with us for whatever time it took to do our work. The Search and Rescue Technicians (SAR Techs) from the helicopter offered to help us get safely up and down the cliff face. We would then hitch a ride back to Stephenville, and we would be done with that part of the investigation.

Looking over the cliff face, I got confirmation from my nervous system that I don't like heights. It wasn't straight down all the way to the water, but to me the first few hundred feet looked close to vertical. It seemed like if you lost your footing you could tumble all the way down. I was doubly concerned about Dave going down there. Dave was tall and gangly, and the opposite of nimble. I secretly asked one of the SAR Techs to stay close to him.

If I could log mountain climbing time, I would have 4.75 hours. That's how long it took us to get down there, do our work, and climb back up. On our way down we came to small ridges where we could stop and rest and feel safe, but for a lot of it there were near vertical drops where it was best to be hooked to a rope that had been secured by a SAR Tech.

When we got to the wreckage level and met the RCMP guys we were shocked to find out they had stayed on their little perch all night. I asked them how many were there when they bedded down, and they assured me they were the only two. Apparently, they were not predisposed to roll over in their sleep.

As best they could, they gave us a tour of what they had documented, and we spent our time there examining the debris and taking our own photos and measurements. To this day, this remains the only site I have worked at where we could find no wreckage worth recovering for evidence.

There was one piece that we took away with us. Amazingly, we found a camshaft from one of the engines that had survived in completely pristine condition. It was just lying there, among all the devastation, and it looked brand new. It even had shiny oil still on it, even though it was within the burn area. There is no explanation for that, but that's the way we found it. Amazingly, things like that can happen in crash dynamics.

A couple of hours into our cliff climbing episode we got word from above that the helicopter would be departing. There was a fog bank coming in, and they wanted to get out of there before they got stuck. That's very typical for that part of the world. Fog along the coastline is always a threat, and unpredictable. They would come back later, when the fog lifted. It wasn't long before the fog arrived, and the conditions became (as the Newfoundlanders say) "not fit". For the remainder of our time down there we helped the RCMP with their work, recovering what human remains we could find. Then we struggled our way back to the top, with plenty of help from the SAR Techs.

Now we had to decide – would we chance waiting for the fog to disappear so the helicopter could retrieve us – or would we walk out on our own. The RCMP guys told us it was a five-mile hike down an unmarked trail to get to the nearest road. The RCMP guys decided to stay, not wanting to carry their equipment and recovered materials with them. A SAR Tech guy volunteered to stay with them. Dave and I decided to walk out, and the other two SAR Tech guys would go with us.

None of us knew exactly where the trail was, or how we would follow it in the fog, but walking out seemed like a better option than staying there overnight. Before we headed out, Dave – who as a manager always had a strong inclination to lead – gave our walking group a safety talk based on tips from his boy scout days 50 years previous – very educational for the professional SAR Tech guys I expect. To finish with a bang, Dave cautioned that we were in an unforgiving environment where many people had died making a lesser attempt.

We were only two minutes into our epic trek when we met a group of five young teenagers hiking the other way. They said they were from the local area, and were on their way to have a picnic overlooking the ocean. We told them about our comrades being there, and we wished them a fine evening, and we went on our way. It was comforting to know that if we came to any of the harms Dave had warned us about, these young people would find us on their way back out.

We analyzed the data we collected about the accident flight, and we concluded that they had made a critical mistake when they programmed their Loran C. They had mistakenly set their autopilot to start with Leg 10 instead of Leg 1. They thought the autopilot was taking them to their first leg that was way out over the water, but instead it took them on a track direct to the cliff face. We checked the weather, and it confirmed that when they approached Table Mountain on the accident flight, it had been shrouded in fog. To confirm our theory, I rented an aircraft that had a Loran C (we didn't have an aircraft with Loran C in the government fleet) and I programmed their coordinates. The autopilot flew me exactly to the impact point where they hit.

Back in the 1980's, Roy and I did an accident that had a different element to it. We were at the office when we got notice that a Bell 206 helicopter had just crashed in Cape Breton, Nova Scotia. It was attempting a quick positioning flight, but it crashed short of its destination. The pilot, who was the sole occupant, was killed. Normally, it would be a five-hour drive to get to that part of Cape Breton, but with Roy driving we could get there in four, so we took our response truck.

When we got there, we found there was a lot more interest than normal for a single fatality accident. That was because the helicopter was being used to apply herbicide to woodlots in the area. In fact, the company had a contract with woodlot operators to spray herbicide on large swaths of forest, at numerous locations across the island. Protesters considered the herbicide to be carcinogenic to humans, and some of the citizenry were vehemently opposed to its use. There had been demonstrations, and even death threats, including threats to shoot the helicopter down.

When we met up with the RCMP officers who were working the case, they filled us in. Their initial interviewing confirmed that the helicopter had departed from a nearby motel where the pilot had spent the night. He was on his way to the base camp they had set up for the day's spraying – where they had parked their resupply vehicles full of fuel and herbicide. The accident flight would not have lasted more than about five minutes, based on how far it had travelled from the motel to where it had crashed.

The officers told us they had been to the site, but they hadn't disturbed anything. They said the wreckage was in amongst trees, and that everything was badly burned. We agreed that we needed to work together with them so we could determine if this was an accident, or if it could have been a criminal act. We don't get involved in criminal investigations, but they would certainly need our help with helicopter expertise.

An obvious first question – did anyone hear gunshots? No. Did anyone see the helicopter hit the ground? No. But there were witnesses who watched the helicopter depart from the motel and head off in the direction where it was later found. They said it stayed at low level, and then disappeared from their view in the distance. They said the overall weather was good, but where they lost sight of the helicopter there was some patchy early-morning fog or low cloud.

The helicopter had sat unguarded overnight. We would have to look for any signs of tampering with flight controls or other systems or structure. We would need to check for contamination in the fuel and oil. We would have to look for signs of an explosion, or an incendiary device. And, of course, we would look for bullet holes. We would make sure the autopsy looked for signs of foul play, such as bullet wounds, or poisoning – we would need a full toxicology report.

The accident site gave us lots of evidence. This was a medium-density mixed forest environment, with maximum tree heights of some 50 to 60 feet. We went first to where the main structure of the helicopter came to rest, and as we had been briefed, we saw that it was severely burned and mangled.

We could see that the charred remains of the pilot were in the cockpit area. The crows had already gone after the parts they go for first. The body was shrunk into a fetal position. That happens when it is exposed to intense heat over an extended time. The heat causes the big muscles in the arms and legs to contract, and they pull the limbs towards the torso. The same thing happens to the fingers – they are drawn toward the palms, making the hands look cupped. There was nothing for us to learn from the body in situ, so we took our own photos and gave our approval to recover the remains – we left that to the RCMP.

We could see that the rotor blades had sliced off a number of trees as the helicopter cut its way to its final resting place. We walked back along the trail and found the first tree that had been hit – the top was sliced off cleanly. We wanted to determine the height above ground of the first impact. I was getting set to use the method where you fold a square piece of paper to give you a 45-degree angle to use as a sightline to the top – then measure from where you are standing to the base of the tree. Roy had a quicker and more accurate solution to measure it. He used his axe, and he cut the tree down.

We used my less destructive measuring method to document the other struck trees, and our plot plan confirmed the helicopter was at a normal cruise speed when it first hit. That told us it had not come to a hover and then crashed vertically. It also told us that the engine was producing significant power – no engine failure here. We noted that the wreckage trail was on a gentle upslope, producing conditions where the pilot – in poor visibility – could have been in level flight and still flown into the trees as they came up to meet him. That became our working hypothesis, but we still needed to investigate for other possibilities. In accident investigation, if you don't have definitive proof of what happened, you must find evidence to eliminate all potential scenarios – the objective is to be left with only the one that fits.

There was not enough left in the wreckage to check out the flight controls or instruments. Roy got some samples of fuel and oil out of what was left of the engine – he did that just for completeness – we knew from the tree damage that the engine was running. We could find no evidence of any projectile passing through the cockpit/passenger outer skin structure (what was left of it) – basically, no bullets going in, and no explosion fragments going out. This had been a very intense fire, but we could see no evidence of there being an extra hot spot that might point to an incendiary device.

All that was left was to get the autopsy done, and we would be finished with the field work part of the investigation. That turned into an issue. I had been to one autopsy previously and had promised myself I would never do that again. But because of the high interest in this investigation, the RCMP officer who was assigned to attend requested someone from CASB be there to confirm there were no signs of foul play – then he would officially turn the investigation over to us. Roy and I both went.

Unlike our last autopsy experience, at this one we were observers only. Again, it was educational to see the techniques used to complete the work on a badly charred body – like how to stabilize and remove the upper and lower jaws to facilitate identification through dental records, and how to find and extract toxicology samples when most everything has been burned away. But to me, there was not enough useable education to make up for the uncomfortableness of the experience. After this one, I vowed that if I was ever to show up at another autopsy it would be my own. I have never been to one since.

There was nothing suspicious found in the toxicology, and no signs of bullets or other forms of foul play. In our report we attributed the accident to flight into poor visibility at low level. A contributing factor was that he was headed directly into the rising sun. This was a CFIT accident – the pilot unwittingly flew a perfectly serviceable helicopter into the rising terrain.

When CASB was formed in 1984, they were given the responsibility for investigating incidents within the air traffic control system, which at the time was run by Transport Canada. Prior to CASB, when there was an occurrence, TC would form what was known as a "Fact Finding Board", and they would look into it themselves. Functionally, it meant that ATC investigated itself – never a good plan. But of course, in their view, that worked just fine – they felt like they had the expertise in that specialized field, and nobody else did.

As I briefly described earlier, in the high-level airspace above the Atlantic Region we had (and still have) one of the world's busiest air route structures. At the time it was called the North Atlantic Organized Track System. All the aircraft travelling back and forth between North America and Europe were funnelled right over top of us – many hundreds of flights each way, every day. The eastbound flow to Europe was overnight, and the westbound flow to North America was during the day (it still works that way). The control centre in Gander, Newfoundland controlled the western half of the North Atlantic Ocean airspace, where it gave way to Shanwick Oceanic Control, based in Ireland and Scotland.

A big problem for CASB was that they (we) were given the investigation responsibility by legislation, but we started up with no in-house experts who had ATC experience. Probably you can guess where this is going – guess who was the very first CASB investigator in Canada to be sent to do an ATC investigation – me – all by myself – sent to Gander to look into an incident that happened out over the ocean. A controller had made a mistake that allowed two airliners to fly too close to each other – it was a "loss of separation".

Before I left for Gander, I called head office for input. Basically, they told me to figure it out as I went. My only solid instruction was to avoid doing anything that might lead to a labour dispute. As was usual, ATC was having management/union issues at the time.

When I arrived at Gander ATC it was awkward for everybody, including me. Basically, everyone knew that this situation had been forced on all of us, and we would all have to make the best of it. I didn't know anybody, and nobody knew me. Thankfully, Newfoundlanders are a welcoming people on a personal level, so that helped.

The way I got through it was this. I asked for an introductory meeting with representatives from both management and the union – we all sat down in the same room. I told them my marching orders – I was to conduct an independent investigation into the matter – I would get all the facts and evidence – I would use that to make safety recommendations if I felt any were necessary, and they would be made public – I would write a draft report – all involved parties would have an opportunity to review it for accuracy – it would be fixed up if necessary – then CASB would make it public. All this was in the new CASB Act, so that's what the law called for, and that's what was going to happen.

I told them that I had a big red badge in my pocket that allowed me to look at whatever I wanted to look at, and talk to whoever I chose to, and if anyone withheld anything, or told me an untruth, they would be held accountable under an act of parliament. I told them that up to now I had never had to take that badge out of my pocket, but I could show them the badge if anyone wanted to see it. All this was done in the "down east" style of communication that we were all used to, with the occasional laugh and twinkle in the eye – but they knew I meant business.

I told them I would start by getting a tour of the control room and the specific workstation used during the incident. Then I would interview the controller who was working the flights that lost separation. Then I would interview any other controllers who might have information. Then I would interview the shift supervisor. After that I would determine if I needed to interview anyone else, based on what I found out.

Everyone thought all that was a good plan. The centre manager informed me that he would have a management representative sit in on all the interviews. I informed him that he would not. I told him that only two people would have a say in who was there – me, and the person I was interviewing. The union representative said that he would have a representative there, and I told him that would only happen if the individual controller wanted someone there on his behalf.

I explained that all my interviews would be confidential and fully protected under the new CASB Act. That way, the person being interviewed had the freedom to speak openly about what had happened. Nothing they told me could be used against them in any way. I would make up my draft report based on the collective knowledge that I gained during my investigation, and I would never reveal anything that could be traced back to an identifiable individual. That's the way CASB was set up – to give us the best chance to get to the truth so we could identify anything that needed fixing.

167

The most nervous individual I have ever interviewed was the controller involved in this event. His body was literally shaking as he entered the room – he was accompanied by the union guy. This whole process had gotten to him. He had messed up – he had made a mistake that led to the near miss and potentially multiple fatalities – he knew he had made a mistake – it was the first one on his record, but he was still scared he might lose his job. Then he was faced with this new investigation process. He was overwhelmed by it all.

After I introduced myself, and I had assured him his secrets were safe with me, I asked him if he was okay with the union guy being there. He said yes. I told him that if I ever found out that the union guy had spoken to anyone about what was said in that room I would have him shot, and I had the right to do that. I told him that I was not a controller – I was a humble pilot – so before I could understand anything about what happened to cause the incident, I needed someone who knew the procedures very well to educate me about how the system worked.

I asked him how long he had worked there – 17 years was his answer – and I told him he was just the man I was looking for to give me my education – and I asked him if we could start with that, and he said he would try. With that, he launched into a detailed description of everything he did every day at work. He got right into it. Before long it was just pouring out of him – his nervous energy was burning off – he was a wealth of knowledge.

I told him about being on the other end of the ATC conversations – the pilot end – I had imagined how it must work at the ATC end – now, through his explanations, I knew I was wrong about many things. Of course, we had a few chuckles along the way. I asked him if we could go to the work station where he had been during the incident so we could look at the actual aircraft data blocks he had used to track the incident aircraft – and he said sure, no problem – and we sent the union guy off to set that up.

The three of us went into the operations centre and walked over to his work-station, where he continued with his teaching of me – quietly, of course, this was an active control environment. I was a bit of a slow learner, so he had to explain more than once what had gone wrong, and how he could have done things differently. We talked about how this incident could be used to make changes to the overall procedures – in their operations manuals and training – things that would make sure all the others in that control centre would not make the same mistake.

When we got back to the interview room, I thanked him very much for all the great training. I told him there was really no need for me to do an interview. I already had all the information I needed from him. He was most relieved.

Then I asked if the two of them would do something for me – and that was to explain to the other controllers that I would very likely be the one doing the investigations in Gander Centre from then on, and that I would need their help to figure things out, and that I was no threat to them so long as they told me the truth, and that I would be interviewing enough people for each incident that I would always be able to tell if someone was fibbing, so don't even try – and that if we all worked together we could make changes for the better and everyone would benefit.

Over the years, I did a good number of ATC investigations, both at Gander Centre and at Moncton Centre – both are facilities that handle the North Atlantic flow. Before I leave this subject, I'll make mention of one notable investigation – I wasn't the IIC of this one, but I played a prominent role.

For this one, I remember writing the first draft of the CASB report, including the first paragraph in the Synopsis, which reads as follows:

"Delta Flight 37, a Lockheed L-1011 en route from London to Cincinnati at flight level 310, deviated south of its assigned track after passing 30 degrees west. The aircraft crossed the track of Continental Flight 25, a Boeing 747, flying from London to Newark, also maintaining flight level 310. The front half of Delta Flight 37 passed beneath the rear fuselage of Continental Flight 25 with less than 100 feet vertical separation."

I'll explain it in non-aviation language. The two aircraft were both at 31,000 feet over the ocean, cruising westbound towards North America. To keep them apart, they were cleared on parallel tracks that were separated laterally by 60 nautical miles. While still on the ground in Gatwick, the pilots of the Delta flight had made an error when they inserted their track (route information) into their navigation system, and they never caught it. After passing their 30 degrees west longitude waypoint, their automatic flight system turned them off course, and they drifted over and crossed the track of the Continental flight. We calculated that they actually missed by only 30 feet. Combined, the two aircraft were carrying 589 people. They all came that close to a disaster.

On that one, my duties included investigating the ATC facilities – the one in Gander, and the one in Prestwick, Scotland. On my way back from the UK, I accompanied the pilots of my flight as they went through all the flight planning procedures, and I flew in the jump seat (a cockpit observer seat) – this was the same Delta flight out of Gatwick. I got a first-hand look at Delta's procedures.

There was a very distressing side to this investigation – remember, all this happened way out over the ocean. The flight crews of several other aircraft in the vicinity of the near miss were aware of the near-miss incident. When the Continental pilot indicated over the radio that he would have to report the occurrence, they all engaged in a discussion about whether that was the right thing to do. (Thankfully, those discussions were recorded by a military flight in the vicinity.) What I remember most was that the remarks were exceptionally unprofessional – to me they were shockingly unprofessional. I would never have thought that my fellow pilots could be so unconcerned about aviation safety. They took it upon themselves to guide the Delta flight back on course, saying nothing to ATC. They were not aware of the location of other aircraft on the track, and as a result, they could have created a hazard to other aircraft.

In the end, the pilots of the Continental flight reported the incident to their company dispatch as they approached New York. As it turned out, it would not have been a secret for very long anyway. Dozens of passengers in the Delta flight had spotted the other aircraft in very close proximity, and everyone on board felt a huge jolt as they flew through the turbulence from the Continental flight. It was "big news" in the USA for the next while.

During that investigation we worked with the NTSB in the United States to get some very good recommendations to improve flight safety procedures on the North Atlantic routes. It was handy for me that I had all that previous experience investigating at the ATC facilities, and had built up such goodwill with the controllers and management.

17

A MAJOR MOVE — TO HEAD OFFICE

As I've mentioned, working in the regional office of CASB in Moncton was a dream job for me. I couldn't imagine doing anything different. In March of 1990, CASB morphed into the Transportation Safety Board of Canada (TSB) – the significant difference being that CASB was strictly for air investigations, whereas TSB was responsible for air, rail, marine and pipelines. I thought that one day I might like to be the Atlantic regional manager for TSB, so I started thinking about what I would need on my resume to win that job when Dave Owen left it.

One box to tick would be head office experience. For a couple of summers, I had volunteered to work out of head office to help them catch up on their report processing. That also worked out for my youngest daughter, who was into figure skating. I was able to be close by while she took summer training in Ottawa with top-level coaches.

When my wife came to visit, and we got to look around, we realized that Ottawa would not be a bad place to live, at least for a while. After I had worked the summer of 1990 there, in the fall we took the plunge and moved our family to the big city. It didn't take long before all of us got used to our new environment. It's a great city, and we all still live in Ottawa to this day.

I gave up on my idea of being a regional manager. And I quickly put aside any thought of trying for a management job at head office – that didn't appeal to me at all – there would be just too much bureaucracy, and not enough field work. And besides that, all the supervisory jobs at TSB's head office were bilingual positions (English/French), and I was not bilingual.

The story of my life as an accident investigator wouldn't be complete if I didn't include more about my interactions with Travis Hunter. Remember him? When I was the training pilot for TC in the Atlantic Region, Travis was the top manager there, and by design he flew exclusively with me. We had developed a unique relationship during those times, and it expanded further when we both joined CASB in 1984 – me in Moncton, and Travis at head office. Now, in 1990, here I was transferring into the lion's den where Travis was a senior lion.

Before I relate how our reintroduction at head office went, I need to put some context to how Travis and I got along during the six-year period we were interacting at CASB, where we had 750 miles of separation. Even with that physical distancing, it was hard to isolate from Travis's ineptitude. It was recognized in all the regions that CASB, and now TSB, functioned in spite of his leadership, and not because of it.

Occasionally, Travis would visit our regional office as part of his strategic management plan to keep all the regions equally agitated. It always ended up the same. Travis would lead a meeting, ask for comments, and someone would say something negative about one of his dumb policies. Then he would launch into a rehearsed rebuttal that made no sense. The session would end when he won, his victory signaled by the last malcontent recognizing the hopelessness of it all, and falling silent.

Given our unique history and relationship, Travis would always find a way to have a one-on-one with me. He would ask me how he did at the meeting, and I would tell him that he should listen more, and he would say that he would listen if it was more than just whining. I would tell him that regional investigators felt he was not supporting them, and that was causing low morale. Then he would get angry and tell me I just didn't understand the big issues. I would remind him one more time about how I operate – if you don't want an honest answer, don't ask me the question. Then Dave Owen would hear our raised voices and come to rescue me.

That's the context for my move to head office. Now I would be working in my little cubicle not far from Travis's big corner office, but thankfully there were still two levels of management between us. It would not be an exaggeration for me to say I could write an entire book about our encounters at head office, but you'll get the idea if I relay only a couple of our first ones.

By military protocol, after a couple of days to settle into my new workspace, I was escorted by Travis's direct underling (the manager of my supervisor) to meet Travis, the big boss. This underling had no idea that Travis and I had a long history, and that I knew Travis much better than he did. We approached Travis's office with due respect, and we were invited to enter – Travis was like the emperor, motioning for us to "approach". I was introduced as the first investigator from a region to ever transfer to head office (you can only imagine why nobody else had taken the plunge).

Travis went on about how important my arrival was to him. I was to be his voice from the regions. In the pageantry of the moment, he must have forgotten he had no interest in what the regions thought. In typical Travis fashion, to impress his underling manager he asked me to brief him on the most pressing regional issue at the time. Even for Travis that surprised me. I told Travis that I had been travelling and moving my family and hadn't given it much thought, so I would prefer to think about it and get back to him. I was very deferential and nice about it. The underling manager took the opportunity to signal that we should leave, and we started to shuffle our way to the door to slip away quietly.

Now here's what made Travis unique, and our relationship unique. Travis had asked me to do something, and that didn't happen, and in front of his underling manager he couldn't let that happen. With the pursed lips, and using that slightly raised voice I had heard so many times before, Travis directed us back to our previous positions. Unlike the underling manager, I knew exactly where this was headed, and it wasn't going to be pretty.

Travis asked me again to reveal the relevant regional issues. Again, I tried to convince him this was not the time and place for that. Right on schedule, his face got red and his voice got louder, and he demanded that I address his question properly. Having been pushed into it, I decided to give him his way. I told him the biggest issue in the regions was terrible morale. He had his answer, but of course that wasn't good enough for Travis.

Travis asked me what I thought he could do about the poor morale. I replied that it was a complicated issue and maybe we could talk about it another time. Then, in typical fashion, his bullying ways got the better of him. He said something like, "you don't understand, I'm not asking you to give me an answer, I'm ordering you to give me an answer – what can I do to improve morale in the regions?". My answer was, "the best thing you could do would be to resign".

That was one of the few times I saw Travis taken aback. This was not going well for him in front of one of his managers. He took some time to respond. Then he calmly agreed that maybe this could be taken up again later. The underling manager moved quickly to get us out of the room. I don't think he had witnessed anything quite like that, but of course he hadn't seen Travis and I in action before. This was not at all new for us.

The following week I sat in on my first staff meeting at head office, with Travis presiding. Let me preface this story by telling you that as the first agenda issue unfolded, I became convinced that it was a setup for me, the new guy, and soon everyone would start laughing and I would be let in on the joke. It sure didn't turn out that way.

Travis led off with an issue involving the TSB jackets that had just been issued to replace the CASB ones. They were really nice jackets, with the TSB name and logo. Regional investigators were proud to wear them. Travis noted that at head office many of us were wearing them to work. He said he'd been thinking about that, and he had concluded it was unfair to the taxpayers. Why should we get the privilege of wearing government issued jackets to work when regular taxpayers didn't?

Then Travis went around the table to get input. Everyone agreed with Travis that there was at least the appearance of unfairness, and something had to be done. Someone observed that the military let their employees wear their uniforms to work. Travis said that was irrelevant. That was their tradition. And more importantly, without uniforms that showed everyone's rank, no one would be able to figure out who was smarter than who.

The discussions went on. The jackets had to be available for an unexpected dispatch to an accident site. Should the investigators keep them at home? Or at the office? Maybe we should carry them back and forth – hidden from the taxpayers. Maybe everyone should have two jackets. I scanned the room. Nobody was laughing – there was not even a hint of it. Another thing came to me. If I didn't count myself, nobody in the room had ever worked at an accident site where they had actually gotten their boots dirty.

I was pretty sure this was an initiation joke on me, but I wasn't 100% convinced, so when Travis asked me whether regional investigators wore their jackets only to accident sites, I decided to tell him the truth. I replied that accident sites were the only places they never wore them, because they wouldn't last half a day there before being ripped to shreds. They wouldn't stand up to the wear and tear. At accident sites, we had to wear protective work gear. We wore these nice jackets everywhere else, to proudly show off the colours of the new TSB.

That's when I thought everyone would break the charade and welcome me to head office and thank me for being so proud of our organization and so on. But there was a long silence. Finally, Travis spoke. He said the minutes of the meeting would show that a discussion of the use of jackets took place, and that he would immediately issue an instruction letter to all investigators that TSB jackets were no longer to be worn except on official business, and it would be mandatory for investigators to wear them on accident sites. I couldn't believe it – this was no joke – the next day the letter came out.

I have to tell you quickly about the next item on the agenda for that meeting. The TSB had a mandate to set up a confidential reporting system to accept tips from the public about safety issues. There was no way to do that on the internet back then, so they put self-addressed and stamped envelopes in strategic aviation-related locations for the public to use. Very few tips were coming in, so Travis wanted ideas to get the pace of input quickened. The investigator filling that confidential reporting role suggested the following. He said that it was his practice to check the mail once a day. He would immediately start checking the mail twice a day. Travis accepted that as a solution, and we moved on.

Whenever Travis got close to being tripped up or exposed, he turned to put-downs and bullying. I saw it many times where people had to sit there and take it, in deference to his power position. What he failed to realize was that everyone knew him for what he actually was – someone who had to be tolerated and accommodated and worked around. It was amazing to watch him leave an encounter feeling so proud of himself for dominating, not realizing that everyone had him pegged as a dud.

In my investigation work, I use Travis as a marker when looking at management issues. People can make their way into management positions even when they are unsuited to the position. I have seen it in lots of investigations – whenever you have a management style that includes put-downs and bullying, you'll find safety issues that result from it. There will be unsafe shortcuts and workarounds that will be factors in your investigation.

When I moved to head office in September 1990, I started in the section called "Audit and Review" (we called it Audit and Redo). There were four of us who were charged with reviewing and fixing all the draft reports submitted by the six regional offices (or from head office for high-profile cases). We had to go through all the associated files and evidence, and make sure each investigation was complete, and each report met the investigative and editorial standards of "The Board". The term "The Board" was used in two ways – it referred to the organization in general, and also to the five political appointees who had the legislated authority to make each report public.

The board members sat at the top of the quality assurance pyramid, but the real work was done by us folks at the working level. In the years I did that "redo" job, I literally worked on hundreds of draft reports that needed upgrading. Like any other job, the more you did of it, the easier it got to spot things that were wrong. The weaknesses would pop out.

You could tell when the investigation itself was incomplete, or when relevant information was left out or misrepresented. You could pick out flawed analysis and findings, and you could identify needed safety recommendations. The easiest thing to spot was poor writing. I would spend countless hours rewriting technical gobbledygook and disjointed analysis, putting it into language that could be understood. Occasionally, it was necessary to pretty much reinvestigate, and that could take weeks or even months. All this, of course, was a tremendous learning experience for me, giving me in-depth exposure to countless numbers of investigations.

As I mentioned, I worked out of head office from September 1990 until I re-tired from the civil service in January 2009 – almost 20 years. I got to work on some very interesting investigations during that time. I actually got to work my first head office investigation just before I started working there. I got called up from the region to be the Deputy IIC on a crash in Dryden, Ontario that happened on 10 March 1989 – still in the days of CASB.

That was the crash of a Fokker F28, operating as Air Ontario Flight 1363 from Dryden to Winnipeg, Manitoba. The pilots tried to take off with ice and snow contaminating the wings – very similar to the Cessna Caravan I talked about at the beginning of this book. They got airborne – just barely – but the aircraft wouldn't fly, and it crashed into a forested area off the end of the runway. There were 65 people on board, and 24 of them were killed, including the two pilots.

I was pleased they asked me to help with this investigation, but professionally it turned out to be anticlimactic. First, the CASB major occurrence manual defined a specific role for a deputy IIC, and it was not an investigative role. Most of the job involved being the logistics person – to help set up the travel and accommodation, and the operations room – telephones, workstations, equipment – rental cars – whatever the team needed.

While everyone else was out investigating, I was signing contracts and paying bills and making phone calls and renting things and hiring contractors – nothing I really wanted to be doing. But I was in a position of "management", so of course I got to give my input at the investigation meetings and so on. Actually, it turned out to be a good experience, forcing me to become familiar with how all the support structures are put in place. That exposure served me well in investigations yet to come.

As it turned out, after only 19 days that investigation was taken from CASB and given over to a Commission of Inquiry led by The Honourable Virgil P. Moshansky – the famous "Moshansky Commission" – perhaps the finest piece of work ever done in the name of aviation safety. Unfortunately for me, I had no connection to the Moshansky Commission, so I will not comment on it here except to say I have great respect for what it accomplished. For those who are interested in how such inquiries are run, I suggest you look it up on the internet.

Another subject that I will not delve into here in any detail is the reason that the Dryden accident was taken from CASB. That could be the subject of a book all unto itself – how CASB self-destructed through the 1980's, to where it couldn't be trusted to conduct this type of investigation (or in fact, any investigation).

Very briefly, when CASB was being set up in early 1984 the Liberal government of the day appointed the first board members – political appointees, but in my opinion credible people. Then, an election in September 1984 brought to power a Conservative government that appointed an equal number of its own political appointees, some of which were (in my opinion) not nearly as credible. The new appointees saw their main task to be fighting with the previous political appointees. It became such a circus that it was unfixable.

The main battlefield for the board members was the infamous crash of Arrow Air Flight 1285, a DC-8 that crashed in Gander, Newfoundland on 12 December 1985. That crash killed all 256 people on board – 8 crew, and 248 members of the United States military on their way from Egypt to Fort Campbell, Kentucky. Initially, Dave Owen was named as IIC for that accident, but while he was on his way to Gander, he was notified that head office had decided to appoint one of their own as IIC.

I was on an investigation course at the University of Southern California at the time, so I was not part of the initial response. Later, after I got home from my course, I went over to do some cleanup work at the site. As previously mentioned, (in relation to the Armenian investigation) I did some surveying at the airport, looking at aircraft being refuelled to see if frost built up on their wings – that was determined to have been a factor in the DC-8 crash – that finding was the main point of dispute between the board members.

After fighting about the cause of the Gander crash for more than three years, the board members had such animosity towards each other that virtually every investigation (draft report) that was brought before them was fought over. No report could escape there in a reasonable condition. I had first-hand experience trying to shepherd my reports through that circus – every board meeting I witnessed was an embarrassing spectacle. Even though CASB had some excellent board members, they were all sacrificed when the TSB was formed – thankfully, the TSB got a fresh start with an entirely new board.

Just one quick anecdote from the accident site at Dryden – you remember Travis Hunter – I was at the site one day when he arrived from head office to wander around and look official. I was at the site to negotiate with the insurance adjustor about who would pay for what. The insurance adjustor was a good guy – I had dealt with him before – as we talked, we were coming to an agreement about how much each of us would pay for the wreckage recovery – all standard stuff.

We each had some bargaining power. CASB wanted to take the wreckage to Ottawa for our investigation. The insurance company had no legal responsibility to pay for that. But environmental laws made the insurance company responsible for cleaning up the accident site, and that would be costly. We were headed for a 50/50 split in the cost, but we had to negotiate.

Unbeknownst to me, Travis had snuck up close enough behind me that he could overhear our negotiations. I was asking the insurance guy – how much have you budgeted for? – and the adjustor was telling me he had (I forget how many) dollars – and I was saying why don't we just go 50/50 – and he was saying that would maybe be too much for him – and then Travis stepped right between us and told the adjustor that CASB was not going to pay anything, and that insurance people were always trying to rip people off – and he started up with some other foolish words like that.

I remember this like it happened yesterday – calmly putting my hand on Travis's shoulder and telling him that I would handle this – using a voice that told Travis this was too trivial a matter for someone of his importance – and gently turning him through 180 degrees – and giving him a little push – and I remember him walking away peacefully, with that look he always got when he was sure he had prevailed – and the adjustor asking me who that weird guy was – and me telling him not to worry about it – and us completing our agreement at 50/50. That was the best way to handle Travis when he got in over his head.

On 11 July 1991, ten months after I had transferred to head office, I was assigned to the Canadian team responding to a major accident in Jeddah, Saudi Arabia. Canada sent a team there because this was a Canadian registered aircraft, a Douglas DC-8 (registration C-GMXQ) operated by Nationair, a charter company that was based in Montreal. They were in Jeddah to operate flights on behalf of Nigeria Airways, which had a contract to transport Nigerian pilgrims to and from Mecca for the Hajj pilgrimage.

This was an exceptionally tragic accident, with 261 fatalities, including 14 Canadian crew. During the ground run for takeoff, witnesses saw sparks and smoke trailing from the left main landing gear bogie. When the wheels were retracted after takeoff, a fire started in the wheel well – the fire quickly spread into the fuselage. The pilots tried to return to the airport, but the fire disabled the flight controls before they could land. The aircraft crashed into the desert about 2 miles short of the runway. Wreckage was spread over more than ¼ of a mile of the sand covered landscape.

Our investigation turned up evidence that the DC-8 had been operating for several flights with one tire on the left bogie that was substantially underinflated (that cannot be noticed visually). On each bogie there are four tires, mounted in pairs, one pair behind the other. It was the front inboard tire (tire #2) on the left bogie that was underinflated – this caused the front outboard tire (#1) to assume most of the weight being carried by that pair.

They had to taxi a long distance to get to the runway for departure, and the weather was very hot. The tire carrying the extra weight (#1) overheated, and as it was sped up during the takeoff roll it blew out. Instantly, the underinflated tire #2 was carrying all the weight, and it also blew out. You would think that this would be very noticeable to the pilots, but it wasn't.

There were still two more tires on the left bogy to carry the load, and they held up. The DC-8's engines were so powerful that there was almost no noticeable degradation in the takeoff performance. The pilots did notice a bit of unusual noise and vibration, but it wasn't enough to cause them to abort the takeoff.

Even with all this tire damage, there would have been no accident except for one tragic circumstance with the wheel rim for tire #2. By the worst of coincidences, a piece of rubber from the shredded tire got wedged in a spot where it stopped rim #2 from rotating. For almost the entire takeoff run, that stuck rim was being dragged along the surface of the runway, and it was being ground down. We found the long scrape mark it had made along the runway surface, and in the wreckage, we found a significant flat spot on that rim. You can only imagine how hot that rim got – away above the ignition point for rubber.

The pilots had no idea all this was happening on the takeoff roll, so after takeoff they did the standard thing – they selected the wheels up. As soon as the wheels got into the wheel well and the gear doors closed, the extreme heat from the dragged rim ignited the remaining tires and other flammables in the wheel well. The DC-8 had no wheel-well fire protection or warning devices, so the pilots were completely unaware there was a fire until it was fully developed and spreading, and affecting the controllability of the aircraft.

It was especially difficult to listen to the cockpit voice recording for this one. Our calculations showed that no matter what the pilots might have tried, they would not have had sufficient time to get back to the airport and land safely – the fire was spreading that quickly. We listened to them struggle valiantly to keep control, but the fire progressively disabled their instrumentation and flight controls.

We listened to the flight attendant telling them how bad it was getting in the passenger cabin. The fire burned a hole up through the fuselage, and passengers started falling out and landing in residential areas. The pilots actually got the aircraft lined up with a runway, but when they selected the landing gear down for landing the fuselage lost its structural integrity. They crashed in a huge fireball.

Going to Saudi Arabia was like going to a different planet. Again, the infrastructure looked familiar, but the way society worked was entirely different. On our way over we connected with Saudia Airlines in Paris – we flew business class – very nice. When we boarded in Paris, almost everyone was wearing western style clothing. When we were getting off in Jeddah, almost everyone was wearing the traditional clothing of Saudi Arabia. I found that quite amazing, how so many people could change their attire during the flight.

After we got there, we found out that we would have to do most of the investigating. There was no way that Saudi Arabia could run things. I became the official investigation's Operations Chair, an unusual happening for a foreign investigation, but necessary in this case. Our technical investigators did the bulk of the investigating to figure out what had happened with the wheels, and how the fire had spread.

I can report that this was the hottest crash site I have ever worked at. I'm not sure what the actual temperature was in the direct sun, but I saw the thermometer in the shade at our tent shelter hit 46 degrees Celsius (114 Fahrenheit). Thankfully for me, I didn't have to do any of the on-site work there – my job was looking at operational issues, and I got to work inside where it was air conditioned.

I was also the designated driver of our rental car. The airport in Jeddah was huge, and the highway to the city was modern and flat. It was not unusual to get passed from behind by a car I never had time to see in the rear-view mirror – a Ferrari or Lamborghini going flat out – very startling – and it would be gone out of sight again in seconds. In the city, it took a while to get used to the intersections. If there were two lanes for going straight, and one lane for turning left, the cars stopped for the red light would line up at least six abeam – and more if they could squeeze in.

Some would wait until the light turned green, but many would look for an opening and just go for it. The few pedestrians who ventured into the crosswalks were seen as targets. For those drivers who actually waited until the light turned green, that was the signal for them to decide where they wanted to go. The green light would come on, and all of a sudden most of the cars in the right three rows wanted to turn left, and vice versa.

Strategically (and thankfully), the traffic lights were programmed so that there was never a two-way flow at the intersections. Only one of the four sets of combatants at a time were supposed to be able to pass through the inter-section. This decreased efficiency, but it allowed everyone to practice their horn-honking. It took me three days to figure out that the signs showing the street names didn't show the name of the street you were actually on. Instead, they showed the name of the street that was at the other end of the street you would come to if you turned right at the next intersection. Believe it or not, that kind of made sense after I got used to it – it could point you in the right direction. Needless to say, I did a lot of driving. I would only find the correct route after eliminating all other potentials.

We were there for some two weeks. Nothing gets done fast over there. The Saudis have a very different concept of time. Agreed to meeting times were at best rough estimates. Some days, the main players never even showed up for work. No matter what we asked for, for example a payloader with a driver to move wreckage, the answer would be "inshallah" (God willing). Frequently, God seemed unwilling.

At the wreckage site, one of our technical investigators found a piece of paper that had survived the fire. It turned out to be critical to determining what led to this tragedy. It was a page from a maintenance check that had been done on the aircraft four days prior to the crash. Through forensic work we found that a mechanic had checked the tire pressures and found that tire #2 was at 160 psi – significantly underinflated. Then, another mechanic had written over the original entry, replacing 160 psi with 180 psi, even though no nitrogen had been added (aircraft tires are inflated with nitrogen).

Through further checking, we found that the deployment of this aircraft was done with little in the way of logistical support. The operating environment was one of pressure to keep the aircraft on schedule, at the expense of doing proper maintenance. They had tried to build in time to swap the tires (they were carrying spares), but the scheduling and lack of facilities kept getting in the way. They tried to get nitrogen – they were scrambling to get nitrogen just before departing on the accident flight – but none was available to them in time to keep to the schedule.

I have become who I am as an investigator because I've had the good fortune to be exposed to undertakings like this one in Saudi Arabia. The same is true for my personal development. This investigation, like no other, offered me the opportunity to recognize how my "normal" was so starkly different from some other people's "normal". In particular, it gave me an opportunity to learn more about how institutional control mechanisms can be structured to dictate how individual members of society function, and how human nature can adapt.

To this day, Saudi Arabia is viewed as the most buttoned up and conservative country in the world. I read about how it is very gradually opening up and "reforming", but I would suspect if I were to go back there now it wouldn't appear to be much different. I met some wonderfully friendly individuals there – people who were focused on making a living and raising their families – but their traditions and ways of operating seemed to be very deeply engrained.

From an accident investigation perspective, this tragedy happened because of the actions of Nationair – case closed. And from a safety investigation perspective, Canadian authorities had a responsibility to ensure Nationair had the wherewithal to operate safely, and they failed to do that. There were complications because they were operating in Saudi Arabia, like when they tried to get nitrogen on an urgent basis – that was not going to happen. Things work differently over there, but it was up to Nationair to factor that in.

I will share some more anecdotes from my time in Saudi Arabia. Because they happened in an accident investigation context, they work well for chitchat at an accident site – when we have a let's take a pause time.

On our team from Canada, we had one female member – she was a cabin safety specialist (she was from Nationair – I'll call her Jane). We had to arrange special transportation for Jane because their laws forbid her from being in a car with a man unless they were married. We arranged for a separate taxi for her – she could travel in a taxi with a male driver, but she couldn't be seen in a car with one of us. One of our technical guys offered to marry her – he was already married, but he found out that in Saudi Arabia you can have four wives – she appreciated the offer, but she turned him down.

Our team was given workspace in the main civil aviation office building in Jeddah. Jane was the first female to ever enter that building, and probably the only one to this day. It was awkward for the men who worked there – lots of stares and not much friendliness. The washrooms were not really shielded much from the open areas, and of course they had no doors. Obviously, there were no washroom facilities for ladies. We had to clear the entire area and keep guard when Jane needed to use the facilities.

Jane couldn't go with us when we went on outings to look around the city – that was forbidden. All the eating places had separate sections for women and men. Even families couldn't eat together. We were briefed about how to handle prayer times. At specified times, loudspeakers would signal it was time to close things down and engage in prayer. In Jeddah at that time, the call happened seven times per day. Each individual had to meet their quota by praying during five of them. We were very careful to be respectful during these times – we would find some out-of-the-way place to be inconspicuous.

I recall vividly one event I had during a prayer time. I wanted to buy some gold at the big gold souk in the market district. I went there with one of our technical guys (I will call him Jacob – he was the guy who had found that maintenance page at the crash site). The souk was an open-air market with long alleyways. The alleyways were lined on both sides with the most amazing stalls and kiosks and storefront windows filled with intricately designed gold jewelry. No matter how intricate the design, you paid for your purchase by its weight. This souk was a sight to behold.

Jacob and I were strolling up and down the alleyways – looking in the windows and checking out the prices. Suddenly, but no longer unexpectedly, we heard a call to prayers. With that, there was a mad rush by all the merchants to roll down their security doors so they could leave for prayers – by my observation they typically got back in about 15 minutes. We happened to be standing in front of a window with plenty of jewellery on display, so we just stood there quietly to wait it out – looking in the window.

It so happened that behind us were two women dressed in black burkas, and in the glass window we could see their reflections as they rolled out mats and knelt down to pray. We had been warned to be very careful when out in society – it was very bad form to look a woman in the eye, or even to look in her direction for more than an instant.

I felt a tap on my shoulder, and I turned my head to be looking into the barrel of a military style machine gun only inches away. Aiming it at my head was a member of the Mutaween, the dreaded Islamic religious police – brown uniform and black beard and all. He had two companions with him, equally armed and attired. It immediately came to me that they had spotted us watching the reflections of the women praying, and that we were in deep trouble.

The rifle barrel pointing at me motioned for us to start moving to our right – out towards the exit of our alley. We could see there was a brown open-top military jeep parked there. We saw two additional members of this virtuous gang. They started climbing out of the vehicle as we got closer – it most certainly looked like they were making a place to put us.

I will admit that I was scared. I had visions of us disappearing, never to be heard from again. At the very least, we would be the initiators of a diplomatic embarrassment that would do us no good. Jacob, who thankfully had more of his wits about him, looked straight ahead as he spoke just loudly enough for me to hear him say, "when we get to the end we'll turn left and just keep walking, no matter what – and don't look back". That's what we did, and nothing more came of it. It seems they were content to just get us out of there. I remember with every step wondering what it would feel like to get a bullet in the back.

We didn't work on Fridays – the official day of rest. We were briefed to not leave the hotel on Friday mornings. Apparently, in Jeddah that was the most common time for the public punishments to be carried out, and they delighted in rounding up stray foreigners to be witnesses to the festivities, placing them right up front for the best views. I never ventured out on Friday mornings, that's for sure. At the hotel, every day we got an English version of the local newspaper, and Saturday's paper described all the punishments carried out on the previous day.

It read like fiction, but it was all too true. I remember one account where they described the method of execution to be, "he was thrown over a cliff". There was a story about a fight between two men on a 7th floor balcony that resulted in the loser falling to his death. The winner went to trial, and the newspaper story told of how the court adjourned to the same apartment, and how the accused man happened to fall from the same balcony. I remember reading an advertisement offering execution services. If you had a loved one who was sentenced to be stoned to death, you could hire these guys to come with one huge stone to drop on your loved one's head – to save them the trouble of suffering – an act of great kindness.

I'll end this part with a newspaper story that at the time I found to be most bizarre – having to do with witchcraft – straight out of the middle ages. I cut the story out of the newspaper and smuggled it out with me (that was against the law back then) because I thought nobody would believe me. I still have that newspaper clipping – here's what it said – this is a direct quote.

THREE-YEAR JAIL TERM SLAPPED ON CONVICTED WITCH

JEDDAH, Wed. (Al Ummah Al islamia)

SHE comes from the land of witchcraft, wonders and snakes.

The accused is an Indian woman. The charge: witchcraft.

The complainant is an Indian man. During a court hearing, he pointed to the accused and said "Prevent her evil from me, my family and the society as a whole. She cast an evil spell on my brother, his sons and family because of a quarrel between him and his wife, who is a daughter of the witch."

The witch stood and looked at him in anger. She denied all that the complainant had said.

Speaking in broken Arabic, the complainant went on: "Her evil extended to my sister, and this was authenticated by the sheikh who read the Quran on her to save her from the witch."

He presented the evidence written and signed by the sheikh who read verses of the Holy Quran on his sister.

The case moved to the attorney-general who demanded that the penalty for witchcraft be upheld against the woman as stipulated by the Islamic Sharia.

The woman denied again the accusation levelled against her and requested the attorney-general to present to a higher court the proof he had.

The attorney-general did as requested, and the case moved to the higher court.

During the court hearing, the accused was astonished when the sheikh who read the Holy Quran on the bewitched woman presented himself and gave evidence against her. He told the court: "I give evidence in the name of God. This woman is a witch. I became aware of this when I was treating the bewitched woman. The

185

damage caused by her witchcraft have extended to the man who divorced her daughter."

The attorney-general presented another evidence, written by some other sheikhs who demanded the deportation of the witch woman.

Before the court session was adjourned, the complainant brought his sister to the court. She was shown the accused. She pointed at her immediately and said that indeed she was the woman who bewitched her.

The accused replied: "This woman is suffering from lunacy, as has been disclosed to me by her mother six years ago".

Evidence was also given by the son of the bewitched woman. He denied that his mother suffered from lunacy and said he had never seen any behavior on her part to prove that she was suffering from lunacy.

The complainant spoke again and said that the witch woman had bewitched him when she gave him a glass of juice to drink, after which he felt a compassion of love towards her daughter, whom he married under this circumstance.

He went on: "One of the sheikhs promised to read the Holy Quran on me until I became well. I have a little son and I think that he had also been bewitched by her."

Noting that the accused had denied any connection with witchcraft, the court by a majority vote sent her case to the emergency court.

Her case was placed before Judge Sheikh Ibrahim Al Khudairi who sentenced the accused woman to a term of three years imprisonment and 1,000 lashes, so be divided to 20 times at an interval of 15 days each time.

The term of imprisonment started from the first date of her appearance before the court.

At the time of this writing, the evidence is that punishment for witchcraft still takes place in Saudi Arabia, up to and including execution in all its grotesque forms. Needless to say, my time in Saudi Arabia has left an impression on me.

The most northerly accident site I ever worked at was in Tuktoyaktuk, in the far north of Canada. The accident happened on 3 December 1993.

A Britten-Norman Islander (a light twin-engine aircraft) operated by Arctic Wings and Rotors crashed while trying to return to the Tuktoyaktuk airport following a failure of the right engine. The pilot lost control, and the aircraft hit at high speed into the ice-covered surface of a lake about eight miles from the runway. The pilot and his six passengers were killed.

I was there to help the investigators from our western region, based in Edmonton, Alberta. It was great to work with them, and they did a good job. By examining the wreckage, we found the reason for the engine failure – a worn magneto impulse coupling. We also found a major contributing factor in why the pilot lost control. In trying to deal with the asymmetric yaw force resulting from the loss of one engine, the pilot had mis-trimmed the rudder.

When the right engine failed, he would have had to press hard on the left rudder pedal with his left foot – he would use the rudder trim wheel on the ceiling above his head to trim away the foot pressure – in the stress of the moment he turned the handle the wrong way, and actually multiplied the pressure, up to about 250 pounds.

As a result of this accident, better magneto inspection procedures were mandated – a good result for accident prevention. We had put out a recommendation about that, but that would have happened anyway, recommendation or not – the safety issue was evident without us pointing it out, and the fix was relatively simple.

But the fix for the magneto problem was not the big safety prize for this one. We were looking at the fact that the pilot was not able to deal with the failure of the engine. Why was that? In flying, you have to be able to handle whatever comes your way – an engine failure is just one of many things that could go wrong. Was this pilot ready to handle emergencies? Could we come up with recommendations that would make sure every pilot doing these kinds of charters was fully trained and prepared? Don't think when I ask this that I'm blaming the pilot for this one – far from it – he was doing the best he could, given his background and experience.

Our recommendations pointed out that Transport Canada was slack in its audit oversight of the operator. We challenged why TC let these flights operate using visual flight rules that require only one pilot. Even though the accident flight met the technical requirements for visual flight, there was no way our pilot could have flown without relying almost solely on his flight instruments – it was cloudy and dark, and he was flying over featureless terrain. The visual flight plan was just a convenient money saver, saving the cost of a second pilot. We pointed out that our pilot had not received his required night training, and that the TC audit hadn't caught that. The required night training was only 1.5 hours per year, and that was totally inadequate.

We pointed to problems with "grouping" of aircraft types – pilots were expected to be current on a number of different types of aircraft at the same time – this can lead to "transfer errors" where a pilot defaults to a procedure applicable to one type while flying another type – this happens, especially in periods of stress or high workloads (an example would be turning a trim wheel in the wrong direction).

We made a bunch of recommendations based on what we found. That was our job, and in my opinion we did it well. But let me use this accident to explain more about the real world of accident investigation. There are accidents that you can categorize as "typical" – this was one of them. It sounds callous in the context of such a tragedy. But it's a fact of life, and not unique to aircraft accident investigation. For major crime investigators, there's a typical murder – the spouse did it. There's a typical traffic accident – a drunk driver caused it. There's a typical house fire – the stove got left on. These types of typical events happen on a regular basis. Even if you figure out exactly what happened, that doesn't mean your efforts will prevent the next one.

You know going into an investigation like this that there will be expectations among some of the bereaved that this tragedy – the death of their loved one – will put a stop to this kind of accident forever. They need to believe their loved one did not die in vain – nobody else should have to suffer like they are suffering. It simply doesn't work that way. For a typical accident, there is very little chance of getting some overarching safety action that will prevent another similar one.

As an investigator, the best tactic for trying to get big picture safety action is to use your single event to string together a pattern of similar events – to show how the safety deficiency you identified is at work in many other flights, and is therefore putting large numbers of people at risk – not just the people on your airplane. Sometimes, if you work hard enough at it, your typical accident may just be the one that breaks the camel's back – the one that brings about systemic safety improvements. If that doesn't happen, then you just have to wait for the inevitable next accident and try again, using the "I told you so" argument.

This is a good place to insert some more reality about how aviation works – stuff that I've learned after all this exposure. I'll use the Tuktoyaktuk accident for context, but my observations are about these kinds of operations in general. In one form or another, operators like Arctic Wings and Rotors exist in all parts of the world – some are bigger, and some are smaller. These are the kind of operators that find ways to keep going no matter what gets thrown at them.

It's a gross understatement to say that the people who died in this accident didn't get the level of safety they deserved. But it's not too big a stretch to say that the operating environment to which they were exposed was what inevitably should be expected. Here is reality. This was a company whose sole source of income was flying people and freight using a mixed fleet of light aircraft in a sparsely populated area of the far north. They were providing a needed service, with limited resources. This was not, and could never be, a sophisticated and detail-oriented operation.

In the aviation industry there are a few people/operators who put safety completely aside – some because that's their nature, and others because they simply don't know any better. I have interviewed people like them after an accident. Inevitably, they're not the nicest of people – these words just came into my head "disrespectful", "authoritarian", "impolite", "pompous", "slippery". Thankfully, over the years I've seen fewer of them. They tend to get weeded out, hopefully before they do too much damage.

Here's what I've seen more of – people/operators who get incrementally squeezed into corner cutting. Again, some resist more strongly than others, but through my interviews over the years I see people who are trying their best to be the safest they can be. They eventually find that to be able to operate at a profit they have to back off from the safest possible course. In some areas they get to where they're simply trying to meet the minimum standard. In my world of accident investigation, I get to visit them when something has (knowingly or unknowingly) dipped below that minimum standard.

Just a couple of final notes from the Tuktoyaktuk accident. We reviewed the recorded communications with the aircraft. A spectral analysis of the background noises gave us the exact time that the engine failed, and the rpms of each propeller throughout the flight – we could track what was happening to each engine that way. It's always tragic to listen to the final transmissions from a flight that's in dire circumstances. For this one, the final transmission, which lasted 15 seconds, ended with the impact – that terrifying transmission from the pilot is one that has stayed with me.

This investigation was unique for me because it was my only experience being in conditions of 24-hour total darkness. At that latitude, at that time of year, the sun never gets above the horizon. In fact, it remains so far below the horizon that all you see of "daylight" is the slightest bit of brightening in the southern sky at around 1:40 in the afternoon. That soft brightening lasts only a short time, and you wouldn't really take notice of it unless you looked for it.

In October of 1996, Roy and I had another chance to work together as the Hallmark Team. I was called from head office to be the IIC of a tragic and high-profile accident in the small community of Eel River Crossing, New Brunswick. I was headed back to familiar territory in my former region. The twin-engine Piper Chieftain was carrying one pilot, and seven passengers – all citizens of the United States. Everyone died in the crash. We knew before we got there that the pilot had reported a power loss on one engine, and he was attempting to divert to a nearby airport when the crash happened.

What made this particular accident so high profile was that five of the seven passengers were police officers – four from the city of Lowell, Massachusetts, and one from nearby North Reading. With two other friends – a father and son – they were returning home from their annual hunting trip to Anticosti Island, just off the coast of New Brunswick. Two entire communities, along with police departments everywhere, were shaken by the tragic loss of these individuals. Nineteen children lost their fathers. For this one, there was lots of media attention, and extra interest in our investigation. As we always did, we threw everything we had into figuring this one out, looking to provide answers for those who were left to grieve.

Your familiarity with the Tuktoyaktuk accident will make it easier to see how this one fits into my "typical" categorization. Again, we'll see why it's hard to get universal safety actions out of these tragedies – to get barriers that would guarantee another accident like this could not happen again. For me personally, this has been a frustration throughout my career – but that frustration is made up for by the satisfaction of getting to the truth about what happened.

This was yet another accident that was set up by questionable decision-making by the operator. As you follow through this, I'm sure you will see how easy it was for them to slip up, even though they thought they were running things safely. Telford Aviation Inc., based in Waterville, Maine, was a well-run and respected operator with a mixed fleet of 19 aircraft. They had operated for 14 years without a single fatal accident. Roy and I checked out their facilities, and we were impressed with how well they maintained their aircraft. Everything was done to a high standard – much higher than the minimum required.

On the flight operations side, they were also better equipped than many other operators in the "small aircraft charter" category. They had low staff turnover, and experienced office people who handled all the bookings and assigned aircraft and pilots. These office people were not required to be trained as dispatchers – dispatchers have specific knowledge to help pilots with such tasks as weight and balance. It would simply be cost prohibitive to require operators like this to employ licenced dispatchers. They would have to charge too much for their flights, and that would drive away their business.

One thing this operator specialized in was transporting hunting parties to and from Anticosti Island. They chose which type aircraft in their fleet to use based on the number of passengers, any unusual baggage or cargo, the number of seats in the aircraft, and the operational range of the aircraft. They would drop off the hunting party, and then five days later go back to pick them up. On the flights to Anticosti Island, they had to stop in Gaspe, Quebec to clear Canadian customs. They also refuelled there, because there was no fuelling facility on Anticosti Island. On the return flights to the USA, they landed in Bangor, Maine to clear U.S. customs.

This hunting party had been taken to Anticosti Island in a Swearingen Merlin aircraft, which was large enough to carry everybody, and all their gear. When it came time to pick them up, they couldn't use the Merlin. The timing would have required the aircraft to stay overnight on Anticosti Island. It happened that there was unusually cold weather, and in the morning the Merlin would need external power to get its engines started – something they didn't have on Anticosti Island. With that, the office staff chose to send two aircraft to bring this hunting party home – they would use the Chieftain (with its seven passenger seats) to carry the passengers, and a Cessna Caravan (which had no passenger seats) to carry all the other stuff.

Here's where their safety system broke down. For the return flight, the Chieftain only had enough fuel range to make it all the way to Bangor if they filled it full of fuel when they stopped in Gaspe – so that's what they did – they filled it up. But with that much fuel, plus the weight of these passengers, it would be overweight departing Anticosti Island. That's not saying that the aircraft wouldn't lift all that weight – it would – and it did – but it wasn't legal, and it wasn't safe. When one engine lost power, being overweight was a major factor in why the aircraft couldn't maintain altitude.

It was the responsibility of the pilot to catch this. He should have done a load calculation for his return flight before accepting the assignment. The company should have given him the actual weights of the passengers – they should have had the passenger weights from the previous flight. Even a quick calculation would have shown that for the aircraft's gross weight to be okay, the passengers would have to average less than 150 pounds each – not likely for seven adult males. Either the pilot never even bothered to calculate the weight, or he was willing to accept the risk that he would be overweight.

You can bet that this accident pilot purposefully never did an actual weight calculation. He recognised that for his flight home he would be heavy – he had nothing to gain by figuring out exactly how much overweight he was. He would have dismissed the only two options he had to stay underweight. His first option would be to cut down on how much fuel he uploaded in Gaspe – that would mean a stop for fuel on the return flight to Bangor – his second option would be to leave a couple of the passengers behind on Anticosti Island – how likely do you think that would be? No – he would accept the risk of being a bit overweight, and play the odds that an engine wouldn't fail.

Actually, those aren't bad odds. Engine failures are very rare. I have over 12 thousand hours of flight time, and I've only had two actual engine failures. Many pilots go through their entire career without having any. You get lots of simulated ones in your training, but you almost never get actual ones.

This is the story of accident investigation. You look for the chain of events that lead to the outcome. Inevitably, you find a whole bunch of conditions and decisions and actions where everything had to be lined up just the way it was, or otherwise the crash wouldn't have happened. Here's a summary of the chain we came up with for this crash in Eel River:

- Telford Aviation didn't have a way to monitor weight and balance control – the FAA should have made sure they did, but the FAA didn't have enough staff to conduct audits.

- The pilot decided to accept the risk of flying the aircraft in an over-weight condition (as discussed above).

- The pilot had not received any recurrent training on the Chieftain since his initial type training some four years prior to the accident – this was allowed by the FAA for this type of small aircraft charter operation.

- The turbocharger on the right engine of the Chieftain failed in cruise flight – it seized up and caused a substantial loss of power from that engine.

- The loss of power occurred just about directly overhead an airport, but just by chance that airport (Charlo, New Brunswick – which is close to the ocean shoreline) was shrouded in a very localized fogbank coming in off the water – everywhere else, for miles around, was clear.

- The pilot chose to divert to Charlo, obviously believing that he would not be able to make it to anywhere else. He was setting up for an instrument approach to runway 13 when the crash occurred.

- For some reason (it was lack of training), he failed to conserve altitude and use it to his advantage. Instead, he let the altitude bleed off quickly until he descended into the top of the fog bank – at that point he tried to level out, but he discovered that the aircraft wouldn't stop descending.

- The crash was now inevitable – the airspeed bled off as he tried to stop the descent during his final turn towards the runway – the aircraft stalled aerodynamically, and the asymmetric power rolled the aircraft inverted before it dove into the ground.

Do you see how everything had to be lined up? This tragedy could so easily have not happened. If only the FAA had done a base inspection – if only they had taken action to ensure better weight and balance control – if only the turbocharger hadn't failed – if only it had failed 30 minutes later, when they would have been closer to another airport – if only the fog bank had stayed off shore – if only the pilot had better judgement from better training – any one of these things would have stopped this chain of events.

I finished writing the accident report on this one in September 1997. In 1996, the United States had enacted the Aviation Disaster Family Assistance Act, giving the NTSB responsibility to look after the needs of the families and friends of those killed in an airplane crash. Along with a colleague at head office, I was asked to develop a TSB equivalent to what the NTSB was supposed to be doing for the families, and to use this accident to try it out.

With that, we set up procedures to keep the families and loved ones informed about the progress of the investigation. We committed to giving them a full in-person briefing prior to the release of the report, and we set that up for the end of September through the Lowell Police Department.

The gathering was well attended, and from the feedback we received it was very much appreciated. The families had no idea what to expect, but it was apparent we hit the mark – they liked the Canadian way of doing things.

There was plenty of emotion. There were lots of questions, and it was good to be able to address them head on with answers that might not jump out so clearly from the report. We learned much that we took back to pass on in our training workshops.

A final note regarding Telford Aviation. Telford Allen II, founder of the company, was killed in August 2010 when he crashed his floatplane while landing on a lake in front of his house in Rockwood, Maine. His Cessna 185 had amphibious floats with retractable landing gear. Unfortunately, he forgot to retract the wheels after he took off from a runway, and when he touched down on the water the drag from the wheels flipped him over. I had met him when we were investigating the Eel River crash – a very nice man – he was only 64 years old when he died.

On my investigation training courses, I'm frequently asked to talk about what it's like to be on an investigation in United States. Operators from all around the world fly into the U.S., and they see cultural and logistical and legal differences in how things operate there. They want me to brief them (or maybe to alert them) about the American way of doing things. They want to know what they should expect if one of their aircraft has a mishap in the U.S. It's the same for government investigators who might get to the U.S. as accredited representatives for their country – everyone wants a heads-up about what they should look out for.

Because of how my career has worked out, I'm in a pretty good position to answer their questions. I've worked many cases in the U.S., and I've worked with U.S. investigators in many other countries. I did a lot of that work when I was with the TSB, and I've done quite a bit more since I became an investigation consultant. Consulting has given me a whole new insight into how the American litigation system works. I've seen how their politics can come into play, even to where it can influence their safety investigations. I can give those on my training courses some insight into all of that – I'll do the same for you in later chapters.

That's what happened in 2014 when I went to Seoul to do an investigation course for Korean Air. They lined up their entire Go Team to be trained, including the Fleet Managers for all their different aircraft types. They had lots of scheduled flights into the U.S. Just as significant, many of their aircraft were either built in the U.S. or had engines or other components made in the U.S.

This meant that no matter where in the world their accident might happen, they would inevitably be dealing with U.S. authorities. We talked a lot about U.S. issues.

One of my favourite examples of a typical NTSB investigation is the one I went to in Teterboro, New Jersey in February 2005. TSB sent a Canadian Accredited Representative (me) because the aircraft that crashed was a Bombardier Challenger, built in Montreal. This was a high-profile occurrence, mostly because of where it happened, not because of a high fatality count. In fact, nobody was killed, and there were only a few serious injuries. Having no deaths always lessens the intensity (me and my small Canadian team had a lot of fun on this one, to tell you the truth).

Here are the basics of the accident. This was a business jet that had been hired to take eight passengers from Teterboro Airport to Midway Airport in Chicago. There were two pilots, and the operator had assigned one cabin aid (an unofficial flight attendant) to the flight, so there were 11 people on board. The aircraft was loaded in such a way that its centre of gravity was away too far forward, meaning that the aircraft was very nose heavy.

When they reached their takeoff speed, the pilot pulled back on the control column to lift off, but the nose wouldn't rotate up. He had no choice but to abort the takeoff attempt. Unfortunately, they were already too far down the runway to get stopped, and they went off the end of the runway still travelling at about 110 knots (126 mph). They went through an airport perimeter fence, then across a six-lane highway (Route 46 – where they struck a vehicle, seriously injuring its two occupants), then across a parking lot (where it struck five unoccupied vehicles) – all that before they impacted a building and drove the first 1/3 of the aircraft through the wall.

The aftermath made for great live coverage in one of the world's most intense media markets, greater New York City. It happened at 7:18 in the morning, so there was significant traffic disruption. It drew lots of response from every emergency responder in the eastern United States – or at least that's what is looked like when we got there that afternoon. For me, this one holds the record for most emergency flashing lights visible at the same time.

From Canada, we were a team of four. One was our newest head office investigator at the time, a great guy named Yves, who over the years became a very good friend of mine. We also had a representative from Transport Canada – that was standard – his name was Brad (another great guy who eventually joined TSB) – and we had a technical advisor from Bombardier named Andre (yet another great guy who was very competent and easy to work with).

This was a really easy assignment for me. Yves was just getting started in the business, and this was his first time out. To ease him into it, I told him I would look after everything myself – all he had to do was watch and learn. I gave Yves just one assignment – I told him he was to keep track of anything he found to be particularly important. With that setup, I never had to do much of anything. We left there with dozens of pages of notes, and photocopies, and photos and the like, none of it collected by me. As expected, Yves had found everything important. He was driven to leave no evidence behind, which is the number one task at any investigation. With his assignment, he was launched on his way to becoming a first-rate investigator. When we got back to head office, Yves was able to give an exceptionally detailed presentation to our comrades – it was a great start to his career.

As I said, I use investigations like this to give people on my courses a taste of what they will encounter in the U.S. Everybody who is not from the U.S. is aware of the uniqueness of operating there, but it's hard to get a handle on what makes it different – to put that into words – but during the training I do my best. I tell them that any high-profile investigation, no matter where it is in the world, starts with organized chaos. But in the U.S., there can be a different feel to it. Intermixed with the chaos, there can be a higher degree of friction. In the U.S., it takes longer to start feeling like part of a cohesive team – one that's working together towards a single goal.

You sometimes see that the individual Americans are in a kind of competition against one another. To me, it's like everyone is role-playing – like they're trying to show each other up – they're testing to see who stays dominant and who can be intimidated. Their standard form of putdown is a body-language message showing a sarcastic dismissal. It's like, I'll show you what I think about you for not agreeing with me, or for not knowing the answer to the question I just asked you – I'll give you an eye roll and a wave of my hand, and I'll turn abruptly and walk away shaking my head (and for good measure, I hope everyone sees me doing it).

I explain to my students that all this will fade away as the investigation settles down. I tell them that they just have to get through the initial phase of it. They'll find that on a one-on-one basis, most Americans are very personable and helpful and sociable. But when they are together in an accident environ-ment, many of them initially take on a different and edgy demeanour. You can hear it in their tone of voice and see it in their body language. I find it strange to see people I know quite well start to act that way. I honestly think that they don't know they're doing it.

This Teterboro accident was a perfect example. We arrived at the makeshift operations room to find many who seemed to be there only because they had a right to be. It was the same at the wreckage site – lots of hangers-on. They were from any number of agencies – people from several different police jurisdic-tions – chiefs of this, and heads of that – it seemed everyone was sticking around so they could say something at the evening meeting. This would be the type of environment my students could find when they arrive, so I spend some time preparing them. With my students, I cover a lot more on this subject when I am leading them through the various investigation examples I use in my training.

After saying all the above, I'm pleased to report that the NTSB's investigation into the Teterboro crash was first rate – very thorough and hard-hitting. For anyone interested in how an investigation report should be written, I recom-mend that you look up the NTSB's report on this Teterboro crash. It is a shin-ing example of what the NTSB is capable of. They uncovered a rat's nest of shady operations – workarounds and loopholes in the ownership and control of charter aircraft that led to unsafe operations – untrained and unlicensed pilots – inadequate surveillance by the FAA – a whole litany of failures in the oversight of these types of operations. Many important safety recommendations were made, and important changes resulted. As I mentioned, this showed the NTSB at their finest. I ask that you remember this paragraph of praise when you read later about the other side of the NTSB.

As for our little group, we were quite content to monitor what was happening. As observers, we had no direct role in the investigation activities. Sometimes it happens that you have to help out (like in Saudi Arabia), but that never happened on this one. Thanks to Andre, anything the NTSB asked for from Bombardier was made available to them right away. The bottom line is that we were not big players in the Teterboro investigation.

I always find it interesting to compare how the various investigation agencies set themselves up to handle different aspects of the investigation. One way the NTSB differs from the TSB is in how they handle the media. Here in Canada, the IIC is given that task. In the U.S., especially for the higher profile cases, they send an NTSB board member to be the spokesperson for the investigation. At Teterboro, that person was Deborah Hersman. At that time, she had been with the board for only a few months, and this was her first time out for something like this. I spoke with her only briefly, but I was impressed with how she carried herself. She was quick to absorb the information she needed to know before walking out to face the press. She did a good job – very smooth.

From previous investigations, I already knew quite a few of the NTSB investigators working this Teterboro one, including Bill English (the IIC). I know they were also impressed with Ms. Hersman. I was not surprised when, in 2009, she was appointed by President Barack Obama to be the NTSB chairman – she served in that role until 2014. I have always been impressed by her obvious dedication to safety. In my experience, many people who get political appointments have far less dedication to their actual mandate. Again, I ask that you remember this paragraph when you read later about another interaction I had with Ms. Hersman – that one did not go as well.

Here are two of my neat memories from our Teterboro visit. Very efficiently, they reopened Route 46 later on the same day as the accident. But the traffic congestion was even worse than normal, with passers-by slowing to get a view of the aircraft embedded in the building. On our way to the site on the morning after the accident, we got stuck in this heavy traffic – me (driving the rental car) and Yves (in the right front) and Brad (in the back seat). Eventually, we got close enough so we could see the damaged building in the distance, but we were making almost no headway.

Ahead of us was an intersection we had to pass through – it was being controlled by a traffic cop. After a while, Yves suggested we give up and go for breakfast – we could just turn right at the intersection, go find a restaurant, and come back later when the traffic had died down. I agreed with Yves, but Brad didn't want to chance missing them moving the airplane – he had a better idea. He said he would walk up and talk to the cop and convince him to let us through. Brad said that should be no problem, given our status as part of the investigation. We tried to talk him out of it, but he would hear none of it. Out he got, and he made his way past the other cars to the intersection.

Yves and I were laughing as we watched Brad in conversation with the cop. After a bit we saw Brad dig out his Transport Canada badge, and before long he was waving it around. It was really funny to watch. Then we watched as Brad strode back to our car. As he opened the rear door, we heard him say, "let's go for breakfast". As they say, you had to be there – it was really funny – me and Yves were bent over in our seats laughing. We had great fun at breakfast extracting Brad's logic for thinking that a Transport Canada identification pass would impress or intimidate a cop in the middle of that intersection in New Jersey.

When we finally got to the site, we were pleased to see they had not yet started to extract the aircraft from the building. It would be entertaining to watch that. They had lots of equipment, including a large crane. They had put a number of straps around the fuselage, and it looked like they were ready to get on with it. They had the perimeter of the parking lot marked with yellow do not cross tape. We could have gone in for a closer view, but that would mean another round with one of the dozen or so armed police officers on guard. We decided to stay outside the yellow barrier tape – we could see just as well from there anyway.

Yves pointed to an elderly lady who was walking along beside the road – not on the sidewalk – she was coming through the part of the parking lot that was outside the barrier. She was moving very slowly, using tiny steps to make her way. She had on a long winter coat, and a bandana headcover. There was some snow on the ground, and she stared straight ahead as she walked. Behind her she was pulling one of those small two-wheel pull carts with a couple of plastic bags in it, probably groceries. She never broke her pace as she approached the yellow tape, and she ducked under it.

We watched as she made her way in a straight line all the way through the entire secure area. Nobody stopped work, and nobody there took any notice of her. It was like she was invisible, even to the guards. She never glanced at the wrecked airplane, or at any of the equipment. She just kept her head fixed, and her stare straight ahead. She passed close enough to the crane that she could have reached out and touched it, but she just kept walking. Eventually, she came to the barrier tape on the other side, and she ducked under it, and she kept going apace until she disappeared from view. I think that was the weirdest thing I have ever witnessed at an accident site.

If I was forced to pick the single funniest story about something that happened to me, this would be it. First, I need to give you some background, so you can appreciate why this is the one. I'm a huge fan of the comedy of Peter Sellers, particularly as Clouseau. My all-time favourite scene is the one in *The Pink Panther Strikes Again* where he's checking into the hotel, asking for a "reum" – where he wants to pet the little dog in the lobby – and he asks the old guy behind the counter "does your dog bite?" – and the old guy says "no" – and Clouseau goes to pat the dog and it bites him – and Clouseau says to the old guy "I thought you said your dog did not bite" – and the old guy replies "that is not my dog" – to me, that's the funniest scene of all time, and obviously, the type of humour I enjoy the most.

My story happened in France when we were there to investigate Air France 358. We started with meetings in Paris, and at lunch on the second day I got a sandwich that contained a mixture of E. coli, salmonella, giardia and norovirus. I got violently ill with the world's worst ever case of diarrhoea – with a side order of extreme nausea. But I'm a trooper, and somehow got through several meetings and visits over the next couple of days. Then we had to go to the Airbus Training Centre in Toulouse to do some test flights in their A340 simulator.

There were three of us, and we rented a car to drive down the A20 to Toulouse – a 7-hour drive. If anything, my condition had worsened, mostly because I mixed up the instructions on the two sets of pills I got from a pharmacy (I don't read French) – every 2 hours I took one of the pills I was supposed to take only once a day, and vice versa – my innards didn't take well to that.

We stayed at a hotel on the way to Toulouse. The next day I was barely alive when we arrived to start the simulator work. Somehow, I made it through the two days in Toulouse, but my condition never improved at all. I was now faced with the journey back to Paris, a prisoner in the back seat of that rental car. About three hours into the drive – which was two hours past my "I need a toilet" time, I was in a fetal position in the back seat hoping the grim reaper would

200

soon arrive to collect me. I remember moaning towards the front seat to stop at a hotel for the night – they spotted one – a quaint little establishment (to put it nicely) – and pulled in. I unloaded my roller suitcase and my computer bag, and lugged them to the check in counter, where I was greeted by the same old guy from the Clouseau movie (it was either him, or an exact lookalike – he even had the same pipe).

The hotel had 5 floors, and he gave me a room at the top. The key was one of those electronic ones that look like a credit card. I put that in my pocket and headed for the elevator, hoping not to explode before I got to my room. The elevator was barely big enough for me and my suitcases, but I got everything loaded in and pressed the top button. When it stopped, it was only on the third floor – that's as far as it went – getting to floor 5 required climbing two flights of stairs.

In my condition, climbing those stairs with the two bags was pure torture, but I made it and found my room number. I reached into my pocket and pulled out the key and guess what – it wouldn't work. I tried it every which way – no luck. I thought about leaving my luggage there to go back down, but quickly thought better of it, and took both bags back down the stairs, and then down the elevator – back to the check-in.

Handing the old guy my electronic key, I mustered up my best Clouseau French accent and said to him – "ziss key does not work for zatt reum" – he glanced at the key, took a puff on his pipe, and replied – "zatt key is not for ziss hotel".

Instantly, I recognized this skit to be the most hilarious thing I have ever been a part of – it was right up there with my comedy hero, Peter Sellers. I reached into my pocket, and discovered that in there I had an entire collection of electronic keys – one for each hotel we had stayed at. I laid them all out on the counter, and I asked the kind gentlemen "which of zeese keys is for ziss hotel?" He pointed, and replied, "ziss one". I thanked him for his assistance.

The next number of minutes were the longest of my life – suppressing laughter and extreme bowel urges – getting back up the elevator, and to the stairs, where one more time I had to listen to those luggage rollers go clunk each time I conquered a step. As I anguished my way along, I was actually running a movie skit in my head – Peter Sellers was playing me. I'll reveal that I made it to my "reum" without soiling anything, and I will say no more – other than it would take quite a story to top that one.

18

THE CRASH OF SWISSAIR 111

Peggy's Cove, Nova Scotia
2 September 1998
McDonnell Douglas MD-11
229 Fatalities

Without doubt, the most significant and influential experience of my professional life was my participation in the investigation of the crash of Swissair 111. I was the Deputy IIC for the TSB's investigation. Starting on the evening of the crash, that investigation consumed my life for an astounding four years, six months, and twenty-six days – until 27 March 2003 – that was the day we released the final report. For the first 19 months of that time, I was away from home, living in a hotel and working at our temporary facilities in Halifax (Shearwater), Nova Scotia. It's not an exaggeration to say that this project was all consuming. It was basically 7 days a week, for 238 weeks – that's 1,668 days, and I worked 1,606 of them. A typical workday was 10 to 12 hours, but many were much longer.

I was part of an incredible team – an amazing group of people who put their private lives aside to accomplish what I hereby claim to be the world's greatest aviation accident investigation project of all time. I know that's a lofty claim – it's something I've never claimed before in public. But now is the time – I'm getting too old to hold back. The Swissair 111 project deserves that recognition. From start to finish, it stands above all others in size, scope and complexity. It ranks highest in all categories – team effort and sacrifice, compassion for families and loved ones, interdepartmental and international coordination and cooperation, independence, openness, and above all, results. There was universal support for the outcomes, which led to significant advances in safety, and a lasting legacy for a job well done.

Let me offer a bit more context for my claim. In all the history of aviation, only 33 occurrences have resulted in 200 or more deaths. Among those 33, there is only one that even comes close to Swissair 111 in complexity. That is the investigation into the crash of Air France 447 – an Airbus A330 flying between Rio de Janeiro and Paris that crashed into the Atlantic Ocean off the coast of Brazil. I take nothing away from that investigation – it was amazing – but in my opinion, it takes second place to Swissair 111 in every category. None of the other 33 even come close.

The "UN Shuttle" – that's what they called the daily Swissair service between New York and Geneva – the two cities that are the main centers of United Nations activity. The shuttle flights carried many UN connected passengers, and lots of other high-profile people. They were also noted for transporting large amounts of valuable cargo, including cash, jewelry, diamonds, and artwork.

It worked this way – every morning, Swissair Flight 110 would leave Geneva for New York. It would join the westbound flow across the North Atlantic, and transit overhead my old region in Atlantic Canada before arriving in New York in the early evening. Every night, Swissair Flight 111 did the reverse – it would leave New York to join the eastbound flow over Atlantic Canada, and it would arrive in Geneva in the early morning. As was typical, Swissair 111's route on the night of 2 September 1998 took it on a track over the southern coastline of Nova Scotia.

It was less than an hour into the flight when the pilots smelled some smoke in the cockpit. They decided to divert to a nearby airport – Halifax, Nova Scotia was the closest. As they were setting up for the diversion, they were unaware that a fire had started in the overhead ceiling above and behind them – at the rear of the cockpit. The fire was already spreading uncontrollably. Within 13 minutes, the fire started to disable critical systems in the aircraft. It took only a couple more minutes before the aircraft was completely unflyable. Swissair 111 crashed nose first at high speed into the ocean off Peggy's Cove. Upon impact, the aircraft fragmented into more than two million pieces. The destruction of everything, and everyone, was complete.

Before I go on to talk about my role in the Swissair 111 project, I would like to emphasize that I was but one of thousands of people who each had an intimate connection to this tragedy. They came from some 50 different agencies, or they volunteered as private citizens. Each one of those thousands could provide an interesting and moving account based on what they did or saw. Of course, I can't capture anyone else's personal story – I can only tell my own – but I want to clearly acknowledge that my story is but one of many. I don't put it forth as being any more compelling than any of the others. I was not everywhere, and I did not see everything, but I did have a unique role where I was totally immersed in all aspects of this project from the start to the finish. In keeping with the purpose of this book, I will focus mostly on explaining how this 4 ½ year commitment became a pivot point in my life – when I look back over my existence, I see the pre-Swissair part, and the post-Swissair part.

Also, before I go on, I need to talk about Vic Gerden, the TSB's IIC for the Swissair 111 investigation. Vic's background was quite different from mine. He had flown fighter aircraft in the Air Force, and had retired from the military as a Colonel, joining our regional office in Winnipeg as its manager. He didn't have much experience as a field investigator, but he had ten years of connection to how we did things. It turned out that our backgrounds were complimentary.

On Swissair, Vic and I were the closest of working partners for those 4 ½ years. I had/have tremendous respect for him, and I know (because he has told me) that he felt the same about me. We shared the same small office in Shearwater, and the same workspace when we moved the investigation to Ottawa. We were always driving towards the same goals, and we trusted each other completely. We weren't like best friends – we were more like professional soulmates. It's hard for me to find a way to better describe our relationship, but in the spirit of this book I will try.

Imagine the countless numbers of times that Vic and I were in a stressful situation together – with a time crunch – where the pressures were all but unbearable – where we were two guys carrying the weight of the world on our shoulders – where we had no good options, but we had to decide anyway – where we found out that one of us (or both) had messed something up – where we had to fess up about something we should have done differently – where we needed to protect each other. Here is what speaks volumes about our relationship – not once, over all those 4 ½ years, was there ever a single angry word said between us – not a single word. Nor was there ever a single word expressing disappointment – one of us in the other. I bet I could not have had that happen with the Pope, or the Dalai Lama, but I had it happen with Vic.

Vic is the most even-tempered individual I have ever met. That's one of the traits that made him the perfect choice for IIC of such a major investigation. Not only was he fully competent, he had the demeanour of an individual who could be trusted no matter what. People just knew instinctively that with Vic in charge, this investigation would get to the truth if that was at all possible. And they knew he would present that truth to the families and to the public without outside influence.

For TSB management, and for the politicians, Vic could be trusted with the purse strings. He projected what he actually was – professional, competent, careful, conservative, cautious, and incredibly trustworthy. It was because of Vic's trustworthiness that we continued to get funding over the years. That support got us to the truth about what happened and allowed us to close out the investigation with no outstanding issues.

I'll give you a sense of the size and scope of this incredible recovery and investigation project. It involved tens of thousands of people. At about 10:30 on Wednesday night (2 September, the night of the accident) the people who lived along the coast near Peggy's Cove heard the aircraft fly over at low altitude. Shortly after, from out at sea, they heard and felt the explosive force of the crash – so forceful that it registered on the Richter scale that measures earthquakes. Local fishermen responded with their own boats to try to rescue any survivors – over 150 boats were out there on the first night. They found a large area of floating debris, and they started recovering what they could – it was a gruesome task.

Soon, they were joined by vessels from the Canadian Coast Guard – big and substantial ships with names like the Hudson, the Mary Huchens, the Simon Fraser, the Earl Gray, the Matthew, and the Sambro (which was the first government vessel on the scene). The Coast Guard sent an additional 14 fast rescue craft, and some 15 Auxiliary vessels, and numerous helicopters. The RCMP also brought in their own vessels, and their personnel took charge of securing the human remains and personal effects.

The Royal Canadian Navy ship HMCS Preserver happened to be in the area, and it was made the on-scene commander. The Navy deployed additional assets, including search and rescue helicopters, and a submarine. They scouted out the main debris field on the ocean floor, using divers and remotely operated vehicles (ROVs). The water depth was about 185 feet. Most of the wreckage had sunk to the bottom and piled up in a confined area of about 400 feet by 300 feet, but there was still plenty of floating wreckage that was being scattered by the wind and water currents – much of it ending up on the shoreline of the mainland and various small islands near the coast.

A massive effort was launched to scour the shorelines, with volunteers coming from all parts of Nova Scotia and nearby provinces – I heard they numbered somewhere near 3,000. They picked up some 10,000 pounds of material that had come from the aircraft, and untold amounts of human remains. Many of these people were traumatized by what they were finding, not only by the body parts, but from handling personal items, including children's toys and clothing. Being exposed to all that brought home the reality of what had happened. Many would need counselling – same for those people who continued to search on the water. The effects of that time have stayed with many to this day.

At my home on that Wednesday night I saw the breaking news about a crash into the water. I fully expected that we would launch our go team immediately – that we would travel overnight to get to Nova Scotia as quickly as possible. I knew that my former regional office colleagues would have responded, and they would need immediate help. But we never left that night.

By morning, this had become a world-wide story. It was being covered live from Peggy's Cove by all the major news networks. Amazingly, I went to work Thursday morning to find a debate happening at the management level as to whether we even needed to go right away, given that the aircraft had not yet been located. To me that was crazy talk.

I was informed that Vic Gerden was to be the IIC, and that I was to be one of two deputy IIC's, the other one being Joe Jackson, a guy who had been my first supervisor when I moved to head office. I was good with that. I didn't know Vic very well, but I knew he would need someone like me to help him out, both because I knew the region very well, and because I had a pretty strong background from all my field investigation work. I had worked with Joe a lot in head office, and I was also his deputy when he was the IIC at the Dryden crash back in 1989. I knew Joe had a special interest in computer setups and all that, so we could rely on him for that aspect of things (he would do the same job I did for him at Dryden).

Eventually, wiser heads prevailed at head office, and we arranged to get a government aircraft to fly us to Halifax as soon as possible. Vic was on his way from Winnipeg, and he would join us on the flight. Our go team was from head office and from our engineering facility. We knew we would need to do a press conference right away, so we took our Chairman of the Board, Benoit Bouchard, and our press guy, Jim Harris.

When we landed at the airport in Halifax, they had a military helicopter waiting for us. Four of us – Vic and me and the Chairman and Jim Harris – went on the helicopter to Peggy's Cove. As we flew over to set up for landing, I saw what we were about to face. Peggy's Cove is a small coastal community of about 60 people, with a magnificent lighthouse. Everything is clustered on a huge rock base that rises from the sea at the shoreline where the rocks gets pounded by the waves that come in from the open water – from out where the aircraft had crashed. On this day, it looked from the air like a huge movie set – vehicles of every description, everywhere – police cars – network broadcast trucks with huge satellite dishes – military equipment – huge tents full of supplies – emergency response vehicles – people going every which way – it looked like chaos on steroids.

The four of us had talked about what the Chairman could say at the news conference – nothing much really – he could express his condolences – say that we would do everything possible to figure out what happened – outline the basics of an investigation and talk about its objective – all the standard stuff. We knew that the pilot had reported to ATC that he had a fire on board – what caused the fire would be a focus for our investigation – but we warned the Chairman not to get into any speculation about all that. Vic would accompany the Chairman at the news conference.

When we got off the helicopter, the others went to prepare for the press conference. I went to look for our regional TSB guys. At that point, I didn't even know which of them had responded. I spied a trailer that looked like it was in the middle of the action, and I went over and looked in. That's when I spotted Roy, my Hallmark Team partner. I will always remember the greeting I got from Roy – a very indelicate version of "where have you been?". Roy had responded to Peggy's Cove immediately – he got there at 3 a.m., and he had been going flat out ever since. With him, he had only one other TSB guy, and that guy was relatively new. Roy was exhausted. I apologized for the typical head office dithering – I felt so sorry for Roy, and so embarrassed for not being able to convince head office to get there sooner.

In came an RCMP Sergeant who was the site commandant – he was in charge of site logistics, and he controlled who had access to the trailer. Everyone called him by his nickname, "Bucket". His greeting was even less delicate than Roy's – he asked me who I was and what I was doing there – he used a minimum of words. It crossed my mind to tell him that I was from head office and I had come to take charge, but I thought better of it. Bucket was just like many of the RCMP people I had worked with out in the wilderness at accident sites – rough and ready – I would wait for him to warm up to me. Roy convinced Bucket to not throw me out.

For the first time, I had an opportunity to absorb what was going on. I observed that things were happening on multiple fronts. This was still a search and rescue exercise. Officially, they were still looking for survivors, even though it was apparent there would not be survivors. They can't call off the rescue phase before all hope is lost. That meant that at this point the investigation could not be turned over to the TSB – that only happens when the rescue phase is over. And even when the site was turned over, control would first go to the coroner who was responsible for the bodies, and then to the RCMP – it would stay with them until it was confirmed it was not a criminal act. That would give us a time window to get our feet under us.

For me, this was watch and learn time. I needed to figure out where we needed to have TSB representation. One place was out at the crash site on the ocean – we would have to get a couple of our investigators out there on the control ship pretty quick. I found out they were taking the recovered material to the military base at Shearwater – that they had already secured a couple of hangars there – one for the wreckage (Hangar A) and one for the human remains and personal effects (Hangar B). We would set up our technical experts in Hangar A.

Our team had to be divided up to gather all the standard information we would need – to get interviews from people who had seen or heard the aircraft fly over – to get the ATC records, and to interview the controllers – to get the maintenance records, and to interview the technicians who had last worked on the aircraft – to get the pilots records, and those of the other crew members, and to chase down their 72 hour histories. Fortunately, we had lots of very experienced go-team members, and a well-developed checklist for them to follow. Other than the sheer volume of it all, we were in good shape.

We would need our own operations room – Joe was in charge of that. He set us up at the Holiday Inn in Dartmouth, where he turned their ballroom into the setup we needed. He got us computers and phone lines and work-stations – enough for us, and for all the advisors we would need – experts from Boeing, Swissair, Pratt & Whitney the NTSB, the FAA, TC – lots of people.

In Peggy's Cove, I started to get a sense of who the various players were, and what roles they had. The biggest player for us was the RCMP. They had re-sponded with hundreds of people – to me, they were exceptionally well organized, but I bet some of them didn't think that – anyway, they were the agency calling the shots. They were also helping the Chief Medical Examiner – I would dare say not just helping him – they were doing much of the job on his behalf. The other big players for us were the Canadian Forces, and the Coast Guard.

I found out that the Chairman had agreed to do a one-on-one interview after the news conference – it would be live across Canada, on our main national net-work. I found Jim (our media guy). He asked me to meet with the interviewer (Peter Mansbridge) to make sure he knew what kind of questions were best for right then – what kind of questions the Chairman could answer at that time, and what he should avoid getting into. Peter was very good about it – he recognized that this was not a time to put our Chairman on the spot in front of all the world.

That evening at the Holiday Inn, Vic and I sat down to figure out how this was going to work. It was huge, and we were about to get smacked hard by as much as we could handle, and more. This was an aircraft accident, and the TSB had a mandate to be in charge of aircraft accidents, so we were going to soon be (by legislation) in charge of all of this. Our big pressing issues right then were two – the media, and the NOK – they would both have to be briefed daily.

We recognized that we had a bit of a reprieve. Other than the bits of floating debris, the vast bulk of the wreckage was under water, and it would be there for some time. This would give us time to get organized to where we could process it. And thankfully, we would have the tremendous support and resources of the RCMP. As I recall, in those early days we had about 30 people with us from the TSB – the RCMP had well over 300. For the wreckage, our technical investigators could coordinate with the RCMP to get the proper facilities set up to receive the wreckage as it was recovered – to get it from the ocean to Hangar A.

Right from the beginning I found it amazing how well Vic and I came together. We weren't really alike – he had a military background – I was civilian. Vic was reserved and careful – he rarely decided anything on gut instinct – he had a hard time making quick decisions. I was far less reserved, and more likely to act on instinct. Vic was an officer – he didn't know many of our investigators personally, and he had not worked in the field with them. I had come up through the ranks, and I knew almost all of our investigators there – I had worked with them, and on an equal footing.

It seems like Vic and I balanced each other off. This might sound corny, but I'm going to say it anyway because it's absolutely true (I know, because I've thought a lot about it) – Vic and I came together as a team because we each had an intense desire to succeed – we were going to do this right – for the families – for all those agencies and volunteers, for our organization, for the local community, for our country, and for aviation safety. This was the time for Canada to perform on a world stage, and the two of us were going to make sure it didn't get messed up.

On a personal level, I was confident in my own ability, and I had lots of confidence in the TSB team that we had, but I will freely admit that a main motivator for me was a fear of failure – that old phobia of not wanting to be embarrassed.

I will add a quick anecdote here – in the early days of the investigation, high-level officials from the United States government offered us the opportunity to delegate this investigation to their NTSB. They flat out said that they weren't sure we would be able to handle it. Can you imagine? Talk about condescending. At that time, they still hadn't finished their investigation into TWA-800 – that was the Boeing 747 where the fuel tank exploded after takeoff from New York – where the aircraft dropped in a number of pieces into the water near East Moriches – the investigation where there was constant conflict between the NTSB and the FBI and the Terrorism Task Force – and conflicts with the families – and conflicts between the parties to the investigation – and they wanted to bring that circus to Canada – no thanks.

On the personal side, this was a very inconvenient time for me to be away from home. My wife Charlotte and I had a project underway. In 1998, I was still 10 years from retiring, but I was already looking for something to transition into – and I found something. It was an established franchise that was for sale – a learning centre – a facility that offered after school and summer tutoring for kids from kindergarten to high school. Charlotte was a retired teacher. This would be right in her wheelhouse. She could run the school, and I could run the business side. I could do the banking, and the payroll, and pay the rent and all that. Running this would be something we could do together, and if it worked out it would give us some extra income.

We put in an offer, and it was accepted. We would take over the business on September 1st. Charlotte started working there during the summer to get trained on the programmes. It was an up and running business, with a staff of some 12 people, mostly part time. They had lots of students enrolled for the fall – it would be an easy transition over to us.

I went there after work on our first day of ownership, and again on our second day. There were a few hiccups explaining the new ownership to some long-time customers, but everything got off to a great start. Swissair 111 crashed on our second day of ownership – Wednesday, 2 September 1998. The next day I left for Halifax. I told Charlotte that I would either be gone for two weeks, or two years. What an incredible circumstance this was for us – so stressful for both of us, with me leaving her to run this business on her own. She had no preparation for running the business side – even I had precious little – but at least I was supposed to be there with her.

It would not be possible for me to exaggerate the amount of activity we had going on in Halifax in those first few days. It was absolute pandemonium – trying to get ourselves set up – to get our own team of investigators organized – to put some structure in place to accommodate all the accredited representatives and their technical advisors who were arriving – to organize how Vic and I would divide the management duties – who would be the main contact with each of the dozens of other players – who would go to which meeting.

We planned, and we did the best we could, but much of the way it evolved just seemed to happen along the way. Vic and I became very much inter-changeable. We tried to stay together for the biggest meetings, but when that wasn't possible Vic concentrated on the "up" stuff (interagency management issues) and I concentrated on the "down" stuff (activity to do directly with the investigation). I don't remember us talking about structuring it that way, but for the most part that's how it worked out. All I know is that by the end of each day we were both exhausted – so was everybody else.

It was in this environment that I tried to call Charlotte when I could. An issue arose with our franchise purchase. We had all the financing in place long before the closing date, but by Friday (4th Sept) our payment to the previous owners had not been released. I had done all of the financing work, so Charlotte had no background to investigate what had gone wrong. I called our bank and found out there was a banking technicality holding things up – an old, unused, and long forgotten line of credit that needed to get closed out – and of course, it needed my signature. What a mess. We went into the Labour Day holiday weekend with this unresolved.

One positive thing had come out of the TWA 800 investigation. Their inept handling of the families had energized the U.S. government to pass the Aviation Disaster Family Assistance Act. This legislation forced air carriers and federal agencies to develop procedures that put a priority on the needs of families and loved ones.

Swissair, and Delta Airlines (which had passengers on this flight under a code share arrangement) had just put in place their new procedures. To me, their new procedures worked amazingly well. As early as Friday morning, they were bringing NOK to Halifax by the hundreds, putting them up in the Lord Nelson Hotel. The NOK had to be a major focus for Vic and me. We knew that if we ever lost their confidence, it would be a major blow to our chances for a successful investigation.

Another major priority – it seemed we only had major priorities – was the media. For the sake of the investigation, we also had to keep them on our side. The RCMP and the military were coordinating the setup of a major media hub

at the Metro Centre – there were over 100 media entities – over 300 reporters – there were five satellite trucks – everyone wanted information and access.

With our partners, we settled on a daily briefing time for the
NOK – 4:30 p.m. – that would be at the Lord Nelson Hotel. We would follow
that up with a media briefing at 5:30 p.m., at the World Trade and Convention
Centre. Our policy was that anything that was about to be released to the
media would first be released to the NOK. We agreed that Vic would do the
TSB's part at the media briefings, and I would handle the TSB's part with the
NOK. In deference to the families, Vic (as IIC) would do the first couple of
NOK briefings – then I would take over.

At 10:30 on Friday morning, Search and Rescue announced that they were
ending their search for survivors. This would now be a search and recovery
mission. Overall control was given to the RCMP, who would take the lead
on the basis of a criminal investigation. That was perfectly acceptable to me
and Vic. We were not about to fight them for the title of "in charge". They
had the resources and command structure for this level of event, and we most
certainly did not. We knew that at some point it would all be turned over to
us, but now was not the time.

Over the long weekend, the major focus by the NOK, the media, and the
outside world was on the search for human remains. Some families clung to
the hope there could still be survivors. There was also lots of interest in the
search for the main part of the wreckage, and for the black boxes. As the divers
and ROV's did their work, it became clear that there was no classic "wreckage" to be found. There were no large identifiable pieces of the aircraft left,
other than the three separated landing gears, and the engines. There was no
cockpit, no fuselage, no wings, no tail, no cargo hold, no passenger cabin, no
intact seats – there were only millions of small pieces of what used to be the
aircraft. And there were no bodies – only shattered remains of bodies that were
unidentifiable except by extraordinary means.

This is what had to be explained to the NOK, and to the media. The painful
part of that messaging to the NOK was done at the weekend meetings by the
Coroner, and by the briefers from the RCMP, and the Coast Guard, and Search
and Rescue. They could give first-hand descriptions of what was out there – the
NOK deserved to know, and they were told. Among the NOK, attention had
not yet shifted to what had caused the crash. They were consumed with shock
and grief, and a disbelief that they would have to wait an indefinite time to see
if their loved ones could even be identified. They were being tasked to provide

items associated with their loved one that would be useful for identifying body parts through DNA.

Vic and I, and our operations investigators, were working from the ops room at the Holiday Inn. Our technical investigators (other than the ones we sent to sea) were working in Hangar A, getting ready to accept the wreckage that was being recovered from the shorelines, or recovered by the boats. I went to check out Hangar A. It was impressive.

With the RCMP, our people had set up a grid pattern on the hangar floor where they were placing wreckage pieces according to their station number in the aircraft. Any location in an aircraft can be defined by its distance rearward from the nose (the Y-axis), its lateral distance from the longitudinal center-line (left or right) (the X-axis), and its vertical height above the "waterline" (the Z-axis) – in the MD-11, the waterline is arbitrarily located at 18 inches above the cabin floor. That grid pattern on the hangar floor was a good start for the wreckage that was coming in at the beginning, but it would need to be modified many times over the months to come.

On Friday, we got word that the U.S. Navy was offering the services of the USS Grapple, their most modern rescue and salvage ship. It had been used in the TWA 800 wreckage recovery. It had a lifting capacity of 300 tons, 32 experienced divers, and high technology sonar to help map the ocean floor. How could we say no to that – we accepted their offer right away.

But let me give you some behind the scenes thinking about our use of the Grapple. From what we knew about the nature of the crash, we were confident that the Grapple was not what we needed to recover the wreckage. We knew that Swissair 111 had crashed at high speed. We knew the type of hydrodynamic forces that would result. The water would instantly invade into the fuselage and explode the aircraft from the inside out. There would be nothing left but small pieces. We didn't need a ship that could lift a 300-ton piece – we needed something with a much different capability, and we started looking for alternatives right away.

On the Tuesday after the long weekend, I called our bank to see what could be done about getting the money released to pay for our learning centre. I explained why I couldn't get there to sign anything, and they understood. I told them it was urgent that they release the money, and they assured me they would make that happen. I called Charlotte to give her the news. She said she was worried because the lawyer for the seller had threatened to take some action to prevent us from opening for classes at 4 p.m. That would be absolutely terrible, and from where I was, there was nothing I could do about it.

At our operations room, Tuesday was another day filled with one issue after another. I had developed a tracking system for putting context to my stress level – a fictitious gauge in my head that showed "decisions per minute". All that Tuesday, it was pegged. We were now fully up and running, with all the parties to the investigation in place – each needing something or other – and meetings, meetings, meetings.

This was to be my first day replacing Vic for the NOK briefing at the Victoria Hotel – it was set for 4:30. This was the day we were prepared to release the aircraft's track, based on recorded radar returns – kind of a big deal. It was the first solid information to show what the aircraft was doing prior to impact. Our Operations Chairman, Mark Clitsome, helped put together a PowerPoint presentation, and a narrative description to go with it. In 1998, this was a pretty new way of doing things – it was very impressive.

Now I will tell you about the sequence that was the most stress-inducing I have ever encountered. At the pre-arranged time, a car came to take Mark and me over to the Victoria Hotel – it would take about 15 minutes. On our way, I was familiarizing myself with the narrative that Mark had written up. We were about halfway across the bridge over Halifax Harbour when I got a phone call from Charlotte. She told me that the sellers had still not received their money, and I needed to do something right now to get it released – either that, or our learning centre would not be able to open for the students – the students had already started to arrive.

Charlotte had no idea what kind of situation I was in. Here I was, just minutes away from arriving at this huge auditorium where there were now more than 600 grieving and upset family members waiting for a briefing. I knew she was in an extremely stressful situation too, but there was nothing I could do to help her. I had to tell her that she was on her own, and that I had to hang up right now. I felt sickened for having to do that.

Mark and I walked into the auditorium, and onto the stage where places were designated for representatives from the military, the RCMP, the Coroner, Swissair, and the TSB. Before everything started, Mark set up our PowerPoint presentation, and I took my seat. The Swissair representative went to the podium and opened the briefing by expressing his condolences. He committed to offering Swissair's continued support for the families. It didn't take him very long. When he finished, he introduced me as the next speaker.

As I was walking to the podium, the big screen we were going to use for our presentation went completely blank. The computer had gone into sleep mode. I had no idea how to get it back awake – Mark came to my rescue. In the meantime, here I was standing in front of 600 plus grieving family members with only the scripted notes that needed the slides to make sense. I apologized for the technical difficulty, and offered my personal condolences for their loss, and condolences on behalf of the team that was working as fast as possible to get some answers for them.

Mark got the computer out of sleep mode, only to find that the projector had now gone into sleep mode. As I write this I can feel a low-dose version of the same sensation I felt back then – this has to be some kind of dream – maybe I'll just wake up any second now – it was so unfair – it was all too much – how could this be happening at the exact same time that my wife was explaining to our customers that there would be no classes for their kids tonight. My natural default when I get into a stressful place is to try to make fun of it – to say something funny to take the edge off of it. Obviously, this was not the time and place for that. I was sleep-deprived, mentally exhausted, stressed beyond belief from every direction, and being stared at by 600 grieving people who were devastated and looking to me for answers. I challenge you to try to top that story for stress.

Then a thought came to me. If I could somehow get through this moment, forever after I would be able to tell myself that it was possible to get through anything that might be thrown at me. As that thought registered, I felt a great relaxation come over me. I took the presentation notes, and I explained that we would soon have visual depictions for them, but I could describe what we had found out about the track of the aircraft – and I launched into an explanation that filled the time until Mark got everything back in order. So far as I could tell, it all went seamlessly – soon I had the visuals to use, and I got through that, and I finished with a promise that Mark and I would stay there after the briefing for as long as necessary to answer all their individual questions.

To this day, I have never had any stressful situation come even close to what transpired in that short period of time – from when I was on the bridge talking to Charlotte, to when I sat back down after giving that presentation. It was probably not much more than 30 minutes overall, but every second of it got seared into my experience bank.

That audience of 600 sat through details that nobody should ever have to hear. Their loved ones were gone. They had not just stopped living; they were actually gone physically. Many of the NOK came to Halifax hoping there might still be survivors. That hope got quashed. Now they were finding out that they would have no bodies to take home. It would take weeks, or even months, for the human remains to be found and identified. For some, even that might not be possible.

As promised, Mark and I stayed, and we answered questions. As it turned out, there weren't many questions for us. The main interest from the families was on the recovery of their loved ones, and on the handling and identification of the remains and personal effects. For those issues, they went to the military and the RCMP and the coroner – they were in charge of those aspects.

I remember a young man – maybe 16 years old – standing in front of me – he had a question. He started by telling me that his dad had been on the flight, and his mom and siblings were in the audience. He told me how proud they all were of his dad. He was in the middle of a sentence when he suddenly started to collapse. I reached out and caught him. Instead of letting him down to the floor, I held him tight. After bit I felt him getting his legs back under him, and soon he could stand on his own. He carried on with his question, and I gave him an answer, and he thanked me and walked away. I remember thinking how good it was for me that over the years I had gained some experience with this type of interaction – that would have been a hard one to start with.

Just to close off the story about what was happening with Charlotte at our learning centre, I found out that she was able to open the doors that Tuesday evening – somehow, she had talked her way through it – and the money was released the next day. She was completely on her own, but at least our business was up and operating – she was a trooper.

At a briefing on one of the following days I was approached by a small group of individuals who were inquiring about a passenger from Saudi Arabia. I remember the spokesperson was wearing a thobe – he spoke very softly, and

I appreciated him thanking me for my efforts at the briefings. He had one specific question for me – in my professional opinion, was it possible that the body of the Saudi victim could be in one piece? He made it clear that he wanted an honest answer – not something made up to make him feel better. I told him very directly – there would be no full body. He thanked me for my honesty, and they turned and walked away.

Later that night, back at my hotel, I started to do some research to better acquaint myself with the various death and funeral rituals applicable to the diverse passenger makeup on this flight. This proved to be a worthy investment of my time, as I was then better able to understand the motives behind some of the questions. The circumstances of this crash made it particularly difficult for many traditional rituals to be followed.

Over the next weeks these daily briefings kept going – every day at 4:30 – seven days a week. After a while, they got to be more routine, but they never got much easier. As time passed, the interest shifted more to our investigation. They had lots of questions about what we were finding, and what we were thinking, and what had gone wrong to cause the fire. It was important to keep them informed, and in particular to make sure they were the first to get any new information released by us – they would always get it before we released it to the media.

When Vic and I talked early on about dividing up the duties, we decided that I would take the lead for the TSB regarding wreckage recovery issues. That didn't mean that I was in charge of the overall recovery project – not at all. I had no expertise to run anything like that. The recovery project was being led by the Navy and the RCMP and the Coast Guard. But I was the TSB's voice at the meetings. Everything, wreckage wise, was to end up with the TSB for our investigation, so our input was critical from the beginning – everybody knew that.

In the overall recovery effort, we would have to keep track of the progress by weighing the recovered materials. We knew the weights of everything we were after. There was 285,000 pounds of aircraft structure, 46,000 pounds of cargo, and 14,000 pounds of human remains (the total weight of the occupants was about 40,000 pounds, but 26,000 pounds of that would be unrecoverable liquid).

I think it was on the same day that I did my first NOK briefing that the Captain of the USS Grapple came by, with two or three of his assistants. They were very friendly, and eager to help. The captain told us that it might take them as long as two to three weeks to get all the wreckage recovered. We thanked them for volunteering, and we wished them well. Despite their optimism, we knew they wouldn't be able to make much of a dent in the wreckage pile. In fact, we had already firmed up our plan to launch the next phase of the recovery – the follow-on method we would use to actually get the bulk of the wreckage from the bottom.

On 12 September, the Grapple went to work alongside the Canadian Navy ships that were already working there. The Grapple stayed for some three weeks. Together, that team did amazingly well, helping to document the site with ROV's and sonar. Canadian divers recovered the data recorders, and they all worked together to raise as much as they could from the bottom. Their primary focus was on retrieving as much of the human remains and personal effects as possible – they actually got a small percentage. They got some smaller wreckage pieces, and they managed to get a couple of the larger items too, including a piece of the main landing gear, and (as I recall) two of the three engines.

I was being updated regularly by our TSB guys on site. The more I heard about what was happening, the more concerned I got for the safety of the people doing the work. They were relying almost exclusively on divers, and the water was deep – some 185 feet. This put them right at their dive limit. They could only stay on the bottom for about 20 minutes per dive. There were sharp and jagged pieces of wreckage everywhere – hazardous for direct injury, and for potentially cutting their lines.

Their method for recovering the small pieces was to lower wire cages from the surface, fill them by hand, and hoist them back up. It was exceptionally slow work. Vic and I met with our RCMP and navy contacts, and we all agreed that it was time to call a halt to that operation. During their time on site, they had fulfilled a great need for the investigation to show on-site activity. We reported to the NOK and media that they had hauled up more than 15,000 pounds of material. We didn't highlight that their weight total was significantly boosted by the few larger pieces.

I felt sad for what those individuals had to endure. The Canadian and American divers recovered material that was extremely stressful to handle – all that material was processed on the decks of the vessels where everyone was exposed to it. I recall that the average age of the crewmembers on the Grapple was something like 22 years old. It would have been cruel to let that operation continue, and it was kind of a relief when they sailed away.

Normally, when you recover wreckage, you take great care to not cause further damage to it. That's because you want to examine it later for things like witness mark evidence. In this case, we had to abandon any thoughts of being delicate. We had to get a huge pile of wreckage from the bottom, and we wanted to do that quickly before the winter weather moved in. And we had to do it without getting anybody hurt. The only practical method would be to use a crane, mounted on a barge. The crane would use long steel cables to lower a huge open clamshell bucket down to the pile. Then, the clamshell would close and scoop up as much as it could, and it would be pulled up by the crane to where the contents could be dumped.

The barge we hired was called the Sea Sorceress – that's the one we put the crane on. We also contracted for a smaller barge we could tether next to the Sea Sorceress. We used that one to deposit the wreckage on. We made a plan to run that operation full time, 24 hours a day, using teams of about 20 people each. We ran the teams back and forth from land to the barge using a small boat. There were no living quarters close to the launch point for the small boat, so in the tree-covered wilderness we constructed an entire workcamp from scratch. The teams would sleep, eat, and get cleaned up there. We had that workcamp built and ready to start operating by 13 October.

We needed TSB representation on the Sea Sorceress, to be part of the oversight. Vic and I talked it over, and we decided that I needed a break from the long days in Halifax, so off I went to sea. We needed two of us to cover off the 24-hour operation, so my good buddy Randy went too. Randy had joined the investigation from the Winnipeg office – same as Vic. We took 12-hour shifts, switching off at 4 a.m. and 4 p.m.

Randy and I had the easy work. We basically helped to figure out when and where to reposition the barge according to what was coming up from the bottom. We were using a grid pattern, and they could dynamically reposition the barge with great accuracy to cover the entire sea bottom area we had marked off by using the ROV's. It was the people on the wreckage barge who had the most miserable work you could imagine.

Over a period of 11 days, we recovered 150,000 pounds of wreckage. As each load came up and got dumped on the deck, the teams would separate all the material. Mixed with the rocks and ocean bottom sediment, there would be aircraft related material – human remains, personal effects, priority wreckage, normal wreckage, cargo – everything mixed together. Randy and I watched all this happening from our vantage point – we would either be in the bridge, or outside on the first or second deck of the Sea Sorceress. We watched as a Coast Guard ship came every day to collect up the recovered material and take it to Halifax – the material would soon be in Hangar A, or Hangar B.

It was quite the adventure for me to live on that barge. I was there for eight days, and I gained eight pounds. They served full meals every six hours, and the cafeteria never closed for snacks. It was my go-to hangout. Every day I swore I would only eat two full meals, and every day I ate at least four. They made the desserts overnight, and at our 4 a.m. changeover the cook would bring Randy and me fresh samplings – lots of them, and there was no way to resist.

I remember one member of the crew – a big guy from Newfoundland who weighed well over 300 pounds. He weighed himself once a week, and if he saw that he'd lost more than five pounds he'd head straight for the kitchen and tear a strip off the cook, and write him up for dereliction of duty. He told me that he and his wife ran a jewellery store back in his hometown. During his off time, he made jewellery – I watched him do it. He had fingers as big around as my wrist, and he made these awesome and dainty little pieces of jewellery – amazing.

I could write many more pages about life on that barge, and the characters I met there, but I will share only a couple more stories involving Randy, who by the way is one of the top investigators I ever worked with. He gave me his plan for making one pair of socks last for eight days – the rotation went like this – left foot, right foot – turn inside out and repeat – then trade with me. I assessed that as a good plan, but not a great plan.

We wanted to have better communication with our guys on the other barge, so Randy came up with the idea of ordering a pair of walkie-talkies. They were delivered by helicopter with the daily supplies. They were top of the line – I remember they cost hundreds of dollars – an unbelievable sum. Randy set up the plan to get one of the walkie-talkies to the other barge – he would toss it across the gap between the barges, where it would be caught by Wray, a very fine investigator from our Edmonton office. We went out to the deck, and I watched Randy give it a toss, and I saw Wray wave his arms in a catching motion, and I watched the walkie-talkie bounce off a stanchion pole and fall into the water and disappear.

There is nothing more useless than one walkie-talkie. The investigator in me went through a reconstruction of the events – an assessment of what had gone wrong. The facts were these. Due to an accident in his youth, Randy could see from only one eye. Wray wore coke-bottle glasses with really thick lenses. Together, they had only one good eye between them. These were the two who were tasked to do the walkie-talkie toss. I placed the blame on management – that was me. I found it amazing that even though we recovered almost all of the wreckage from the sea bottom, we never did recover that walkie-talkie.

I left Randy to finish the final three days of barge supervision on his own. I had to get back to give Vic a break. I remember when I got off the shuttle boat at the wharf – I climbed the ladder, took my first step, and fell flat on my face. I had completely adapted to my sea legs. It took three days for me to stop swaying around. It was especially noticeable in the shower – I would literally bounce off the walls. I also remember having to pay special attention using the urinal.

As the barge operation was winding down, we knew that significant amounts of wreckage were still on the bottom. With the RCMP and the Coast Guard, we decided on the next phase of recovery. We would use a scallop dragger – we would recover wreckage the same way they fish the ocean floor for scallops. They use a boat to tow a rake that scrapes the seabed and kicks up material – scallops included. That material is collected in a chain-link mesh net. They worked that boat 24 hours a day, from late October to the end of January – 2 ½ months at sea – 1,839 tows across the target area – they recovered 75,000 pounds of airplane material – again, including everything imaginable. Two of our TSB investigators worked on that vessel – Doug McEwen and Peter Rowntree – they became heroes of mine for doing that.

Back before I had left to go to the barge, on my computer I had started to set up the outline of the TSB's public report. These major reports follow an internationally recognized format that goes like this: Synopsis – History of the Flight – Injuries to Persons – Damage to Aircraft – Crew Information – Aircraft Information – Meteorological Information – etc. etc. etc. – then at the end, Analysis – Conclusions – Safety Action – it's all very formal – the order you follow is all laid out. I assigned myself to start populating the various sections. I got a quick start by stealing the "History of the Flight" and some more boiler-plate stuff from Mark – he had drafted that up already, to use in his Ops Report.

For the entire length of the Swissair 111 project, the draft copy of the final report resided on my computer. I spent countless hours during those 4½ years crafting and refining all the word structures and sentences and paragraphs and sections. While researching for this book, I used that final report to refresh my memory. Amazingly, after all these years, I can still stop on any page of that 338-page report and remember putting those words and paragraphs together – that's how incredibly intense it was back then – the drafting and redrafting to get the words just the way they needed to be. Some of the sections were very technical, and I remember the effort it took to put everything into understandable language.

There was method in my madness for becoming the designated report writer. I figured it was the best way for me to help Vic keep control of everything. To compile the report, I would need information about all aspects of the investigation. I'd get that information from each of the investigation groups – I'd be working regularly with all the investigators, both ours, and all the other ones brought in by our partners. I got to poke my nose into everything – that was a perfect way to keep track of what was happening. On an ongoing basis, I got to find out who was making progress, and who needed help. It was also a great way to check up on everybody's mental health – to see how they were coping. I could lighten the load for them, if need be.

By the end of January 1999, we had been in Halifax for five months. The scallop dragger had finished its work. We had tens of thousands of pounds of recovered wreckage that needed sorting. In Hangar A, we were putting recovered pieces of the front section of the aircraft on a life-sized frame (we called it "the jig") that we had built to the exact dimensions of an MD-11. We were reconstructing the cockpit area, and the forward part of the first-class cabin. We knew that the fire was isolated to the overhead ceiling above the cockpit, and above the drop-down ceiling in the forward passenger cabin. We saw where the fire had eventually burned through the cockpit ceiling, just above the pilot's seats. We knew that about six minutes before it crashed, the aircraft had become unflyable for two reasons – the fire had knocked out critical systems, making control impossible, and the heat from the fire had made the cockpit environment all but unliveable.

Our focus was on finding the ignition source for the fire. We had already figured out what the main fuel for the fire was. The interior surface of the fuselage, and the air ducts in the overhead area, were both covered with insulation blankets – these blankets gave protection from the outside environment (from the heat and cold), and they also absorbed sound. We discovered that the cover material on these insulation blankets was exceptionally flammable. We were looking for the ignition source that caused this cover material to ignite.

The heat damage patterns on the metal structures in the area of the fire told us that the fire had started in a specific small area – at the right rear of the cockpit, above the cockpit ceiling – just inside the bulkhead that divides the cockpit from the passenger cabin. In that area, the only potential ignition source was electrical wiring. We had recovered electrical wiring we knew to be from that area, and sure enough, some pieces of wire showed signs of electrical arcing. We were sure that the insulation blanket cover material was ignited by an electrical arc in that area.

Let me get technical for just a bit. A wire will arc when its insulation cover material gets compromised to where the copper conductor inside is exposed. If that copper conductor comes into contact with something metal, that will cause a high-energy flash (an arc), like what you see from a welding rod. A high-energy event like that will typically pop the circuit breaker protecting that wire. If you examine the point where the exposed copper conductor made contact with something metal, you'll find (at that spot) a bead of solid copper – a bead that has re-solidified after getting melted during the arc.

In the wires that we recovered, we found a number of these beads that showed there was arcing, but in every case we found that the damage to the insulation cover on the wire had been caused by the fire – the heat had caused the insulation cover to melt away exposing the copper conductor. We needed to find an arc that had occurred prior to the fire – where the insulation cover on the wire had been compromised in some other way – such as being chaffed by rubbing on a metal structure piece – if we found something like that, it would be our lead event – that would be the electrical arc that lit the insulation blanket cover material on fire.

This is a good place to explain some more about a dynamic that I mentioned earlier – one that is part of nearly every safety investigation, from the biggest to the smallest. Safety investigations are done for accident prevention. You look for safety deficiencies – you point out them out, and fixes are put in place to prevent the same accident from happening again. During most investigations, you'll get to where you recognize that going further with the investigation will not be cost-effective from a "safety" point of view. That's where we were at the five-month point with the Swissair 111 investigation – let me explain.

We knew that the fire started from an electrical arc on a wire. We knew the location where that arc had occurred – not the exact location, but we had it pinned down to a very small area. That small area had dozens of wires running through it. Most of the wires were installed when the aircraft was built – they powered aircraft systems. But that small area also had other wires that had been installed later – they were part of an after-market in-flight entertainment network (IFEN) that had been installed by Swissair (they used sub-contractors). Which wire started the fire? Was it a ship's wire, or an IFEN wire? That would make a huge difference, liability wise.

But to look at it purely from a safety perspective, it shouldn't matter which wire it was. The threat to the aircraft actually wasn't even from the arc. The real threat to the safety of the aircraft was from the flammable material that had been installed. The arc, by itself, was no threat to the aircraft – an arc wouldn't cause a crash – at most, it would cause an inconvenience. But the flammable material – that was a huge threat – that's what brought the airplane down. That was the universal threat. In an aircraft, any one of hundreds of potential ignition sources could light that stuff up, and in no time the aircraft would be unflyable. After five months of investigating, we had enough evidence to recommend that this flammable material be removed from all aircraft (and that's what happened). No more flammable material equals no more threat – equals no more accidents like Swissair 111 – the removal of that material would satisfy our safety mandate.

It came to be that over the next few months, the good folks at TSB's head office got interested in getting their overall agency more normalized. The Swissair 111 project had borrowed many of their key investigators. Other work was piling up, and it appeared there was no end in sight. We came under pressure to scale back. We knew this to be exceptionally short-sighted thinking.

We knew that if we cut back at that point, we would lose the support of the NOK. That would be a disaster. We had worked so hard to gain their confidence. We needed them on our side. We needed to maintain our credibility. We had plenty more recommendations coming – on various secondary issues that we were finding – we had to sell each recommendation hard – we needed the regulators to be pressured into taking action. For credibility, we needed to find the initiation point (the ignition source) for the fire – we needed to find the elusive single arc that had started everything.

We knew there was still more than 35,000 pounds of aircraft structure on the ocean bottom, and there was more of everything else too. Doug McEwen, who had been on the scallop dragger, was convinced that most of what remained was still in the initial area where we had been with the barges. He was convinced this material was imbedded in the sea bottom where the scallop rake couldn't get it. One of our big-ideas guys – John Garstang – did some research, and he came up with the idea of dredging the sea bottom in that specific area. That would bring up anything that was still there.

John discovered that a vessel that could do the task was working not far away – a vessel called the Queen of the Netherlands – it was working in the oilfields off the coast of Newfoundland. It was spanking new, and it was a monster. It could easily dredge at 185 feet down, and surgically recover all the material in a specific area, to whatever depth we wanted. I still held my title as "lead" for the wreckage recovery issues. With the confidence I had in Doug McEwen, and with the encouragement of John Garstang, I became the main promotor for hiring that vessel.

I can tell you that not everybody was on board with it. Some of our people thought it was overkill. In our reconstruction jig, we already had plenty of wreckage pieces that pointed to what had happened. But for me, I didn't just want more evidence – I wanted the sea bottom cleaned up. I was the one who had gone to the meetings with the fishing captains who had their boats tied up because of our exclusion zone around the recovery area. I had heard firsthand their demands for ongoing compensation – they wanted annual compensation, indefinitely.

I heard their worries that nobody would buy the lobster they caught, because people were apprehensive about the lobsters potentially feeding on the remains that had not yet been recovered. I was the one who heard the stories about relics from shipwrecks migrating to shore after being on the bottom for decades – there was stuff still showing up from World War 2. I was the one hearing from treasure hunters who wanted access to the site – the ones who offered to recover wreckage for us, but were actually looking for valuables, including a shipment of diamonds that was on board – they would risk their lives if we let them. I was the one hearing about the potential for personal effects migrating to shore – bit by bit – if we just left them there. Some would be discovered every year – that would go on indefinitely. To me, it was a no-brainer – we had to clean all this stuff up.

I will relate to you how this issue came to a head with head office management. The owners of the Queen of the Netherlands agreed to make the vessel available to us, but only if their schedule permitted. They had a potential window in the fall of 1999 – they projected having a few days between jobs – that could happen only if they had no weather delays on their present job. They offered no guarantees they would show up, but they would try. Also, they would need good weather at our end – rough seas would not work for such a delicate operation (delicate in their world). Their fee would be $4.5 million. There was another issue. The specific pipe they would need for our job was not on their vessel – it was in Europe. To ship it over would cost $150,000, and the shipping had to be arranged right away. That cost would have to be paid by us, regardless of whether they got to do our job.

In one of his updates to head office, Vic outlined this plan to senior management. Up to this point, we had managed to keep them out of our decision-making processes, but they took a keen interest in this one. To put it mildly, they were not supportive. There were too many variables, there was too much risk, we simply couldn't justify risking the $150,000 – they had a strong desire for us to put a stop to all this. I remember getting ready for their call that was to come in at 4 p.m. to our office – me and Vic at our end, and four or five of our finest senior managers at the other.

They opened with a barrage of their best rationale for cancelling the initiative. I countered with our intention to sign the contract. They told me to change my mind – that was their decision. I told them if that was their decision, then I would go with it – I would cancel the project the very minute I received written and signed instructions from them to do so. They said that was not in their plan – I was to make the decision to cancel. Once again, I responded to say I would be happy to make that decision, as soon as I got the written and signed instructions. It was tense – lots of loud voices from their end. It ended with a stalemate – we never received any instructions from them, and we went ahead with the contracts. I knew all along that's the way it would end up.

I have to admit it was a tremendous risk. There were so many things that could go wrong. And to make the project work, we had to get started building a five-acre containment area alongside the dock in Sheet Harbour, east of Halifax. This would be where the Queen of the Netherlands would offload the recovered material. That major construction project would be as useless as the dredge pipe on its way from Europe if the Queen of the Netherlands was unable to show up, or if the weather on their day of opportunity turned out to be unsuitable.

Here's a brief description of how all this was designed to work – the Queen of the Netherlands parks over the target site – the pipe is lowered to the bottom – using high speed water flow it sucks up (like a vacuum cleaner) all the material from the area that we designated on the sea bottom, down to our desired depth (we asked for five feet) – it gets everything on the bottom down to that depth (mud, rocks, etc.) – mixed in with the rocks and mud is all of our aircraft-related material – everything gets pumped into the hopper in the ship's belly – the extra water goes back overboard – the solid material stays in the hopper – the ship transits to where it pulls up alongside the containment area – they run a discharge pipe from the hopper into the containment area – the pumping is reversed – seawater gets pumped into the hopper – then everything in the hopper gets mixed with the water – the mixture travels up the discharge pipe and into the containment area (in a great plume of water, with the sea bottom stuff mixed in) – the solid material settles to the bottom of the containment area (which is lined) – the water is discharged out the far end of the containment area (after it passes through a sluice gate with steel grates so we don't lose anything) – the water goes back into the ocean, and we have our material – all we have to do is sift it through mechanical sifters – tens of thousands of tons of it – and then we run it on a long conveyor belt, where crews separate out the aircraft-related material we want – they do that by hand.

That was our plan. We hired crews of local people to work on the conveyer belt. Before they started, we brought them to Hangar A, where I briefed them on what we were looking for. I showed them tiny pieces, like little circuit breakers, and I told them items like these could hold the key to what happened. We told them about the human remains they would find, and the personal effects. Basically, we wanted them to separate out anything that was not part of the sea bottom. They were highly motivated. Everyone in Nova Scotia wanted this Swissair 111 project to be world class.

I had many a sleepless night waiting for the day to come when the on-site dredging was supposed to happen. It turned out like this: the Queen of the Netherlands came available – it arrived as scheduled – the pipe had arrived from Europe – on the day the Queen arrived at the dredge site the sea was smooth and calm, something that was unheard of for that time of year – the offloading went perfectly – everything in Sheet Harbour went according to plan. The local workers were fantastic. We got an additional 28,000 pounds of wreckage, and we recovered more human remains and personal effects. It was a total success. I was happy.

We finished the sifting and extraction effort in Sheet Harbour on 3 November 1999. All the recovered aircraft material was brought to Hangar A. The last of the sorting in Hangar A finished on 4 December 1999, 15 months after the occurrence. It was a tremendous milestone – the effort put into that by our TSB folks, the RCMP, the experts from Boeing and Swissair, and all the others, was unreal. I remember standing next to the sort table as the last piece went through. I made a comment to the documentary crew (we had authorized a made for TV documentary) – I told them, "now the hard part starts – the analysis".

I witnessed something in Sheet Harbour that I found quite amazing. As the material was being pumped out of the ship's hopper, they would have to stop the ship's pumps periodically to allow the water to drain out of the containment area. Whenever they stopped the pumping, there would be materials stuck to the end of the discharge pipe (it had a couple of metal braces that things would get tangled in – mostly clothing). This one time when the pumping stopped, one of our guys, Manny Soberal, walked out to remove some tangled clothing, and he came back holding a Timex watch. Unbelievably, it was still running. Not only that, it had kept the right time, and it showed "today's" correct month and day. Can you imagine? That watch had survived the crash into the water, 14 months underwater at a depth of 185 feet, then being sucked up by the suction dredge and being deposited into the hopper, and then being sucked up out of the hopper to get stuck at the end of that discharge pipe. All that, and it was still running and keeping time. Back in the day, Timex ran television advertisements where they showed torture tests on their watches – they used the slogan "Takes a Licking and Keeps on Ticking". No torture test they ever imagined could top that one.

Swissair 111 was carrying a shipment of diamonds in one of its cargo holds. We had not recovered any diamonds, and we were interested to see if any would show up in Sheet Harbour. The RCMP checked with experts who told them that any diamonds would be mixed with the sea bottom material – that would make them all but impossible to spot on the conveyer belt. Apparently, diamonds are like little magnets for dirt – dirt clings to them. They would simply pass by on the conveyer, disguised as specks of rock. That seems to be what happened. Not a single diamond was spotted. It's almost certain that all the diamonds were removed by the suction dredging – therefore, they would have ended up in the tailings that we discarded in Sheet Harbour. I was told that it would cost more to try to "mine" them from the tailings than what they were worth, even though that was reported to be millions.

We did find other jewelry in our Sheet Harbour sort – many items of personal jewellery that we could reunite with the grieving families. That part of it was especially gratifying. We also recovered more of the shipment of money that was on board. Throughout the recovery, significant amounts of paper money and coins had been pulled up. It was good to get all that out of the ocean.

The best part was that after the dredging was complete, we were able to lift the exclusion zone that had kept all marine traffic out of the area around the crash site for so long. Fishing resumed, and there were no long-lasting aftereffects. There were no treasure hunter casualties. There was no ongoing issue with items washing up on shore. The entire disruption from having wreckage out there was put to rest – there were no residuals to deal with. It had been money well invested. I never heard another word about it from our senior managers.

The caregivers who worked with the NOK were amazing people. Over the entire time we were doing recovery operations, we kept finding more human remains and personal effects. Any family member who wanted to come was brought to Halifax (by Swissair and Delta). We offered them the chance to visit Hangar A, and many of them came. We set up a wreckage display table at the front of the hangar to show them how we used the wreckage pieces to put the puzzle together. They could see the progress of the reconstructions. I did many of these family briefings in the hangar. The visits were always scheduled. They would show up in a limo provided to them – spouses, siblings, grandparents, aunts and uncles, children who lost parents, parents who lost children, relatives who lost entire families. It was always a sombre mood in the hangar when these visits were happening.

Families were very appreciative of what we were doing. I heard this frequently from them – if this had to happen, we are so thankful that it happened in Canada, and in Nova Scotia. It was heartwarming to hear. They were interested in what we were finding, investigation wise, but inevitably their questioning came to one place – what was it like for their loved ones in the last minutes – what would they be aware of, and for how long – what would they see, and what would they be feeling – in other words, were they scared, did they know they were going to die, and did they suffer?

Here's what I told them, based on solid evidence. As passengers, they would have been informed that the flight needed to divert because of a technical issue – they were told to get ready for a landing – the smoke was isolated away from them – there was no smoke or fire in the passenger cabin. Up until the very end of the flight, they would not have experienced any unusual flight maneuvers.

They would have had no indication by looking outside that they were descending over water. They would have still expected to land at the airport until just a few seconds before the aircraft rolled steeply to the right. At first impact with the water, everyone was killed instantly. Some of the NOK told me they had had visions of their loved ones being alive and being trapped in the sinking aircraft – they told me about horrible imaginings – I was able to give them solid evidence – I helped them get to a better place.

The vast majority of the recovered wreckage was not stuff that we needed to examine closely. We were concentrating on the forward section – we kept that in Hangar A. We had a compound for the bigger stuff, like the landing gears, engines, a few bigger fuselage and wing skin pieces, and so on. The big volume of recovered material was made up of the two million small pieces. We kept those in big triple wall cardboard boxes called tri-walls. We had enough material to fill more than 700 of those boxes. We labeled them so we could find any particular one if we needed it.

We had a special structure built to hold the tri-walls. It was a temporary fabric covered building – it was on the Shearwater base, not too far away from Hangar A – we called it J Hangar. Most of the visiting families wanted to go there. I encouraged them to do that, because it was there that they could get the true picture of the total destruction of the aircraft.

It was in J Hangar that I had my most heartbreaking family encounter. I was there with a family, including a mother and her little son. The dad had perished in the crash. We had Helene (from the RCMP) with us as an interpreter – these people spoke French. The little guy was about three years old, and he was running around like little people do. His mom was having an especially hard time taking in what she was seeing. As we slowly went up and down the massive rows stacked high with tri-walls, we passed by the boxes that held the remains of the passenger seats. They all took some time to stare at those.

When we got close to the exit door, I asked if there were any more questions. Helene relayed that in French. I heard the little boy speak – Helene said he asked, "is this daddy's airplane?". He was looking at me, and I nodded yes. Then he asked, "why is it in so many pieces?" I came really close to losing it – I feel tears in my eyes even now as I write this – I asked Helene to tell him, "that's what we're doing here, trying to figure that out". I wanted to pick him up and hold him close, but of course I didn't – we just left. From then on, whenever I felt my energy waning, all I had to do was think about that little guy and his question – he deserved an answer.

We had a lot of visits to Hangar A. I remember the Prime Minister came – Vic showed him around. There were numerous tours for other dignitaries, mostly done by Vic, accompanied by someone from the RCMP. It was important to keep the politicians and senior executives informed and interested, and Vic was perfect for keeping their confidence high in what we were doing. The visitors couldn't help but be impressed. What we were accomplishing was world-class work, and it showed. In every corner of the hangar there was amazing investigation work happening. Visually, it was overwhelming to everyone who got close to it. People could sense the tragedy of what had happened. But they also recognized that we were putting the puzzle together to explain what had brought it about, and all this was being done in an environment of dignity and respect for those who were lost.

There was one briefing I gave that caught me off guard – I think it was a visit connected to the first anniversary of the crash. There was a reunion of the caregivers (we called them the huggy-bears) who had been there at the beginning to help look after the NOK and first responders and so on. There were maybe 50 of them for the tour – wonderful folks – very kind people. I had met quite a few of them in the early months of the investigation. Some of them were the ones who had been designated to run the emotional support debriefings for our investigators. Part of what they were doing at this reunion was checking on each other to see how they themselves were coping at this point.

Not many of them had actually been into the work areas of Hangar A, or into J Hangar. As the tour progressed, I could tell that they were reliving the enormity of the overall project. It was quite different for them to see up close what the aftermath of the crash looked like. I allowed them to actually walk into the jig, including the reconstructed cockpit with the little pieces of aircraft hanging on the wire frame. They saw up close the mangled pilot's seats with the burn spots on them.

I remember talking to them at the end of the tour. I was in front of the re-construction jig, standing on a wooden box so they could see me. I was sharing with them how appreciative I was of their work, and how we needed people like them who were strong in times of great grief. I shared how hard it had been for me sometimes, especially in meeting and talking to some of the little kids who had lost members of their family. I specifically remember one point where, as I was talking, my focus was over their heads – I was looking out the big hangar doors that were at the far end of the hangar. As I was speaking, I happened to look down into their faces. It caught me by surprise when I saw that many of them were crying – some were consoling each other with hugs. It took me aback. I wasn't expecting that. This tour had been a lot for them to take in.

Two other visits were especially meaningful for me. In mid-May of 1999, my oldest daughter, Tanya, brought her fiancé, Bill, to Moncton to introduce him to her grandparents (my mother and father). My other daughter, Laraine, and my son Andrew, joined in. They all drove down in my car from Ottawa – the car I wasn't using. On 21 May, they came to Shearwater – they brought along my nephew, Ian, who lived in Moncton. It was great to have the opportunity to show them what I had been doing during all that time away from home. A month or two later, my mom and dad came down from Moncton for a visit. It's difficult to find the words to describe how proud and emotional I felt in having them there. Actually, I just decided I'm not even going to try to find the words.

When we came back to Hangar A after Christmas, we knew that we had to put a plan together to get the investigation shifted to our Engineering Branch facility in Ottawa (the lab). But there was no way we could take the huge reconstruction jig with us. Our work in the jig was still the main focus for tracing back to the exact point of origin for the fire, and it would be hard not to have ready access to it. But as time passed, the detailed work shifted to a smaller (but still dimensionally correct) reconstruction, one that zeroed in on the wiring that ran through the area of interest. That one could be moved to the lab, so that's what we prepared to do.

The circumstance of the Swissair 111 crash gave us a unique opportunity from an investigative perspective. We had an active fire that had disabled the aircraft, but that fire had been extinguished instantly when the aircraft struck the water. By rebuilding the area of the fire in the jig, we got to study a snapshot of the fire in progress. When you think about it, that diving into the water scenario is about the only way that a fire in progress could be stopped in a split second. We couldn't find where this type of investigation had ever been done before. What we were doing was groundbreaking. There was no clouding of the evidence – the fire damage had stopped happening instantly – that would not happen if the aircraft had crashed on land – the fire would have just kept on burning – thereby destroying evidence.

Here is just one example of how we documented the fire spread. We got sample strips made of the same aluminum used in the aircraft. We had them painted with the same green primer paint used on the inside of the fuselage, and on the air ducting. We heated the samples in controlled conditions (in an oven), using different time/temperature combinations. We saw that the green primer paint went through a number of colour changes over time at the various temperatures. We made a display board of all the heated samples – then we took our burned wreckage pieces to the sample board and found the closest colour match. Then we "built" the fire area in a 3D computer-aided design (CAD) model showing the temperature variations. That's the type of work that gave us a map of the fire. We knew exactly what had happened in the timeframe the fire was propagating, up to where it was instantly extinguished.

Our team was concentrating on getting every bit of information we could from the wreckage. My goal was to make progress on the draft final report. In fact, report writing had become my main preoccupation. I spent countless hours at my computer, getting the information organized for public consumption. Thankfully, when I had a question or needed information, all I had to do was find the right individual in the hangar to get my answer. And if they had no answer, I could make sure my issue got worked on. I always got good cooperation because I was the one who signed their overtime sheets.

In those last months working in Hangar A, everything became much more of a routine. There were far less NOK visits, and of course no more new wreckage was coming in. One day ran into the next – still seven days a week, and we worked long hours. I kept to my familiar routine. I would get up at 5 a.m. and go to the exercise room at the hotel – then go for breakfast – then carpool with the gang to Hangar A. Lunch was most often at the Shearwater Base cafeteria. We would quit for the day anywhere between 6 and 8 p.m., then go for dinner somewhere – then back to the hotel. I would be in bed by 9 p.m. – 10 p.m. at the latest. It was the same thing every day.

The stress was still very high, but by now it was a different kind of stress. There was much more stress related to not having the "lead event" nailed down, and not knowing if we would ever find it. It was hard work trying to document everything in the final report format. We knew that the lead event was a tiny arc on an electrical wire, and we knew where the arcing happened, but we couldn't find the specific wire. Was it hiding in the 250 miles of wire that we recovered? We had already looked at every inch of it. Maybe the little section of wire with the magic arc on it was still out on the ocean bottom. To me, it was incredibly important that we find it. It would give us significantly more credibility – it would help us sell our safety messages. It would also help justify the effort and expense of this project. And it would give that little 3-year-old boy in J Hangar his answer.

One morning I was walking across the hangar – I was on my way back to my office from the washroom. All of a sudden, I felt the entire core of my body start to ache and go weak. I had to stop. I couldn't figure out what was happening. I forced myself to start walking – very deliberately – and I got to my office chair and sat down. I remember Vic was not there that week – I was alone in the little office. It didn't take long for me to figure out that my head wasn't right either. I had suddenly become hyper anxious, and worried, but I couldn't put my finger on what I was so concerned about. My mental condition wasn't just a reaction to the unexplained physical pain – I soon figured out that the physical pain I was experiencing was a by-product of some kind of mental stress – it wasn't the other way around.

I remember sitting there for quite a while, thinking this through. I wouldn't ask for help – that's just the way I am (I know, I know … that was dumb!). I knew it wasn't a stroke. I was up on strokes, having recently witnessed one firsthand – a guy from Boeing had recently had a stroke right there on the hangar floor – it was serious – he was completely disabled, and they took him away in an ambulance. I was convinced mine was not something like that. No – I was having some kind of stress event, and I figured I could get rid of it as soon as I could figure out what was causing it (I never did figure that out – there was nothing specific, I guess).

It came to me that I had experienced one other event like this. That one had happened when I was in Saudi Arabia, after I'd been there for seven days. I remembered that one night – in the middle of the night – I woke up absolutely drenched in sweat. I had the same kind of body aching and mental stress. I remember getting out of bed and trying to pace around the hotel room, but having trouble walking because of the pain and disorientation. I was panicked, and I remember telling myself not to go out on the balcony. I remember that in Saudi Arabia it had taken three or four days for all that to go away. I remember writing it off as a reaction to a gamma globulin injection that I took before I left Canada. One of the guys from Nationair had told me about people he knew who had a delayed reaction to that injection – he said that it typically happened about seven days on.

235

In Halifax, it took the same three or four days for my pain and mental anguish to go away – it got gradually better each day. I stuck to my routine – exercise, meals, sleep pattern, work. It was a struggle though. I'm not good at tolerating pain. I came to realize that what I had experienced in Saudi Arabia had nothing to do with gamma globulin. It had been some kind of stress attack, the same as this one in Halifax. Those are the only two events I've ever had like that, thankfully. They sure opened my eyes to how much suffering, physical and otherwise, can be caused by mental distress. I was exceptionally grateful to have the routine of travelling with the gang in our carpool – the car was always alive with stories and jokes – great for stress relief.

Moving the investigation to Ottawa after nineteen months was good for everybody. Most of the people left working the case lived in Ottawa, and it took away the stress of being away from home. But in another way, at least for me, it added some different stresses. I still had to work the same hours, but in Halifax I had nothing else to do except work. Being home suddenly reintroduced family related duties.

On top of that was the learning centre that Charlotte was still running on her own. She had been working almost as many hours as me, keeping all that together. I still couldn't help her much – I didn't have enough time or energy. We talked it over and decided we would have to sell it. Somehow, in early 2001 fate intervened, sending us a gentleman who showed up looking to see how he could get his own franchise. It wasn't long before he owned ours. I was relieved it was gone, but at the same time sorry to see it go. I would have liked to see how it would have worked out in the longer run – into my retirement.

At the Engineering Branch, we set up two rented trailers in the wreckage compound to use as offices for those of us who didn't already work in the main building. We worked in those trailers for another three years, studying the evidence and putting the various reports together – including the final report, and all its attachments. It was a tremendous grind – we had so much to analyse, evidence wise.

One Sunday morning, I think it was in late 2001, I got to experience the most wonderful feeling I have ever had connected to an investigation. I was in the trailer working away on my computer when Jim Foot came in and asked me to go with him into the lab where the wiring reconstruction was set up. Jim was our wiring specialist, and he was an exceptionally talented investigator – one of our road warriors who had been a main player in Hangar A.

Jim pointed to the microscope and asked me to take a look. I recognized the short section of wire he was examining. It was about two feet long – a length of wire that had been part of the in-flight entertainment wiring. We had already figured out that it had run through the area where we knew the fire had started. Jim had the microscope's lens focused on a part of this wire. We had looked at this wire many times before. We knew it had an arc on it, but we knew that arc we had found was caused by the fire (the fire had burned through the wire's insulation covering, and that caused a short circuit). The arc we knew about was powerful enough that it would have tripped the circuit breaker, making the wire electrically dead. That arc could not have started the fire.

But the microscope lens was pointed at this other part of that same wire – what was Jim showing me? When I looked, I couldn't believe my eyes. I was looking at a tiny little arc that we had not found before. Instantly, I knew this was the arc that had started the fire – this arc had to have happened prior to the fire – this was it – the lead event – Jim had found it – I almost fainted. I gave Jim a big hug, and I would have kissed him if he had let me.

Jim told me that he had been doing his final documentation of that wire when he decided to open up some damaged strands at the end of it – the strands had been bunched together when the wire broke during the impact. He hadn't tried to straighten the strands out before, not wanting to alter the overall evidence piece. Now, while he was looking at each tiny strand under the microscope, he found the tiny arc – it was much too small to see with the naked eye – it took significant magnification to see it.

There is a vast amount of detailed technical information to explain how we concluded that this tiny arc was our lead event – it's much to detailed to try to duplicate it here. But if you have a keen interest, you can read all about it in the TSB's final report. I remember how long it took to construct that section and put all that logic together.

That Sunday morning, Jim asked me to keep his finding a secret – to keep it just between the two of us until he checked, and then double checked, everything. This was so huge a find that he was almost scared to announce it to the team – maybe someone would see some flaw in the logic. We actually kept it between the two of us for two or three days – then Jim showed the tiny arc to the core team. Everyone was on board – it was all magnificent. We all pledged to keep it within our core team, and we actually did that for several weeks. We wanted to get all the documentation and diagrams ready so we could fully explain it to others – such as to TSB management. Everybody knew what Jim's discovery meant – our investigation would be complete and successful in the eyes of the world.

Let me return to my claim about the Swissair 111 investigation project – I proclaim it to be the best the world has ever seen. It took the combined efforts of thousands of people, and expertise second to none. What we had accomplished far surpassed the established standard for describing something that is all but impossible – the top standard talks about "finding a needle in a haystack". We blew that standard away – we found a tiny speck in the massive ocean – a speck that was far too small to see with the naked eye. We found this tiny speck, even though it had been mixed in with two million other pieces 185 feet below the ocean surface. As the saying goes – top that!

We did all this while keeping the families on board, and the media at bay. We published a report with so much supporting information that it was universally accepted, even in the world of litigation. Lawsuit wise, everything settled out of court, based on the fact that our information was irrefutable. Unbelievably, the TSB did not receive a single request under Canada's Access to Information Act. That is a sure sign of 100% success.

I'd like to acknowledge here the tremendous expertise shown by the specialists from Boeing. Their support was invaluable. We worked with them as comrades in every way – there was full trust between us. During that time, we were like family – everyone supported each other. We all had great respect for their expertise. This was Boeing at its best. I would like you to remember this paragraph of praise later when you read some things about Boeing that are not so complimentary.

The Sea Sorceress with the attached barge – 1998

The clamshell bucket depositing wreckage on the attached barge – 1998

Inside Hangar A with a view of "the jig"

Larry with the Swissair 111 Jig

The sort line at Sheet Harbour – 1999

Wreckage pieces from Swissair 111

Larry with his Mom and Dad in Hangar A – 1999

Larry with his kids and family in Hangar A – 1999

Larry with some of the Swissair 111 investigation team members – from the left:
Larry, Jim Foot (seated), John Garstang, Don Enns – 1999

Larry conducting a group tour in Hangar A – 1999

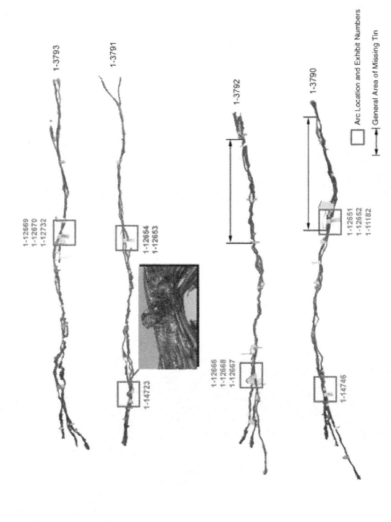

The tiny arc that started the Swissair 111 fire – 2002

1-3793

1-3791

1-3792

1-3790

1-12669
1-12670
1-12732

1-14723

1-12654
1-12653

1-12666
1-12668
1-12667

1-12651
1-12652
1-11182

1-14746

Arc Location and Exhibit Numbers

General Area of Missing Tin

19

TRANSITION TIME — BACK TO THE PRIVATE SECTOR

As I mentioned, the Swissair 111 investigation was a pivot point in my life. To use a sports analogy, we had played in the big leagues, in front of a world audience, and we had finished as champions. I was totally exhausted, but I also felt like I was at the top of my game. I was ready to appreciate some down time, but I knew it would be a hard transition to go back to normal duties at the TSB.

Back when I joined the civil service, on 28 March 1978, I had set a target to retire after 30 years, that would be on 28 March 2008. On the day we released the Swissair 111 report, the countdown to my retirement started — I had exactly five more years (plus one day) to go. Thankfully, I still enjoyed the company of some of the people I was working with. That's what I would use to help motivate me to go to work each day.

The Swissair 111 investigation had cost me the opportunity to own and help run the learning centre, but another interesting prospect emerged when Charlotte decided that we should move out of our big house in the suburbs — she wanted to downsize. By the time Swissair 111 was finishing up, all our kids had departed the nest. I was in full agreement with moving, but my input was that we not just shift to a smaller house in the suburbs. I wanted a change of lifestyle. I had two options — we could go to a downtown condo — or move to a house with lots of property, out in the countryside.

Charlotte had no interest in moving downtown, so with my son Andrew she started scouting out rural properties near Ottawa. They had trouble finding something suitable. They found some nice houses, but without the type of land we wanted. Alternatively, they found some nice land, but without the right kind of house. Eventually, we decided to look for vacant land that we could build on, and that's what we found.

We purchased a 70-acre piece of forested land within easy commuting distance to my work, and to the different parts of the city where our kids and grandkids lived. We had no neighbours — there were no houses nearby, but it still seemed close to everything. On our property we had a contractor build us the house we wanted. And we didn't stop there. We put up a big storage barn, and a separate workshop for both mechanical and woodworking, and a play-house for the grandkids, and a cabin away back in the forest next to a river that our property bordered on. We could cross-country ski on our own trails.

With all that, I had enough to keep me busy. I had always wanted to try country living, and I finally got my wish. I had tractors, and a backhoe, and an ATV, and my own dump truck, and chainsaws, and mowers, and all the attachments to clear some land and make trails – all the outdoor living I wanted, winter and summer. I cut my own trees to make my own lumber, and I turned the lumber into sawdust and other creations in my woodworking shop. I had every tool I needed to do my own work on all this equipment (I wasn't all that good at fixing things, but I was handy at taking things apart).

To go back to my youth, I bought a twin of my first new car – the one I had purchased back in 1970 – and the one I still had when I got married. It was a muscle car – a Plymouth Duster 340, a beautiful B5 blue, with a four-speed manual transmission – it was exceptionally fast. I had loved driving my first one back in 1970 when I was twenty-one years old, and I loved driving its replacement all these years later. I bought a 1990 GMC 3/4 ton dually truck, and a 26-foot v-nose car hauler trailer – I used those to take my replacement Duster to car shows. On one memorable trip, I took the Duster to a huge car show in my old hometown of Moncton – the Atlantic Nationals – they had over 2,000 show cars, and I got a top 20 finish – amazing!

It was in 2003 that grandkids started arriving – the first one on 3 April 2003. She was amazing right from the start. Like her mom, when she was just two years old, she could talk in full sentences. It was pure joy to have her stay over. Four others would follow. It was fun to have them at the property. There was so much to introduce them to – things they couldn't experience in the city. Charlotte and I have been very lucky to have had the opportunity to get close with each of our grandkids during their formative years – lots of one-on-one time with them – for me, they are the great joys of my life.

That's how I got through those years working at the TSB after Swissair 111 finished – that and working on the Air France 358 accident I wrote about earlier. During those years I worked on several other investigations. All were interesting. I remember going out west a couple of times, helping with accidents in British Columbia. I remember traveling through the Rocky Mountains by helicopter to get to an accident site – that is absolutely spectacular territory out there.

There is one accident that I recall as being particularly tragic. It happened on 16 June 2006 at the Carp Airport – the crash of a Bede BD5J – known as the world's smallest jet. The pilot, who was the owner and builder of the aircraft, was killed in the crash. Accidents like this would not normally be handled by head office, but the Carp Airport (in west Ottawa) was just a short drive away, so our regional office in Toronto asked that we respond on their behalf – not as IIC – just to help out. I went, along with Elaine Summers.

We arrived there about two hours after the crash. We met up with the police – they had gathered up some initial information. We were told that the crash happened while the pilot was practicing his routine for an airshow the next day. The routine's final maneuver was a low-speed fly-past at about 500 feet. It was during this low-speed pass that the aircraft rolled sharply to the right and dove to the ground. The pilot had managed to get the wings back towards level, but he couldn't arrest the descent. There were lots of witnesses, two of which were the pilot's wife, and his teenaged nephew.

Elaine and I went to view the wreckage. It was basically all in one piece. We could see that this really was a tiny aircraft – only 12 feet long, and with only a 17-foot wingspan. The pilot's body was still strapped in the seat. I remember looking at a handsome man with a thick black mustache – he looked kind of like Burt Reynolds. He looked much too big to be in that tiny cockpit space.

We could see nothing in the wreckage to give us a clue about what had happened. Elaine stayed to help the coroner recover the body, and to do the documentation at the crash site. I left to do the witness interviewing. I remember thinking that this would be the quickest I had ever met with loved ones after a death. I was amazed at how composed and gracious the pilot's wife was. We had the standard conversation – condolences, questions, answers, talk about the devastation of the loss, how wonderful a man her husband was, how he had played professional football, how he loved aviation. I gave her our commitment to try our best to find out what had happened.

My talk with the nephew was harder. He looked to be maybe 15 years old. He told me about how the pilot was like a second father to him – how the pilot had taken him on as part of the pit crew to help keep the aircraft shipshape. I felt so sorry for this young man – he was devastated. He told me that they transported the aircraft in a trailer, and for that they had to take the wings off and on. The aircraft design accommodated that with quick disconnects, not only for the wings, but also for the flight controls and fuel system.

Earlier that day, they had received an unexpected request to attend a media event with the aircraft. They took it apart, loaded it in the trailer, and went to the event. They assembled it at the event, then took it apart again for the return to Carp, and then reassembled it for the practice run. The nephew had helped with all this work.

There was a video of the flight, and we got to study that. It showed that after the upset the pilot was using the ailerons to try to stop the right roll, but they were not having much effect. The engine was running. We saw that the landing gear was extended, and in the wreckage, we saw that the flaps were retracted.

Elaine arranged for the wreckage to be transported to the engineering branch, where she found out what had gone wrong. During the reassembly prior to the accident flight, the right flap had been incorrectly installed (slightly misaligned) – this misalignment allowing the right flap to retract unexpectedly under an air load. That's what happened during the fly-past – the right flap retracted without command, causing massive lift asymmetry – that resulted in an uncontrollable right roll. The pilot reacted with full countering aileron, and he retracted the left flap, but there was not enough altitude for him to recover from the dive. We were told that the pilot had double-checked everything before takeoff, but obviously he didn't catch the installation mistake.

Several months later, the pilot's wife came to the engineering branch to get a briefing on what we had discovered. They were also there to retrieve the wreckage. With her, she brought a friend of the family who was an airline pilot – he would help her validate our work. Elaine briefed them on the witness mark evidence we had. It proved the wing/flap had not been mated properly. The pilot's wife had a hard time accepting that, believing that her husband would have caught anything like that.

I took the pilot friend to watch the video – the wife couldn't bring herself to watch it. We did freeze-frames to show that the right flap must have retracted as we theorized, and he drew the same conclusion. With Elaine's explanations and logic, and with the concurrence of the pilot friend, the pilot's wife came to fully accept our explanation for what had happened.

We loaded the wreckage into their trailer and watched as they started to drive away. Suddenly, the truck stopped. We watched the pilot's wife searching through the back of the truck, where she found a hat – she brought that hat over and gave it to Elaine. They hugged, and then the wife went back to the truck and they drove off. The hat was a special design, with the logo of the pilot on it. That was an exceptionally thoughtful gesture. What a great gift for Elaine – it was well deserved – she keeps that hat in a safe place.

As best I can remember, that June 2006 accident in Carp was the last one I went out to while I was still with the TSB. In that timeframe, we were still tinkering with the Air France 358 report, but I was losing the battle on getting solid safety action out of that one, as I explained earlier. The Air France 358 report was released on 13 December 2007. According to my long-standing retirement plan, at that point I had only 15 months left to go. That would give me 30 years of pensionable service – I could retire at age 59 with 60% of my salary – good enough for me.

Over the years at CASB/TSB, I had watched as many of the more senior investigators turned into curmudgeons before finally departing. I had a strong desire to not become a curmudgeon, but I could see myself edging towards that. Here's how I knew that was happening. Someone at a meeting would say "we should try this" and my thinking would be that we tried that in 1986, and again in 1992, and again in 1997, and so on – it didn't work then, and it won't work now – and I could either dole out that information like a curmudgeon, or I could sit there and say nothing like a curmudgeon.

Conversely, if I had a good idea that would actually make things better – it would be the same idea I had proposed in 1986, and again in 1992, and again in 1997, and so on – the one that wasn't accepted then, and wouldn't be accepted now – and I could either dole it out like a curmudgeon, or sit there and say nothing like a curmudgeon.

So, you see, no matter what I chose to do, a curmudgeon I would be. I was too close to retirement to be picked as IIC, or for any other important role on the next major. I would be long gone before the investigation was done. And for anything less than a major, there was no benefit in sending me – the newer people needed to go out to get experience on their own. Overall, there was no good fit left for me at the TSB, and I knew it, and I felt it. I had done everything already, from training, to manual writing, to accredited rep – and all different kinds of investigations, from the smallest to the biggest.

There came a day when I finally decided that I would leave – I had to get out of there. I had accumulated more than 400 days of sick leave. We got credit for 15 days a year, and I hadn't used a single day for the first 27 years of service. I was so proud of that, and I started to tell people about it. I thought it was a badge of honour – they all thought I was nuts. It crossed my mind that a doctor's note would take me all the way to my retirement – but I knew my conscience couldn't withstand that. I would retire with all those credit days left behind – just my luck to never get sick.

When I left the TSB on 2 January 2009, I had it set up that I would join up with AIR (Accident Investigation and Research), and that's what happened. I joined with Terry and Robbie, and I've continued with consulting work ever since.

At AIR, they had a policy that everyone had to undergo an Executive Medical. They wanted to make sure they had a base line in case anything was to happen medical wise while out working for them. I finally got around to getting that medical in the fall of 2009. One element of the medical was an exercise electrocardiogram (a stress EKG), something I had not had before.

As a pilot, I had undergone an EKG every six months for many years, and nothing ever showed up. But on this stress EKG, they found an anomaly, and they referred me for further testing. It turned out that I had significant block-ages in some arteries running from my heart – in one artery there was over 90% blockage. That was a shock to me. I had absolutely no symptoms, which is quite unusual with that much blockage.

I was a good candidate for dropping dead. I was 60 years old. I recalled that on my mom's side of the family, I had four uncles who had all died suddenly of heart attacks at the age of 59. In March 2010, I underwent quadruple bypass surgery at the Ottawa Heart Institute, and with that I got a new lease on life. What good fortune I had in getting out of the TSB when I did, and in joining AIR like I did, and in them having the medical requirements they had.

Quadruple bypass surgery is not much fun. I remember being wheeled down to the operating room. It was right next door to the morgue. I asked about why that was. They told me it was because they needed a nice cool place where there would be less bacteria and such. I knew better – they wouldn't have to push me far if it didn't work out. They put an intravenous needle in my arm, and out I went. I woke up six hours later, and I looked to see if I had a tag tied to my toe – I didn't.

They had briefed me that I would be on a ventilator, and sure enough, I had a big tube stuck down my throat. The nurses were fantastic. Everything they told me would happen turned out to be true. After a while, they took the breathing thing out, and I could talk. I told them to move quickly past the morgue door on the way to my room.

For many years, I had paid a premium on my government medical plan to ensure I would get a private room if I ever needed one at the hospital. Guess what – they never had a private room available. All that money wasted. I absolutely hated being in a shared room. I was there for five nights, and I had three different roommates. The first guy moaned and groaned constantly, the second guy snored like a professional, and the third guy was a convict – he literally made drug deals from his bed.

I was scheduled for a five-day stay, but by the third day I had a plan to escape. The final marker I had to meet was to get out of bed, go down the hall on my own, then climb a small stairway, and then do the reverse to return to bed. I talked a nurse into letting me try that early – on day three. It didn't go well. My heart monitor went into overdrive on the stairs, and for my bravado they sentenced me to an extra day – I didn't get out until day six. It took a good four months before I started feeling normal, and an additional three or four months of exercise to get back to where I was before that operation. But the doctor gave me a twenty-year warranty on his work. He said there was nothing wrong with my heart – and he said the arteries they took from my lower left arm should stay unclogged in my chest for at least that long – so I should be around for quite a while yet. Like I told the doctor, he fixed it so now I'll die from something way more serious than heart disease.

I loved the work at AIR. It was all pure investigation, with absolutely no bureaucracy. After only a few days there, they gave me one of their larger projects to look over – it was a case they had been working on for more than four years. As I've mentioned previously, it's not uncommon for litigation cases to last for several years. Our client was Embraer, the big aircraft manufacturer from Brazil. We were working through a major law firm in New York called Condon & Forsyth (our working relationships with both Embraer and Condon & Forsyth have remained strong to this day).

The case involved a major accident that happened in Brazil on 29 September 2006 – a mid-air collision over the Amazon jungle between an airline flight (GOL Flight 1907 – a Boeing 737-8) and an Embraer-built executive jet (a Legacy 600). Tragically, all 154 people aboard the airline flight were killed. Everybody aboard the executive jet survived when the damaged aircraft landed safely at a remote airport.

This accident had been investigated by Brazil – specifically by CENIPA (Brazil's investigation agency), which is their equivalent to Canada's TSB.

Because of the heavy U.S. involvement (they had the Boeing aircraft, and the American crew on the Legacy), CENIPA had significant assistance from the NTSB. The NTSB's accredited rep was the same investigator who was the IIC on the accident in Teterboro where I was the Canadian accredited rep – remember the one where the old lady walked through the recovery site – that's the one where I gave high praise to the final report for an investigation well done.

AIR's task for the one in Brazil was to provide our client with an independent report on the circumstances of the crash. The lawyers would use our findings and advice to assess our client's potential liability exposure. The lawyer's goal was to protect their client, and to negotiate a fair percentage of blame between all the parties who got named in the lawsuits. In this case, our input would tell them whether their aircraft – the Legacy 600 business jet – could somehow be blamed (at least partially) for what happened.

This is another case where lawyer/client relations keep me from going into all the details of my findings, but I can tell you this. In the context of apportioning blame and liability, AIR's investigation turned up nothing to implicate the GOL Boeing 737 aircraft, or its operation – they were innocent victims. Consistent with the findings of the official investigation by CENIPA, we found significant flaws in the Brazilian ATC system that allowed the two aircraft to be flying in opposite directions on the same airway at the same altitude. ATC carried a large share of the blame.

The last part of my investigation was into the company that was operating the Legacy 600, and in particular the pilots on this flight. The purchasers, ExcelAire Service Inc. of New York, were flying their newly built aircraft from Brazil to the United States. I spent many months, and countless hours, going through the sequence of events for the accident flight, starting with the pre-takeoff delivery ceremonies and preparation. Additionally, I studied the cockpit voice recorder in great detail, documenting the actions of the flight crew.

Of particular importance to our client, I found nothing to implicate Embraer's Legacy 600 aircraft – it was not at fault for what happened. In my investigation, I uncovered additional evidence that supported the conclusions reached by CENIPA – that the Legacy's pilots contributed significantly to what caused the two aircraft to collide.

Interestingly, the NTSB chose to attach their own findings to the CENIPA report (which is allowed by international agreement). The NTSB downplayed the role played by the Legacy pilots, concluding that all pilots on both aircraft had acted properly. The NTSB placed the responsibility with Brazilian ATC. To me, it was clear that the NTSB was either unaware of how poorly the Legacy pilots had performed, or they were purposefully deflecting blame away from them. Either way, this was not the NTSB's finest hour. The quality of their work on this Brazilian investigation was in sharp contrast to what they had done on the one in Teterboro.

The bottom line is that when the percentages of payout were negotiated on the mid-air case, our client (and their insurance company) got zero percent of the liability. This was a direct result of AIR's input to their strategy, and the solid evidence they had to prove what had actually led to the collision. Our clients saved multiple millions of dollars, for which they were most grateful. I have worked on many cases for those clients since that first one.

To get a number for this book, I searched my computer files to count the number of cases I've worked on through AIR (and now HVS) – all the ones since back in January 2009. The number is 70, including three that are open and active as I write this.

Here are a few examples of the accidents I've worked on as a consultant. For most of them, I didn't have to travel to the accident site. They show the variety of the work. Most of them are from the earlier times – I'm obliged to keep the later ones confidential.

A Eurocopter AS350 (A-Star) helicopter in Alaska

Many Cessna Caravan accidents, in places like Banning Pass, California – Bellevue, Idaho – Winnipeg, Manitoba – Oak Glen, California – Parks, Arizona – and Pelee Island, Ontario

CASA 212 accidents, such as in the Falsterbo Canal, Sweden – and Robinson Crusoe Island, Chile (the one I wrote about earlier)

Embraer EMB-120 accidents in Darwin, Australia – and Manaus, Brazil

A Hawker Beechcraft BAE 125-800A in Owatonna, Minnesota

Many Mitsubishi MU-2 accidents in places like Terrace, British Columbia – and Carolina, Puerto Rico

Cessna Citation accidents – an example would be one in Egelsbach, Germany

Most of the investigations, including the ones above, require in-depth work to get to the underlying causes, and to ensure our evidence cannot be successfully challenged in court. As I stated previously, we aim to overwhelm any counter arguments, so we always have the winning conditions.

Larry taking his 1970 Duster 340 to a car show – 2014

Larry's grandkids with the 1970 Duster 340 at a car show – 2014

One time I went to a small town in Newfoundland to testify at a coroner's inquest. You weren't allowed into the testimony room until it was your turn on the stand. I wandered into the courtroom next door, just to pass some time. An old gentleman was on the stand, and he was being cross examined by the defense lawyer.

It wasn't going well for this lawyer, so he decided to try something different – a tactical move. Knowing that this was a really small town, he asked, "sir – remember that you're under oath so you have to tell the truth – tell this court whether you know more than half the members of this jury?" The old guy looked them over – his answer was spectacular – "sir, I can swear under oath that I know more than all of them put together"

20

AN INVESTIGATION THAT WAS ITSELF A DISASTER

Near Athens, Greece
14 August 2005
Boeing 737-31S, Helios Airways Flight HCY522
121 Fatalities

This is one of the few major projects that I worked on at AIR that I can talk freely about. That's because we never had a formal client in the classic sense – much of my work on this one was done pro bono – it was the same for the others at AIR. We weren't part of the initial investigation into this crash. In fact, we didn't even get involved until more than four years after the crash.

We were asked to have a look at the conclusions that the official investigation had reached. We agreed to do that as a goodwill gesture for a regular client. For us, it turned into a crusade for justice. We saw that some very good and professional people (these are the people who would become our unofficial clients) were being victimized through incompetence by the international accident investigation community. We couldn't stand by and let that happen. We also saw the devastating results of an unjustifiable intrusion into the investigation by the judicial systems of both Cyprus, and Greece. Regarding the investigation itself, it was evident that it had been mishandled from the start – the conclusions they reached were simply wrong.

I'll start with a summary of the circumstances of this accident – this is information taken from the official report. HCY522 (Helios Flight 522) was a scheduled flight from Larnaca airport in Cyprus, to Athens, Greece. It departed at 9:07 local time in the morning, estimating a one hour and 30-minute flight. After take-off, the pilots put the aircraft on autopilot (that's normal). Four minutes into the flight, they programmed the autopilot to climb the aircraft to its assigned altitude of FL340 (about 34,000 feet). The pilots failed to recognize that there was something wrong with the aircraft's pressurization system – the aircraft was not pressurizing. Spoiler alert – the official investigation got the reason for the pressurization failure completely wrong.

Normally, the pressurization system keeps the atmospheric pressure in the cabin (the cabin altitude) below 8,000 feet. If the pressurization system doesn't

257

work, the cabin altitude will be the same as the actual altitude of the aircraft. Anything above 10,000 feet brings in a risk of hypoxia – a lack of oxygen to the brain and vital organs. The higher you go the less oxygen there is in the atmosphere; therefore, the more dangerous it gets. If you experience hypoxia, it will very quickly affect your judgement – then, you'll become unconscious – then, you'll die.

With the aircraft climbing normally at over 2,000 feet per minute, it took only five minutes for them to climb through the hypoxia danger altitude. As the aircraft climbed through 12,000 feet, the cabin altitude warning horn sounded in the cockpit. The pilots mistook that warning as being for a totally unrelated problem (that same horn is used for a takeoff configuration warning on the ground). The pilots became confused trying to figure out what was happening. They thought they were experiencing multiple unrelated failures – at the same time, they were coming increasingly under the influence of hypoxia. Unfortunately, and tragically, they allowed the aircraft (still on autopilot) to keep climbing.

As they climbed through 16,000 feet, they called their company operations centre to say they had a "Take-off configuration warning", and a "Cooling equipment offline" warning. The captain's technical discussions with a ground engineer didn't make sense – he was obviously influenced by hypoxia. As they climbed through 18,000 feet, the passenger oxygen masks deployed. By design, the passengers have only a 15-minute supply of oxygen – sufficient to last through an emergency descent from a high altitude. Amazingly, the captain remained able to attempt communications with dispatch (we know that because there was microphone keying from his radio recorded on the FDR) all the way to 28,900 feet – after that, there were no more recorded microphone clicks.

The autopilot levelled the aircraft at 34,000 feet and it then flew the aircraft according to the routing that had been programmed into it. When the aircraft got to Athens, the autopilot set the aircraft up in a holding pattern, still at 34,000 feet. While it was in the hold, it was intercepted by two F-16 fighter aircraft from the Hellenic Air Force. One of the F-16 pilots saw that the captain's seat was vacant. Someone was slumped over in the first officer's seat. Motionless passengers were seen with oxygen masks on – their oxygen would have run out long ago.

At one point, during the 10th holding pattern, they saw someone gain access to the cockpit from the cabin area. There was a flight attendant on board who was taking pilot training, and he was the likely candidate. The F-16 pilot saw him sit down in the Captain's seat and put on a set of headphones. It was

258

at this point that the left engine flamed out from fuel starvation. The aircraft turned randomly, and it started to descend.

Amazingly, an emergency call was heard from the aircraft – "MAYDAY, MAYDAY, MAYDAY, Helios Airways Flight 522 Athens … (unintelligible word)". A few seconds later, another "MAYDAY, MAYDAY" was heard – this time in a very weak voice. As the aircraft descended through 7,000 feet, the person in the captain's seat for the first time appeared to acknowledge the presence of the F-16s, and he made a hand motion – but he was unable to take control of the aircraft. The right engine flamed out, and the aircraft entered a rapid descent before colliding with rolling hilly terrain. At impact, there was total devastation.

At the accident site, investigators found a piece of wreckage that they immediately thought revealed the answer to what had happened. What they found was part of the cockpit overhead panel – the part that had the selector knob (Pressurization Management Control – PMS Knob) that controlled the mode for the pressurization system. In flight, the mode selector (it's actually a simple knob) must be set to the AUTO (automatic) position. If that knob had not been set to AUTO, the aircraft would not have pressurized. Sure enough, they found that knob was not set to AUTO – it was closer to the MAN (manual) position. Right away they had their operating hypothesis – somehow, the selector knob had been left on MAN – that would explain why the aircraft failed to pressurize.

To validate their operating hypothesis, they boxed up this piece of the overhead panel with the knob, along with some other wreckage parts, and sent them (in care of the NTSB) to Boeing's Equipment Quality Analysis facility in Seattle, Washington. The examinations took place from the 17th to the 19th of October 2005. The main finding from this testing, which was done by Boeing and observed by everybody else, was this: "The mode selector switch was confirmed to be in the 'manual' mode position". So that was that – the puzzle had been solved – everything else, investigation wise, was just a matter of tidying up. It appears that the Greek investigators had no particular expertise to allow them to assess the testing – they simply accepted Boeing's conclusions.

The Greek Air Accident Investigation & Aviation Safety Board (AAIASB) published their report on this accident in November 2006. It was very comprehensive, coming in at 186 pages with appendices. It was very well written too, having been completed with the assistance of two excellent writers – Ron

Schleede, who had been the NTSB's International Aviation Advisor, and Caj Frostell, former Chief of the Accident Investigation Section at ICAO (International Civil Aviation Organization). Ron and Caj had worked on the investigation – as part of the AAIASB team – under an ICAO contract – they were basically there to help organize the report. (I knew Ron very well – he had served a term at the TSB as Director of Investigations during the Swissair 111 investigation – and I knew Caj also – I had met him a few times along the way.)

Despite the number of pages, the thrust of the AAIASB report was this. They found that on the inbound flight to Larnaca, the aircraft had experienced a pressurization related problem that required a pressure check on the ground – they had to check for any excessive air leaks around an aft service door – this was done by maintenance engineers. To conduct the test, they pressurized the aircraft on the ground by pumping air in through the normal air conditioning system (with the engines running). To allow the cabin to pressurize, they had to close the outflow valve (that's the valve that modulates automatically to regulate the cabin pressure while airborne). To close that outflow valve for their test, they had to select MANUAL (MAN) using the selector knob (the overhead panel the knob is mounted on is just above the first officer's seat) – then they used a toggle switch on that same panel to run the outflow valve fully closed. As mentioned, when the aircraft is in flight that selector knob has to be set to AUTO so the outflow valve can regulate the cabin pressure properly.

The investigation's finding was that after the maintenance guys toggled the outflow valve back to open after the pressure testing, they left the selector knob at MAN. The official investigation concluded that during their pre-takeoff checks, the pilots didn't notice the knob was in the MAN position. That would be an unbelievably bad mistake by the pilots. But the investigation concluded that that's why the aircraft didn't pressurize. That's not what happened (as we found out later), but that's what they came up with – their finding cast the pilots in a very bad light.

All but four of the passengers were from either Cyprus or Greece. Even before that finding came out, people in both of those countries were already looking for revenge against Helios. Now, they were being told that this accident didn't involve some complicated technical issue – instead, it had resulted from simplistic incompetence by the pilots. The next of kin (NOK) and the public wanted action taken against Helios Airways, and in particular against their senior managers. About a year after the accident, Helios Airways ceased operations.

In early 2008, a prosecutor in Athens charged six former Helios employees with manslaughter. Then, on 23 December 2008, the Cyprus Attorney General issued a "Form of Indictment" against certain Helios employees and managers, through the Assize Court in Nicosia – that's a court that tries criminal cases that involve sentences of more than five years. Our soon-to-be clients were criminally charged in two different courts, in two different countries at the same time. Emotions were high. During their first appearance in the Cyprus court, the defendants were attacked by angry relatives of the deceased. Following that, and throughout the trial, the defendants had to be escorted by the police – security measures were ramped up.

I'll share more of my thoughts about the criminalization of aircraft accidents later, but for now I'll say that in my view there's no place in accident investigation for such draconian action. Far better options are already in place. Specifically, the objective of the safety investigation is to explain what happened, and to make recommendations to prevent a reoccurrence. Then, for those looking for retribution, there is civil litigation available to assign blame and liability (that's what lawsuits are for). There's absolutely no space for a criminal prosecution, especially if that criminal prosecution relies in any way on the elements of the safety investigation.

For context, remember that we (at AIR) were not involved in this case at all before these criminal cases started. In the fall of 2009, while the trial in Cyprus was ongoing, we were asked by business associates at the law firm Gates and Partners in London, U.K. (specifically, a very competent lady we had worked with previously named Emma) to review the Greek report to see what opportunities we might find for defending the accused in the Cypriot court. Emma explained that there was no specific funding for this work. Gates was representing the insurers of Helios, but the policies held by Helios didn't cover a defence against criminal charges.

Emma sent us a copy of the Cypriot indictment. Along with Helios as a corporation, it named four Helios executives, the Executive Chairman, the Managing Director and Accountable Manager, the Flight Operations Manager, and the Chief Pilot. Over the next three years, I got to know two of these men quite well – the Managing Director and Accountable Manager, and the Chief

Pilot – and I was impressed with each of them, on both a professional and personal level. As you will see, what all these individuals (and their families) went through, based on an incompetent investigation, was underserving, unfair and unwarranted in every way.

The first thing we did at AIR was to review the Greek report. We saw that everything about their conclusions depended on one finding – that after the crash the selector knob was found to be in the MAN position. To them, this was proof positive that the entire sequence of events started with the ground pressurization check, and then continued with the incompetent pilots not completing their pre-takeoff checks properly. At AIR, we took the "found" position of the knob to be only the starting point to find evidence – we were much more interested in where the selector knob had been positioned prior to the crash (during the flight). Had it actually been set to MAN? Or could it have been set to AUTO?

Without getting too technical, I have to describe a bit about this selector knob. It's a round knob that has a raised part across its middle – you turn (rotate) the knob by gripping the raised part between your thumb and index finger. The knob rotates clockwise and anticlockwise – rotating back and forth between its positions. It is just one of numerous knobs and switches on the overhead panels above the pilots. This one is a three-position knob – it can be rotated to stop in any one of three detent positions – the first position (to the far left) is AUTO – then, if you rotate the knob clockwise through about 30 degrees, you get to ALTN (alternate) – if you rotate it clockwise through another 30 degrees you get to MAN (that's the far right position). The AUTO position is the hard stop on the left, and the MAN position is the hard stop on the right – that's as far as the knob will rotate. The knob is easy to rotate in and out of each slight detent – it takes about the same amount of effort as turning a control knob in your car. In normal flight operations, this knob doesn't get turned very often – it's used only for maintenance – most of the time it just sits there, in the AUTO position.

When we looked at the photo of this selector knob after the crash, it was clear to us that it had not been found in the MAN position at all – the official report even said that. During the crash, the knob had been struck by some-thing, and the strike had forced it to rotate – it was driven clockwise – driven straight past the hard stop at MAN – from the MAN position, it had rotated another 30 degrees or so to the right. It would take quite a smash to do that, but we could see the witness marks on the knob that had been left when it was struck. In fact, we could see two distinct sets of marks on the knob – one set that would have forced it to rotate, and another set (something had hit it from a different direction) that had forced it to move "up" in the direction of the top of the panel.

The selector knob is mounted (using set screws) on a shaft that protrudes through the overhead panel from behind. The back surface of the knob doesn't touch the front of the panel – there's a small gap between the back of the knob and the front of the panel, so there is no friction. On the other side of the overhead panel (behind the panel), the other end of the shaft connects into a control box that contains the electrical connections for each of the three knob positions. These electrical connections send the signals to tell the control system which position (which detent) the knob is in. The Greek investigation put great significance on the fact that after the crash the electrical connections were found in the MAN position.

At AIR, we put no stock in that at all. Given where the selector knob ended up after the crash, where else could the electrical connections be? The knob had been forced to rotate hard clockwise during the impact, and no matter which detent (AUTO – ALTN – or MAN) it had started rotating from, the electrical connections would stop at MAN and be stuck there – physically, that's as far as they could go. The fact that they were found in MAN had no significance whatsoever for determining from which position the knob had started its forced rotation.

What I just outlined is not difficult to understand. When I think back, I'm pretty sure that almost everyone in my grade eight electrical shop class at Sackville High School could have figured that out – that the electrical connectors would get stuck at the last place they were forced to stop at. Same for the guys at the Road Agents Car Club in Sackville (I was an original member there), where everyone had an old car to work on – they had practical common sense – any one of them could have figured that out in no time. But not these investigators who worked on the Helios crash – they were convinced that the Helios maintenance guys had left the selector knob in MAN, and it was found in MAN, and it all made perfect sense, and it seems the investigators never put much more thought into it. It was a quick, and easy, and convenient finding for everybody. It's so easy to blame dead pilots.

At AIR, we knew right away that what we needed to look at was the surface of the panel underneath the selector knob (from here on, I'll call it the faceplate). The damage to the knob told us that the knob's shaft had been bent and twisted by the same impacts that caused the knob to rotate. Those forces would bend/tilt the knob to where the back of the knob would be forced to make contact with the faceplate. Therefore, we would expect to see gouge marks on the faceplate's surface – they would be made during the rotation by the back of the rotating knob as it scraped its way along as it rotated. It would be easy to see how far the knob had rotated by checking out the length of the longest gouge mark.

We knew where the knob stopped after its forced rotation – it was some 30 degrees past MAN. Therefore, if it had actually been selected to MAN prior to impact, the longest gouge mark we would see on the faceplate would have travelled through 30 degrees. By simple deduction, the length of the longest gouge mark would tell us how far the knob had rotated – that would automatically tell us where the rotation had started from – we would know for sure what selection it had been set to prior to impact. Did it start from MAN? Or did it start from AUTO?

It's important to realize that if that selector knob had been set to AUTO, it would totally destroy the findings of the official investigation. If it had been on AUTO, that means it was some kind of system failure that caused the aircraft to not pressurize. And, of course, the prosecutions in both Cyprus and Greece would be invalid.

Emma got us some photos of the faceplate behind the knob. As we expected, we could see circular scraping and gouging, but the resolution of the photos wasn't good enough to see any of the detail – we couldn't follow the length of any individual gouge mark. With that, we had Emma make an official request to the Cypriot Court to allow us to attend there to examine the wreckage pieces they held – the most important piece being the faceplate from underneath the knob.

After some legal wrangling, AIR was given permission to see the wreckage pieces. I was the designated traveller, and I left for Cyprus on 2 January 2010, arriving there to meet up with Emma on 4 January. As we had pre-arranged, Emma brought with her a professional photographer with the very best equipment to get the high-resolution photos we needed.

Even though we supposedly had our permissions in place, it took some extra negotiating to gain access to the "exhibits" held by the court. They were in a side room, guarded by armed individuals with no smile muscles. We had already agreed that we would not touch any exhibit. If we wanted anything turned or repositioned, that had to be done by a designated security guy wearing white gloves. I've never seen wreckage handled so delicately. We were being watched from all angles – by security, and by prosecution lawyers, so we made sure we were conscious of not tipping our hand if we found anything – we would all remain stone-faced.

I didn't start with the faceplate we were most interested in. We looked at a number of other items first – I typed notes into my laptop, and the photographer took his pictures. Finally, we started to examine the faceplate, and what was there was astounding. I examined the rotational gouges under my mini microscope, and I was able to follow numerous scoring marks that showed much more than 30 degrees of knob rotation. The longest one I followed showed a rotation of some 100 degrees. If you were to rotate the knob 100 degrees counterclockwise from the position it had been forced to during the impact, guess where that would put it? You guessed it – exactly in AUTO. The findings of the official investigation were dead wrong. During the accident flight, the knob had been set to AUTO – not MAN – it was a system failure that had triggered this tragedy.

In accident investigation, evidence doesn't get any better than this gouge mark showing 100 degrees of rotation. There is no way to misinterpret it – it's hard physical evidence that is directly and unambiguously connected to the degree of rotation of the knob during the crash sequence.

For those with investigation curiosity, allow me to provide just a bit more detail regarding this 100-degree gouge. Boeing, in later counter arguments, claimed that the gouge could have been made during the aircraft's normal operations by back and forth selections (by the pilots, or for maintenance) – in their scenario, somehow the knob would have had to get mis-mounted on the shaft, thus leaving the knob and faceplate in constant contact.

Here is the evidence to counter that stupidity – the gouging on our faceplate was done in only one direction through its full 100 degrees – the furrow that it created, by digging into the painted surface of the faceplate, had a consistent shiny bottom through its entire length. At its clockwise end point, the furrow had a buildup of material (visible under the microscope and in the hi-def photos) – there was no such material buildup at the counterclockwise end (there would have been buildup at both ends if their back-and-forth theory was correct) – there were no material buildup "dams" anywhere along the length of the gouge (with back-and-forth selections during regular service, there would be identifiable buildups – identifiable under the microscope – at each 30-degree interval, one dam for each knob position) – and here is the most dramatic evidence of all: the arc of the gouge was not perfectly symmetrical – in other words, if continued, the arc would not have formed a perfect circle – the only way a non-symmetrical arc could happen is if the shaft was being bent as the gouge was being created – a non-symmetrical arc/gouge couldn't happen in regular service with a solid shaft – the gouge had to have happened during the crash sequence.

Earlier, I mentioned that I didn't graduate from high school. I failed two subjects – biology, and geometry. Thankfully, I played with my geometry set just enough to understand that I could use the compass to draw perfect circles. Like magic, all you had to do was stick the sharp point into the paper and spin the pencil part around – it would draw you a perfect circle every time – you couldn't miss, so long as the little point stayed put. Perhaps, in their years of university training, the engineers at Boeing learned their geometry on computers – maybe that's why they never figured that out.

I'll throw in another tidbit of information for those with an investigation curiosity. During my investigation of the wreckage pieces in the Cyprus court, I asked to see the damaged selector knob that had been removed from the bent shaft. We had not been provided with any photos of the back side of that knob – we had good photos of the damage that happened when it was forced to rotate at impact, but we wanted to see the rotation marks/gouges where it had rubbed against the faceplate. Guess what they told us? They didn't have the knob – it had been lost! The last place it had been accounted for was at the lab at Boeing. And now it was gone – unbelievable! And somehow, with all the hundreds of photos they took at the Boeing lab, they never managed to take a single photo of the back side of that knob – or at least that's what we were told when we asked for all their investigation photos. What can be said about that? Unbelievable – in every way.

So far as I know, that missing knob has never been found. Examining it would have solidified our evidence, but thankfully we had lots of physical evidence without it. With my in-person examination of the faceplate in Cyprus, I believe that I'm the only one in the world who has ever actually viewed that 100-degree gouge mark with my own eyes. Fortunately, we got lots of perfect photos to prove it exists.

By the time I got home from Cyprus on 8 January 2010, Terry and Robbie had created some amazing graphics based on the high-def photos we got over there.

The long 100-degree gouge mark was easy to see in the photos/graphics – to us, this would be a slam dunk. We would get these photos to the investigators in Greece, and they would reopen the investigation based on this new evidence, and the prosecutors would drop their charges against the Helios executives, and it would all be over.

But amazingly, that's not what happened. The prosecution in Cyprus continued, grinding on slowly. Their presentation of technical evidence amounted to going through the results of the Greek safety investigation. They did this by bringing in expert witnesses, in particular from Boeing and Nord-Micro (the makers of the pressurization control computer) to explain and validate the flawed findings. It seemed it was in everyone's best interest (except the defendants) to stick with the "fact" that the knob had been found in MAN. AIR's input for the Cyprus trial was to help prepare our lawyers for cross-examining the prosecution's technical witnesses.

Here's more of what they did in court. I'll spare you the technical details, but the Greek report contained two additional bits of bogus evidence to support their claim. The first was their acceptance (from Nord-Micro), that the memory chip in the pressurization controller (known as NVM) showed the system was in the MAN mode. The second was their acceptance of a report from a Greek Air Force lab about one of the indicator (annunciator) lights that would have been illuminated if MAN had been selected – they concluded it had been illuminated (in other words, it was ON because it had a HOT filament) at the time of impact.

First, regarding the HOT filament – to come to their conclusion the Greek Air Force lab tested the bulb using a method that had been invented years earlier by (guess who?) – Terry Heaslip – yes, my partner Terry Heaslip – can you believe that! Terry took one glance at their work, and he quickly determined the Greek lab got it wrong. The proof they pointed to, to say the filament was HOT, actually proved it was COLD. This was even further proof that the knob was not set at MAN. So much for their input.

Second, regarding the Nord-Micro evidence – where they said the NVM confirmed the system was in MAN – they got their evidence from the same computer that had experienced the failure that led to the aircraft not pressurizing. How could that evidence be reliable? In assessing evidence, there is no way that NVM from a defective computer can counter the type of physical evidence found on the faceplate behind the knob – it's no contest – even the most junior investigator would tell you that.

267

On 10 May 2010, Terry and I went to London to brief Sean Gates and his team about our findings. They were very happy with what we had found. They had some expectation for a favourable outcome from the Cyprus court – not particularly because of our evidence, but because of some legal arguments they seemed to be winning – it seemed like the case would be dismissed on legal grounds before we had to present a defence. The grounds for dismissal were based on the fact that the airline was fully compliant with all UK CAA requirements, the pilots were properly trained, qualified and well rested. There was nothing to suggest that they shouldn't have been operating that flight.

The Gates people were much more concerned about the charges that had been filed in Athens. It seemed the Greeks were waiting for the results from the Cyprus court before deciding how to proceed. The word was that the Greek prosecution was based almost entirely on the findings of the official safety investigation – something unheard of (and against the law) in most civilized countries.

Everyone knew that the Greek AAIASB investigation was simply a false front for the actual work that was under the control of Boeing, and to a lesser extent Nord Micro. The Greek authorities relied almost totally on the NTSB to be honest brokers to ensure that the findings coming from Boeing were accurate. We would get nowhere in our attempts to have the charges dismissed in Greece without some intervention by the NTSB. We decided to target both the NTSB and the FAA, to prove to each of them that the cause of this accident was still unknown – with an unknown cause, there remained the potential for another accident to happen to another B737 for the same (unknown) reasons.

I remember a meeting I had with Sean Gates in his office. He told me that in his opinion we would get no movement from Boeing, and no cooperation from the FAA or the NTSB in trying to get our evidence accepted. He said they would circle the wagons – he said that our evidence pointed to a technical issue with the aircraft, and that would put up red flags in the United States – he said that Boeing would be protected (by these government agencies) from any potential liability – he had seen it happen before, and he predicted it would happen again.

I told him no way – that wouldn't happen. I told Sean that I personally knew many of the players at the NTSB – I had worked with many of them, during Swissair, and at other investigations – and I knew the investigators from Boeing from similar contacts – I even knew the actual guy who had found the overhead panel at the Helios accident site – he had been at the Swissair investigation – I knew some of the main decision-makers at the NTSB – I had met Deborah Hersman in Teterboro during that investigation – she was a good and honourable person – I was certain that when all these people got the evidence we had, they would act on it and do the right thing.

At that meeting with Sean, we made a bet as to whether the aviation agencies would do the right thing – I was exceptionally confident that they would – our bet was 12 bottles of Guinness. Being a non-drinker, I would be able to give my winnings away to deserving individuals who looked thirsty – I was already making a list in my head about who I would surprise. I was so sure I would win – it was a tremendous shock to me when I didn't.

On 2 September 2011 (by coincidence, the 13th anniversary of the Swissair 111 crash), I sent a formal communication on AIR letterhead to the FAA Flight Standards Office in Seattle (the office responsible for the certification of the B737), with a CC to Deborah Hersman, Chair of the NTSB. In this letter, I outlined the main points of a comprehensive report by AIR (which I attached) that showed the shortcomings of the Greek investigation. I wish there was room here to include that AIR report, with all its graphics and photos – it was impressive – one of the best and most compelling I have ever seen. The evidence we included was overwhelming.

In my letter, I emphasized that the credibility of the official Greek report depended on the validity of three findings – that the knob was in MAN – that the manual annunciator light was ON – and that the NVM data confirmed the system was in MAN. Then I went on to explain how our evidence (in the report I attached) showed each of these Greek findings was completely wrong.

Here are the last three paragraphs from my letter:

REQUEST FOR A MEETING

We are very anxious to have this new information disseminated to all parties who may have an interest in what actually led to the crash of Flight HCY522. For this reason, we are also forwarding this package to the Chair of the NTSB. As we believe that you would have the appropriate contacts, we request that your office forward this information to the Hellenic Civil Aviation Authority (HCAA), the Greek AAIASB, and Boeing – extra copies for forwarding are included. Also, please feel free to release this information to any other party who you believe should have access to it.

By forwarding this to you and the others, we have an expectation that a full and proper reinvestigation will now be undertaken to determine the actual causes of the Helios crash. This should be undertaken immediately, in the interests of justice for our clients who have been charged criminally based on the incorrect investigation findings, and in the interests of flight safety. Any safety deficiencies that might be associated with the continued operation of similarly equipped aircraft must be discovered.

We would also like to ensure there is no potential for misunderstanding as to the validity and substantiation of our findings. Therefore, we request a meeting with you and/or your representatives at your earliest convenience. We ask that you please contact the undersigned as soon as possible to arrange for such a meeting.

As we had come to expect with this case, we got no quick response to my letter – not even an acknowledgement that it had been received. On 21 December 2011, (and as expected) we got word that the Cyprus Court had dismissed the charges against our clients. The panel of judges hearing the case ruled that there was no "causal association between the defendants and the negligence they were charged with for the accident". When the acquittal happened in Cyprus, the prosecutors in Greece immediately launched their trial. Back in Cyprus, an appeal of the acquittal was filed by the attorney general, and a retrial was ordered. But after two months, they dropped the retrial under the double jeopardy rules in the European Union (the trial was by now underway in Greece).

On 18 March 2012, I left for Athens to be a witness for the defence at the trial of our clients. In Greece, they had filed charges of manslaughter against three senior executives of Helios, and one Helios maintenance engineer. This was serious stuff. If convicted, my clients were potentially facing some serious prison time.

I found my entire visit to Athens to be surreal, starting with our taxi ride to the hotel. I had met up with Emma in London, and we were traveling together.

Our taxi driver warned us about crime in Athens – he told us to watch out for shysters who would try to rip us off – especially taxi drivers. When we got near the hotel, he told us it was best to not park right in front. Instead, he would let us out just around the corner – I can't remember why. We thanked him for his sage advice, and after he drove off Emma realized he had conned us out of an extra forty euros for the cab ride. I guess it was his way to reinforce his warnings.

I spent parts of two days testifying. It was a total farce, and a waste of time. There was a presiding judge, with two assistant judges. None of them had the slightest clue about accident investigation matters. There was a prosecuting attorney, and a court-appointed "investigator specialist". This guy was a former investigator with the Greek AAIASB, and I will simply state that he had a medical issue – he was not in a good place mentally. I felt sorry for him – he was completely lost. A primary participant for the prosecution was the AAIASB investigator who had been in charge of the technical investigation. As I have indicated, and will write further about, having someone from the safety investigation testify at a criminal proceeding is flat out wrong.

I testified through a court-appointed English/Greek interpreter, a very friendly and enthusiastic young man who seemed to have trouble communicating in both languages. I never had much confidence that what I was trying to say was being relayed accurately. It didn't matter much though, because the judges had very little interest in my testimony. I could literally feel the contempt they had for me. At one point, a lawyer for the families stood up to accuse me of purposefully insulting the dignity of Greece – he was seething with anger, and his face was glowing red. He suggested that I should be "arrested" (or at least that's the word the interpreter relayed to me – I had a feeling he was protecting my sensitivities).

I tried my best to show the court the evidence that proved the knob was in AUTO and that there had been a system failure. We had spent lots of time and money producing a short video showing how the knob had moved during the impact to produce the marks on the faceplate. The presiding judge would not allow me to show it. You can only imagine how frustrating it was to try to explain the intricacies of basic geometry and physics through an interpreter to an unreceptive audience, using no visual aids. It was hopeless. A recurring theme in the court was that the NTSB did not agree with my evidence, so why should they believe me (or even listen to me).

As things deteriorated, I tried to maintain my composure, and I think I did a pretty good job under the circumstances. But I did take one opportunity – after a particularly uninformed question – to explain how disappointing it was to spend an entire career doing safety investigations only to find there were places in the world where this type of travesty could happen. For the remainder of my time in Greece, I watched my back. They were not happy with me over there – I could tell. For someone who naturally avoids conflict, all that was out of the ordinary for me.

On 20 April 2012, as we anticipated, the Greek Court found the four defendants guilty of manslaughter, and they sentenced each to 10 years in prison. That verdict was appealed, and we set about devising a strategy to get the sentences thrown out. We knew that would only happen if we could get the NTSB to tell the appeal court that there was new information that would need to be examined. Our Greek lawyers said that a communication from the NTSB would burst the bubble – it was their view that the appeal court would have been receptive to a communication from the NTSB – basically, that's all it would take.

Our side launched a full court press. On 11 May 2012, Helios (they were now called Ajet) sent a letter to the Greek investigation agency formally requesting a reopening of the investigation, based on ICAO Annex 13 Standard 5.13 which compels a reopening if new and significant evidence becomes available. The new and significant evidence was in the AIR report, which they attached. This letter was widely distributed, including to all the major players who had a connection to this case, and to others in the international aviation safety business. The addresses included: the Cyprus AAIIB – United Kingdom AIB and CAA – United States FAA and NTSB – the Flight Safety Foundation – ICAO – ISASI – and EASA.

Terry and I met with Ron Schleede and Caj Frostell (the authors of the Greek investigation report), and we convinced them both that our evidence was valid. In June 2012, Ron and Caj sent a very powerful letter to the Greek accident investigation authorities asking that the investigation be reopened.

In the meantime, the NTSB had forwarded our AIR report to Boeing to get their assessment. Boeing's assessment was sent to the NTSB on 9 July 2012. Not surprisingly, Boeing concluded that we were wrong, and that their original findings were still valid. They said that all the markings on the faceplate had been made in service, prior to the crash. That was complete nonsense. But it was enough for everyone (NTSB, FAA, Greece, etc.) to dismiss our evidence.

On 27/28 August 2012, I went to the ISASI Annual International Seminar in Baltimore, where I met up with Ron and Caj. We met informally with NTSB senior staff. Ron, in particular, (being a former high-level employee there) tried to convince the NTSB to have their specialists (along with Boeing and the FAA) meet with Terry and me. Ron went to the highest levels at the NTSB, with no luck.

In our informal meetings, I used AIR's detailed rebuttal of Boeing's "AIR Report Review" (Boeing's rebuttal was some of the most misleading and self-serving investigation work I had ever seen). I told the NTSB people that I was willing to speak to any or all of their technical investigators. I told them straight up that if even one of their NTSB investigators declared our evidence to be wrong, I'd go away and never bother them again. Naturally, they turned down my offer. I expect they knew that any credible investigator without bias would agree with me. It was NTSB management's position that Boeing was to be protected – that was very clear.

In Baltimore, Ron, Caj and I also met with ISASI members associated with the UK AIB, a former Chief Inspector of Accidents, and the current (at that time) Deputy Chief Inspector of Accidents. These were the most senior people in one of the most reputable investigation agencies in the world. They had longstanding reputations internationally for outstanding work in aviation safety. After reviewing AIR's evidence (and Boeing's supposed rebuttal), they enthusiastically agreed that AIR's findings warranted further examination. They tried to use their influence in both Greece, and with the NTSB. We were grateful for their support, but alas it was not enough to change the momentum.

In September 2012, Ron and Caj wrote directly to Deborah Hersman, Chair of the NTSB, asking her to get involved to resolve this ongoing issue. They mentioned our efforts in Baltimore. They reiterated that all she had to do to make things right in Greece, where this sham of a criminal investigation had occurred, was to send a note to the court, or to the investigation agency, saying there was new information. She didn't even have to say she agreed with it – just that it existed. She refused to do even that.

On 26 October 2012, the hearings opened at the Appeal Court in Greece. There were 10 separate hearings that dragged on over several months. On 31 October, Ron and Caj sent a letter to EASA (European Aviation Safety Agency), bringing their attention to the new and significant evidence that should be sufficient to have the investigation reopened. Copies were sent to

Cyprus, Greece, the UK AAIB, and ICAO. You must remember that Ron and Caj were not small players in all this. They had written the Greek report, and they were internationally recognized experts. Not only that, they had good personal relationships with the top officials at EASA.

To show you how bureaucracy works when a coverup is underway, I will include here the total narrative of the EASA response.

> Dear Mr. Schleede,
> Dear Mr. Frostell,
>
> Thank you for your contribution to the above mentioned investigation. As per ICAO Annex 13 standards, the sole independent Safety Investigation Authority competent to decide on the reopening of the investigation is the Hellenic Air Accident Investigation & Safety Board (AAIASB) which instituted the investigation.
> Therefore, I ensured that all elements communicated to EASA are provided to the AAIASB Chairman, Mr. G. Bassoulis, who can decide on the follow-up.
> Thank you again for your support and co-operation in the common interest of flight safety.
>
> Yours sincerely,
> [NAME REDACTED]

What a pitiful response. This came from EASA, a world leading agency that claimed to be dedicated to aviation safety. This was an agency that had adopted, and was promoting, "Just Culture", an initiative to move countries away from criminal investigations in aircraft accident scenarios. In their reply they referenced ICAO Annex 13, which categorically states that accident investigations must not "apportion blame or liability". They told Ron and Caj – who each had authored parts of Annex 13 – that only the AAIASB in Greece was "competent" to decide on what should be done. The AAIASB *competent*? EASA knew this investigation was a sham – they knew what was going on in Greece, and yet they bowed out without even a whimper of resistance. How disappointing – how shameful.

On 30 October 2012, Ron and Caj sent a letter to Deborah Hersman, and to Michael Huerta (Acting FAA Administrator), imploring them to take action.

Their letter explained that they were aware of new and significant evidence that had not been available or considered during the AAIASB investigation. They explained the concern that, "… it was some of the inaccurate findings in the Final Report that led to the conviction of the Helios Airways principals, and their sentencing to 10 years in prison". They went on to explain that this is, "… unjust and unethical, not in keeping with the principles of safety investigations. In many countries, the opinions of the investigation agency, as expressed in the findings and conclusions in the Final Report, are not admissible in judicial processes".

Here is a further extract from Ron and Caj's letter:

> On 30 July 2012, we were informed that the Hellenic AAIASB had made a decision to inform the (Helios) representatives that their request of 11 May 2012 to reopen the investigation of the subject accident was not accepted. We were advised that the Hellenic AAIASB decision was based on a communication with the NTSB.
>
> Subsequently, it was learned that Boeing had reviewed the 9 May 2012 AIR report and in a letter dated 9 July 2012, forwarded an undated, unsigned report entitled, AIR Report Review (Attachment C) to the NTSB. The NTSB forwarded the Boeing review (AIR Report Review) to the Hellenic AAIASB. It is our understanding that the Hellenic AAIASB based its decision not to reopen the investigation on the Boeing AIR Report Review and the NTSB's endorsement of that report.

Ron and Caj went on to explain that they agreed with AIR's critique of Boeing's rebuttal. Here is more from their letter:

> Of significant concern is that from first-hand knowledge we can tell you that the original on-scene investigation team specifically requested an examination of the PMS knob and the mating faceplate to determine the PMS knob position at the time of impact. This requested examination was documented in the NTSB-developed test plan protocol to be used for the technical examinations at Boeing. It is now evident that the requested examinations and analysis were not conducted.
>
> As members of the Hellenic AAIASB investigation team in 2005 – 2006, we find this to be surprising and perplexing. Further,

now that AIR has found compelling evidence that contradicts the original Hellenic AAIASB Final Report findings and conclusions, those investigation agencies, companies and individuals involved in the original testing should step up to ensure there is a re-investigation that takes into account the new and significant evidence.

On December 6th, I was once again in Greece to testify. This time I was only on the stand for one day. I was armed with AIR's full rebuttal of the "Boeing Rebuttal Report". Again, it was like talking to the wall – there were no breakthroughs. They had no hope of understanding anything I could tell them about Boeing's faulty work. Their fallback position for rejecting anything from me was the support given by the NTSB for Boeing's findings, and the lack of intervention from any other authoritative agency.

This time in Greece, I avoided having my life threatened. I left Athens on the 7th, travelling straight to Madrid where we had contracted to run an investigator training course for Airbus Military. I remember being very happy to get out of Greece, and also musing about how many of the "experts" with whom I had butted heads in Greece could have provided any training to one of the world's leading aviation companies – I counted them up – the exact number was zero.

That December, Ron and Caj got their responses from the FAA and the NTSB, written in pure bureaucratese. Having been a government worker for more than 30 years, I am able to translate what they said. They cleverly addressed the "investigation re-opening" issue without actually ever addressing the "incorrect investigation findings" issue. They never once stated that AIR was wrong in its technical findings. They explained that they had fulfilled their "safety mandate", and they rationalized that it was not their mandate to ensure the Greeks got the facts right.

Here is a direct quote from the FAA's letter, a quote that sums up their thinking: "As the regulatory authority for the state of design, we find that corrective actions put in place by the manufacturer and mandated by the FAA effectively address the safety issue, *regardless of the PMS knob position*" (the emphasis is mine) – translation = *they couldn't care less where the knob was positioned.*

By this time, all of the pressurization control systems identical to the one in the accident aircraft had been replaced by updated versions. Basically, the FAA (and the NTSB) were saying that it no longer mattered whether the

Greeks (actually Boeing) got the facts straight – there was no further risk to the flying public, and they were done with the whole mess. The NTSB's letter used the same logic as the FAA – there were no more safety issues, and their work was done.

Neither of these agencies expressed the slightest concern about how this safety investigation had led directly to criminal convictions – nor did they acknowledge their direct roles in that happening. They expressed no remorse for the fates of those who had been convicted by evidence that was incorrect. They gave no thought to how easy it would have been for them to alter the course of the investigation in Greece with a simple letter acknowledging there was additional evidence. They showed they could care less about fairness and decency when it conflicted with protecting one of their own (Boeing) from potential liability and unfavorable publicity.

Having received no input from the NTSB or the FAA, on 7 February 2013 the appeal court in Greece upheld the convictions of negligent manslaughter, and the sentences of 10 years in prison. The convictions were appealed to the Supreme Court, but the appeals were eventually lost because the Supreme Court considers cases only on points of law. However, the higher court gave the defendants an option of buying out their sentences for 80,000 euros each, saving them actual incarceration time. Innocent people remain convicted without any opportunity to clear their names because the agencies that could have prevented that failed to act – that is shameful. To this day, they and their families carry that burden.

So, there you go – I got that off my chest. When all that Helios stuff ended in 2013, I wasn't thinking I would ever write a book, and have an opportunity to reopen this story. But when this book was taking shape, I knew Helios had to be a part of it. Helios was three years of effort for me, and the outcome was the biggest disappointment of my career.

In writing this chapter, I thought about how/why I got so caught up in the Helios case back then. To get my answer, all I had to do was go back and read the section at the beginning of this book – the section where I attempted a description of myself.

With Helios, by my nature I started off optimistic. I trusted that the truth would prevail. Based on my optimism, I made a bet in London that "my" aviation safety community would never willingly let a criminal investigation use material produced for a safety information – and especially invalid information. I was absolutely confident that the NTSB wouldn't let that happen. Then, I kept going with my work on Helios so I could avoid the embarrassment of losing that bet with Sean Gates. Over time, my adversity to injustice kicked in. The way the Helios senior managers were being treated was simply wrong – it was not fair, and I was driven to make it right. Allow me to quote myself from that earlier chapter – "I am driven to make things right, no matter how long it takes. You will recognize some of this 'making it right' happening in this book".

It's funny (actually not so funny) how the world works. Each year, ISASI awards its most prestigious award – the Jerome F. Lederer Award – to "recognize outstanding contributions to technical excellence in accident investigation". Two of the previous recipients were Ron Schleede and Caj Frostell – those were great choices.

Remember that ISASI had been copied on the requests to get the Helios investigation reopened, and ISASI was fully aware of all the facts and evidence that AIR produced. But guess who won their prestigious award in 2019 – the Chairman of the Helios Investigation, Mr. Akrivos Tsolakis. Guess what he named as his crowning achievement – that's not hard – it was his Helios investigation. How sad – during the Helios investigation, his "contribution to technical excellence" was to ask Boeing if their system broke, and then to simply accept their answer "no, it didn't".

MEDIA WORK

Appearing in the media has become a part of what I do these days. I get requests randomly, whenever there's some aviation related topic that's making news. Most of the requests are from within Canada, but depending on the story, requests can come from various media entities around the world.

I'll give you two different spins about my media appearances. Here's the positive spin – I've become "known" in media circles as a source of expertise – someone who can handle questions, speak in plain language, separate fact from fiction, explain how an investigation is set up, and what they are doing, explain what the evidence is showing – all this gives their reporting some credibility. Here's another spin – the media comes fishing for something from me to fill airtime for their segment, and with luck I'll say something that fills in a hole or two for their listeners. Which one is true? Either one could be, I guess. It would depend on the particulars of the request.

As a curious person, I find it interesting when I get to watch (and be a part of) the "news" business from the production side. Over the years, I've formed a pretty favourable opinion of that part of "the media" that goes after a news story to report the latest developments. I'm talking about the producers and reporters who try to dig up information to add to the big picture. I'm not expressing an opinion on the noises made in the media by biased political pundits – or by biased "experts" – that's another side of the media. I'm talking about the news chasers and reporters who work hard to get the news of the day out there.

Overwhelmingly, the people I've dealt with (over many years now) have been honest people trying their best to get good information for their audience. Do they always get it right? Of course not. Do they tend to make the story as "interesting" as possible? Of course. Have I been stung by my words getting used out of context? Of course – that happens. But I haven't seen where these people set out to intentionally twist evidence for some malicious reason – in my experience, that just doesn't happen. I get lots of requests on background – from reporters and producers who simply want to educate themselves – they want to get a better understanding about certain aspects of the story – they want to get the story right. I always help them when I can.

Not being with the TSB anymore allows me to speak freely in the media. I agree to help when I feel I can contribute from a public education perspective, and I decline if I have nothing to add. I also decline if I have a conflict of interest because of a current client, or if I think I might get retained on the case later.

I've told myself many times that I'm finished doing media. It can be very taxing. But then time passes, and another event happens, and I get interested in it, and I start to follow it. Then I start getting requests from some familiar media contacts, and off we go again. For some reason, I find it very hard to say no. So, what's my motivation?

As an honest person I'll admit that ego comes into play. Seeing myself presented in the media as an "expert" makes me feel good. I think most people would feel that way. It's a nice feeling to think that my relatives get to see me in the media, and that they can talk with their friends about having a relative "on TV". Being in the media makes me feel relevant, and that's good for ego boosting. My assessment is that my ego is well under control and normal, so I feel comfortable admitting to having it.

I can assure you that it's not about public recognition. In all the years, I've never once been told by a total stranger that they recognize me from my being in the media. People who already know me might mention that they saw me, but that's it. As someone who appears only from time to time, being on-screen doesn't lead to recognition in public. You don't become a celebrity. There's no ego feeding from that, because it doesn't happen.

Money is not a motivator. I don't receive any renumeration for what I do in the media. In fact, it costs me money when I go to the studios, just normal transportation costs, but I pay for that. I prefer to do interviews from home, via Skype or FaceTime. That doesn't cost me anything in money, and it involves less time commitment.

A good part of my motivation comes from a desire to put out valid information from an investigator's perspective – from someone who has been there and done that. It's important to me to be seen as a Canadian voice, both nationally and internationally. It upsets me sometimes when so much of the expertise appearing in the Canadian media comes from outside our country.

I get questions, so I know that some people are interested in how all this media stuff works. Let me give you an example of one of my media "events" – this one from January 2020 – the crash involved was Ukraine International Airlines Flight PS752, a B737 that was shot down by a missile in Iran. This was a major international story, and it had a particularly high profile in Canada because many of the 176 fatalities were Canadians.

My first media request was for a live interview to be broadcast nationally in Canada. Over the three-day period following the crash, I had over 150 incoming emails and texts from domestic and international media. I did more than 30 interviews for television, and many others for radio and print.

Here is how a typical television or radio interview is set up. The initial request comes in from the producer of a specific show. They give me the name of the host, and the requested timeslot. If I agree to do the interview, the producer contacts me by phone to review what the line of questioning will be.

For live interviews via Skype, FaceTime, or phone, we agree on what time they will contact me to hook into their broadcast. Usually, they hook me in five or ten minutes prior to going live. This allows me to follow the flow of their broadcast. Then they provide countdown time checks until the host introduces me and asks the first question. These interviews typically last anywhere from three to ten minutes – they give an estimate before we start.

For studio interviews, I put on my best business suit. You have to show up in time for makeup. They clean any specks off your clothes, and pluck any stray hairs, and put makeup on you so you don't have shiny spots. For the ones on Skype or FaceTime, I just put on a dress shirt because you're only visible from the chest up. I'm terrible at setting up Skype and FaceTime. I seem to always end up with camera angles that make my face look distorted. Or maybe my face actually is distorted, I don't know. It doesn't bother me though. I have reached the stage in life where I accept what I look like, and I don't really give it a thought.

In high-profile occurrences like Flight 752, it's astounding how fast the media can disseminate information, even from a place like Iran. Things like photos, video, audio, witness accounts and real-time flight tracking are made public so quickly that it's a challenge to stay current. For this one, some of my interviews were so tight together that I had no time to search for what's new. A good trick is to ask the producers about the latest developments related to their questions. Everyone wants the interview to go well, and they will help to make sure I don't get blindsided on the air.

Regarding Flight 752, right from the beginning the crash looked like something other than a mechanical failure. In the first photos of the wreckage, you could see what looked like small puncture holes through wing and fuselage skin pieces. This pointed to either a missile strike from outside, or a shrapnel explosion from inside.

For the first while, the Iranians were insisting there had been some kind of technical issue, suggesting an engine failure. To me, that public declaration by them pointed to an attempted coverup. Their public pronouncements were obviously cooked up by people with no investigation expertise. The Iranian officials who spoke for the investigation had either not consulted with their own investigation experts, or they were ignoring them.

Inside Iran, the authorities would have known very quickly that the aircraft had been struck by one of their own missiles. In putting together their messaging, it seems like they simply panicked. I say that because their coverup attempt was incredibly inept. In trying to sell some kind of technical failure, their choice of "engine failure" was incredibly weak. It simply didn't fit the sequence of events. Here's why.

We know that the aircraft appeared to be flying normally when it suddenly disappeared from radar. The radar returns are generated by the aircraft's transponders. Each of the two available transponders are electrically powered from two independent systems, each powered by one of the two engines. To overcome all of this redundancy would take a catastrophic failure – it would have to be something that could instantly disable the aircraft's entire electrical system. A failure of one engine couldn't cause that, even if it was an uncontained engine failure. The bottom line is that there's no way that an engine failure could cause a transponder failure.

The early information pointed to a sudden loss of control, which led to ground impact in less than two minutes. There had been no communication from the aircraft after the first anomaly. This sequence is not remotely consistent with an engine failure. All the evidence pointed to either a missile strike or an on-board explosion. I was faced with appearing in the media with these thoughts in my head. What would I say?

Please understand – I fully recognize that in the big picture my small role as a media expert commentator was minor at best – I don't want to overstate it. But still, I felt obligated to be extra cautious in what I said. The audience would no doubt include family and friends of the victims. And for sure Iran would be monitoring the intense Canadian media coverage.

Right from the start this was not going to be a normal investigation. Because the accident happened in Iran, everything would unfold in an all-encompassing environment of mistrust and brinksmanship. The complexities were obvious. Even as a non-player, I wanted to avoid blurting out some unwise commentary that could somehow make things worse.

The international community was facing a unique challenge. There was an immediate need for safety investigators to look for any systemic safety deficiency with the aircraft that could pose a risk to other aircraft. From a common humanity perspective, the families needed assurances about the disposition and repatriation of the human remains. Iran needed to be persuaded to show integrity, compassion and cooperation – a tall order. For the longer term, there was a need to lay the groundwork for Iran to take full responsibility, and to pay compensation for the terrible losses.

Initially, the need for cooperation by Iran gave them the upper hand. Within reason, they needed to be catered to. It seemed appropriate to give them some room to get their act together.

My objective in the media was to stick with my normal approach, which is to explain how the investigation process is supposed to work. Initially, I emphasized the requirement to set up parallel investigations – a criminal investigation, and a safety investigation. I explained that a criminal investigation should look for evidence of a missile or a bomb while the safety side looked for something mechanical or operational.

When questioned about Iran's claim of an engine failure, I explained that this had none of the characteristics of an engine failure, but it did have all the characteristics of something sudden and catastrophic – such as a missile strike or bomb. After three days Iran fessed up, admitting that they had mistakenly shot the aircraft down with a surface-to-air missile. With that, my media appearances mercifully fell off, and then disappeared.

On one of the courses I took at the University of Southern California, an old instructor was showing us how testing was done on helmets designed for helicopter pilots. It was interesting to watch them drop things on the helmets they had mounted in test rigs.

Then we turned to testing for helicopter seat belts and shoulder harnesses. One of the bright lights in the class interjected with a question – "I'm a helicopter pilot, and I have statistics that show that over 95% of helicopter accidents happen in the vertical – if that's true, what's the purpose of mandating seatbelts in helicopters?"

The reply was spot on – "It's to make you sit there and take it like a man".

WRITING MY FIRST BOOK – MH370: MYSTERY SOLVED

The one time I was happy to get media attention was in relation to my book about the disappearance of Malaysian Airlines Flight 370, the Boeing 777 that disappeared on 8 March 2014. It was supposed to be a flight from Kuala Lumpur, Malaysia to Beijing, China, but it was diverted, and it flew instead to the Southern Indian Ocean where it ended its flight. Actually, long before I ever thought about writing that book, I had been appearing in the media about all this. There was plenty of media attention – it was being referred to as the biggest aviation mystery of all time – a huge passenger aircraft, with 239 people on board, had simply vanished.

The media requests really picked up for me when a piece of the vanished aircraft washed up on the coastline of Africa – that was in July 2015. As soon as I saw the first photos of that piece (the right flaperon – part of the flap/flight control system) it was clear to me that the aircraft had been intentionally ditched into the ocean. Terry was in full agreement. The recovered piece showed that the aircraft's flaps had been extended, and that the aircraft had entered the water at a normal landing/ditching speed. There had to have been a pilot controlling the aircraft when it touched the surface of the water. It followed that the hijacking of this aircraft was an intentional act carried out by the pilot.

This was completely contrary to what was coming out of the official investigation. They were insisting they had evidence to show the aircraft had flown unpiloted for several hours until it ran out of fuel and spiraled down to strike the water surface at high speed. Their search for wreckage on the seabed was based on that incorrect theory.

Things really picked up, media wise, when another significant piece of the aircraft's flap system was found more than a year later – in May 2016. As with the flaperon, this piece had washed up on the coastline of Africa – it was part of the right outboard flap. The evidence on this outboard flap piece was entirely consistent with that on the flaperon, and I felt entirely comfortable with my position that this event had been a murder/suicide.

In my media appearances, I explained the logic for my contention that there had been a pilot-controlled ditching. I was convinced that the official investigation would soon change their opinion, once they had a chance to examine the evidence from both of the recovered pieces. Soon after the flap piece was discovered, I was contacted by an investigative journalist from Australia named Ross Coulthart. Ross had taken a keen interest in the Australian Transport Safety Bureau's (ATSB) role in the investigation – in particular, their role in the search for wreckage (it was costing the Australian government a fortune).

Ross had a number of contacts with reaches into the inner workings of the ATSB. I educated Ross about some of the evidence on the recovered pieces that showed there had been an intentional ditching (meaning the Australians had calculated their search area based on incorrect assumptions). Ross took my evidence to the ATSB, but they gave it no credence. Ross was a presenter with the Australian TV program *60 Minutes* and he arranged for that show to do a 'Special Investigation' into the disappearance of MH370, based on my contention that the ATSB was ignoring obvious evidence.

On 23 June 2016, I flew to New York to tape segments for that *60 Minutes* program. I remember being picked up at the airport by a limousine, and getting dropped off at the entrance to "The Time" hotel on West 49th Street, in the Theater District near Times Square. That's an area where some of the rich and famous hang out, and passers-by were looking to see who was getting out of this limousine with the dark tinted windows. It was just me, but they gawked anyway (I didn't recognize any of them either).

When that episode of *60 Minutes* was shown on 31 July 2016, it created quite a stir. It was viewed by millions of people around the world. You can watch it for yourself – it is available on YouTube (you can also check it out on my website at HVSAviation.com/pieces).

That *60 Minutes* show cast the official investigation in a very unfavourable light, and the official investigation didn't appreciate it. I had a good number of people from the general public express support, but I got precious little support in a public way from the investigation community, or the aviation community. From the political/official side, I was attacked on multiple fronts. The Malaysians and the Australians were not happy. The official investigation closed ranks – they wanted nothing to do with me or my ideas. They had searched the area where they had calculated the aircraft had crashed, and they had found nothing. There was never a chance that they would find anything. They had wasted millions of dollars searching for a huge debris field that didn't exist. They had based their search area on the incorrect assumption that there was no pilot controlling the aircraft. If they were to suddenly come out and support my findings, they would be admitting that they got it all wrong, and they weren't about to admit that.

In the next months after that *60 Minutes* broadcast, I had many dozens of media requests from all over the world. The "mystery" of MH370 had captivated people everywhere, and my side of things was interesting and controversial enough to attract attention. On 19 March 2017, I went to Tucson, Arizona to tape a segment for a company called "Wall to Wall", based in the UK. They were doing a documentary for a show called "Mysteries of the Missing", hosted by Terry O'Quinn. The episode was to be called "Hunt for Flight MH370". My part was filmed at an aircraft boneyard near Tucson, where we had access to several airliner-sized aircraft, but unfortunately not a B777.

The Wall to Wall people did a good job interviewing and filming, but it was after I finished that little project that I realized that these types of interviews would never allow me to present all the evidence that was available to show the status of the aircraft as it entered the water. There was just too much information, and it was much too detailed and interrelated to be presented in these types of forums.

Now that I was into MH370 this deep, I realized that the only way to do it justice was to write my own "report" – I needed to get everything documented in detail. My plan was to get the evidence recorded in the same way I had done it for years – I would write the equivalent of an investigation report. But a bland technical report wouldn't work – nobody would read that. I needed to write it in the form of a book, with a catchy title – a book that proclaimed that the mystery was solved. And I had to write it in the simplest language possible, for wide distribution to a general audience.

I figured that once that book was available, interested people could absorb the evidence at their own pace, and everyone would see how much evidence there actually was to prove what I had been saying. I was convinced that once the investigators with the official investigation saw the evidence, they would immediately recognize that their theory about a high-speed dive into the ocean was wrong.

I asked Ross Coulthart to press the ATSB for high-definition photos of all the wreckage pieces that had been recovered, and after some pressure the ATSB put some excellent photos on their website. Those photos were a game changer. The clarity was amazing. These photos showed even more dramatic evidence to prove the flaps had been extended when the aircraft entered the water, and that it was a controlled ditching. Terry and Elaine were able to point out and interpret even more evidence that brought everything together. Having those two available to examine the evidence and back me up gave me great confidence that what I had been espousing was 100 percent correct.

Writing *MH370: Mystery Solved* was exceptionally demanding. I started the actual writing part in March 2017, and I finally finished the narrative in May 2018. During most of that time, I worked at it seven days a week, and at the same time I had to fit in all the normal casework I was responsible for. Those were hard days – long days – and I have to admit that there were some days when it was difficult to stay motivated. But the more I worked at it, the more I became convinced it was beneficial, and if I didn't finish it, all this important evidence would be lost to the world. I felt like I was in a unique position to do this work – with my own expertise, and Terry's expertise, and Elaine's expertise – I had the writing skills to make it happen, and I simply had to maintain my enthusiasm.

As I was working on the book, things were still happening with the official investigation. The official search for wreckage had ended, but the Malaysians took it further. They signed a contract with a commercial company to do further searching – they were to search using upgraded high-tech equipment. Through Ross, I had let it be known that we had found even more definitive evidence of a controlled ditching, and maybe this new company might want to know that. But my offer fell on deaf ears – nobody was interested. This new search lasted for an additional five months. Unfortunately, by taking their lead from the official investigation they calculated their search areas based on the high-speed dive theory. They made bold predictions of success, but they had no chance of finding anything.

I kept Ross updated on the evidence we were finding in the photos. Based on this, he set about promoting another special *60 Minutes* episode, this one to be called "MH370 – The Situation Room". Initially, that episode was to focus on the evidence and findings in my book. The plan was to coordinate the release of my book with the airing of that show in May 2018. Alas, that planning got sideswiped when the network failed to renew Ross' contract – he was out. The original producer stayed on, but the storyline changed to where the show was now to be a panel discussion – they would bring in various experts to wax eloquent about what had happened to MH370.

On 1 May 2018, I left for Sydney to tape that show. I was happy to participate in the panel discussion. It gave me another opportunity to explain my position, and to declare that I had actual physical evidence that would reveal what had happened. I was quite prepared to contradict what the official investigation was saying. But with this new panel discussion format, I was once again in the unenviable position of having to explain my evidence in narrative only. I had hoped to be able to use the graphics and photos from my book, but that didn't happen. Without Ross being there, they didn't want my book to be the focus. They thought it would be too complicated for their audience. They wanted the dynamics between the different participants to be front and centre.

They ended up showing 50 minutes of the several hours we taped for that show. They certainly had lots to choose from. I thought it was an okay show, but again, I was disappointed that I never got to present much of my evidence – only my views. You can find that episode on YouTube (you can also check it out on my website at HVSAviation.com/pieces).

That *60 Minutes* episode has been viewed many millions of times, and it has provided me with plenty of publicity for my MH370 book. It also resulted in countless media requests for interviews – requests from all around the world. It seemed everyone was interested in what I had to say. When my book was finally released on 23 May 2018, that publicity gave it a good boost. Finally, in my ongoing interviews I could refer to the real hard evidence, or at least refer people to where they could find it.

It really didn't surprise me when the ATSB failed to change their position after my book came out. It seems they were totally invested in sticking to their previous position about a high-speed crash. They didn't even bother to try to refute my evidence point by point. It's sad to say, but I don't think they had the capacity to do that even if they wanted to. Or maybe they were smart enough to realize that I was right, and to take me on would be a losing strategy. In any event, they simply sat back and waited until the interest died down.

With the passing of time, more and more people have come to accept that MH370 was a criminal act perpetrated by the pilot. Most people now realize that the official investigation got it wrong. I get plenty of feedback from people who have read my book, and they understand and accept that my account is accurate. The feedback I get from readers is overwhelmingly positive. I get great satisfaction out of knowing that my book about MH370 will live on long after I'm gone. Someday, when MH370 is found, everything I said in my book will be fully validated. If I'm not around to accept the accolades, I hope my descendants get to take a bow on my behalf.

While I was searching for links to the *60 Minutes* show, I came upon a five-minute excerpt that they had used as a promotion – they titled it, "Extra Minutes" – I hadn't seen it before. You can check it out on my website at HVSAviation.com/pieces.

The host had asked about conspiracy theories, and the damages that can be done by people who promote them. Below, I have transcribed my part of the answer to her question, where I was expressing my frustration about this issue.

> It's very, very, difficult when a grieving family member comes to you for information, and that family member has taken in information from a source – such as these wild theories that get thrown around – and asks you to disprove that. Because they are clinging to something that somebody has given them as an answer that you can't give them. And they say, now you prove that this – whatever theory – is not correct, prove it to me.
>
> It's not just the conspiracy theorists that are the biggest problem. In my career, what I found the biggest problem to be, are the people with some certain amount of credibility that get invited into the media to give their opinions as the investigation unfolds. And they have a lot more credibility than somebody who says the airplane got sucked into a black hole. It's pretty easy to convince the families that that's not true.
>
> But if you have somebody who has some connection to the aviation industry who goes on a major network and puts forth some theory that's off the scale somewhere, that is quite hard to deal with when it comes to families. And the media people, and the people who put themselves forward as 'experts' and do that sort of thing, I don't know sometimes how they sleep at night. It's just so damaging to the vulnerable family members that it's sad, it's really sad.

If you watch that five-minute excerpt, you'll see that I'm speaking with some emotion – emotion that comes from dealing with this issue over many years. During my career, I have always told the families to look to the official investigation for information, and to not believe everything they hear from "instant experts". Normally, that's very sound advice. But in the case of MH370, here I was doing the instant expert thing myself. Just like with Helios, I was forced into it by a defective investigation.

What's unfortunate when you put forth information in a book, like I did, is that you get lumped in with all the other "experts" who write books. They range from crackpots, to people with some aviation credibility. It's hard to get away from getting lumped in with them. There were dozens of books written about MH370, and there are still more being written. So far as I know, mine is the only one written by an experienced accident investigator. I base that on the fact that I have been on hundreds of accident sites around the world, and I have no recollection of seeing any of these other authors there.

I will give a shout out to one author — Ean Higgins, who wrote a book called "The Hunt for MH370". Ean is a journalist based in Australia, and he did some good work putting his book together. I've decided not to identify any of the other authors by name, or to call out their books, but I suggest that unless you enjoy fiction you stay away from any book with these themes: that there was a fire on board — that the aircraft was hijacked (by anyone other than the pilot) — that it was hit by a projectile — that it was disabled by an on-board explosive device — or that it was taken to some place other than the Southern Indian Ocean. Let me be blunt — the books that make these claims are total crap — they're based on amateurish guesses, and their authors should be embarrassed.

I'll also give a shout out to another trusted source — Simon Hardy — who was a fellow panelist on the second *60 Minutes* show. Simon has done some very good and credible work on projecting where the remains of MH370 could be resting on the ocean bottom. If any further searching for the wreckage is ever done, I hope they start first in the area that Simon has identified.

Allow me to direct you to one more video, where you will see the results of my participation in the Algonquin College Speaker Series. I was asked to appear there to talk about my book on MH370. It was an interesting event for me, and it's turned into an attraction on the internet. You can see it at HVSaviation.com/pieces.

Studio setup for taping "MH370 – The Situation Room"
Sydney, Australia – 2018

A LIFETIME OF THINKING — REMEMBERING — AND LEARNING

My earliest memory is from when I was two years old. My dad worked for the railway, and for the first five years after my parents got married, they moved around a lot. In those first five years they lived in six different houses, in four different communities. I have solid memories of living in five of those six houses. When I was two, in 1951, we were living in a dilapidated old house in Springhill Junction, Nova Scotia. My older sister (who was three) and I were playing on the front porch when I dropped a glass, and it shattered. When I tried to pick up a broken piece, a sharp edge sliced into the index finger on my right hand. I remember it bleeding a lot. I remember sitting on my mother's lap, and my dad driving us to the hospital. I remember being handed off to a nurse, and I remember her carrying me up some stairs.

Then, I guess it would have been a few days later, I remember my grandmother (my mom's mother) taking my hand gently in hers and helping me immerse it in very hot water – she had mixed up some kind of concoction to put into the water – she was famous for her concoctions. It really hurt, but I remember thinking that it must be for the best – otherwise, she wouldn't make me do it. I found out much later that it was my grandmother who realized that my finger wasn't healing properly. She suspected there was a shard of glass left in it – and by soaking my hand in her concoction day after day she brought a shard of glass to the surface and extracted it – that shard of glass had been missed by the doctor. I have the scar from that injury to this day.

I remember my mom finding a dead rat in a trap in the basement of that house. She asked our next-door neighbor Eddie to take it away for her – she hated rats. Eddie went and got the dead rat from the basement, and then he pinned it by its tail to my mom's clothesline. I remember her asking him to take it off that clothesline, and I remember him laughing – he wouldn't do it. I remember thinking it was a great joke for Eddie, but not for my mom.

I have photos that my mom kept from those times. One in particular (dated 1951) shows me sitting on the ground with that old house in the background. I'm holding a long skinny stick that at one time had been part of a small branch on a tree. Attached to the other end of that stick was a piece of string. I very distinctly remember that stick, and that string – that was my first fishing rod. In the photo, I'm sitting at the top of a slope. I remember that whenever it rained there would be a trickle of water running along the bottom of that slope – it was like a little stream – but most of the time, it was completely dry.

I remember that it didn't matter to me whether there was water in that stream or not – that was still a perfect place for me to go fishing. It was perfect because I wasn't really there to catch anything – I was there to sit and think. I remember my dad saying that if you wanted to sit and think, the best thing to do was to go fishing.

So, I would go fishing. I remember sitting there and thinking hard about lots of things. I thought about my grandmother putting my hand into that scalding hot water – not just once – but over and over again. I figured out that she must be trying to help me, because she was putting her hand in there too – it must have been painful for her too. To me, it confirmed that she loved me, and that she cared for me. And I remember trying to figure out whether it was right for Eddie to use that rat to make my mom so scared. I figured out that it was good to make people laugh, but making someone laugh wasn't fair if it made someone else scared like that.

I remember thinking about an argument between my parents – my dad brought home a dog – he said it was for us kids – and I remember that dog running around all excited until it peed on the floor – and I remember my mom being upset about that, and telling my dad to take it back – and I remember her telling him that she didn't like dogs, and that she didn't want one – and I thought hard about whether it was right for her to keep the rest of us from having a dog – and I remember that I thought about it for a long time – and after a while I realized that I didn't much like dogs either, so it was okay – and that feeling about dogs has stayed with me to this day. I never had a dog in my life until after I got married – that's when I started getting outvoted.

My other grandmother (my dad's mother) lived to be 99 years old, and she was a sharp thinker right to the end. I used to love to have talks with her. She had great insights into all sorts of things, and a neat way to tie things together over the decades of her life. She could explain how all the different issues of "today" weren't necessarily new – she could point out how they could be looked at in relation to the issues of "yesterday". When she was in her late 90's, she told me something that she hadn't told me prior to that. She said that when I was just a toddler, I had told her how important it was to just sit and think – I had explained to her that it took time to figure things out – she told me how impressed she was with that. I don't remember talking to her about that when I was a toddler, but I'm very happy that she remembered to tell me that I did.

At the beginning of this book, I wrote a chapter where I tried my best to describe what makes me tick. The purpose for that was to try to show how my basic traits have manifested themselves in my investigation work. You might recall that I wrote this, "I think that these traits have helped me to be a better accident investigator". I've come to realize that my two biggest investigation assets came straight from mother nature – I've had them all my life.

The first one is my ingrained inclination to think. I'm certainly not declaring that I'm a great thinker, or even a good thinker, but there's one thing I will declare – I'm a dedicated thinker. That trait had to have come to me naturally – I was a dedicated thinker at the age of two, and I'm a dedicated thinker now – that's enough to declare that it's ingrained in me. The second natural asset is my heightened sense of curiosity. When I compare my natural curiosity with that of others, I assess mine to be greater than average.

I assess those two traits to be inexorably linked. Mother nature isn't dumb – she wouldn't make someone a dedicated thinker without giving them a boosted curiosity – nor would she give someone extra curiosity without wiring them to be a dedicated thinker. What would be the point? One without the other wouldn't work. And in my case, I got two bonus traits – my natural laziness, and my procrastination tendencies – they help to provide the extra time needed for the other two. These are all good traits if you're trying to uncover and assess the complex issues involved in an aircraft crash.

In that early chapter, I revealed a bunch of other traits that I've been blessed/cursed with. Like everyone else, my traits drive me towards my normal pattern of behaviour when I interact with the world. To stick with the theme of this book, I can say that over the years I've put plenty of thought into which of my instinctive patterns of behaviour makes me a better investigator, and which ones hold me back. I have always looked for ways to enhance the useful ones, and adjust the others.

Here's one of my natural traits that needed a lot of work. Being a natural chicken is not a good thing in an investigation environment. It's even worse in the world of litigation. I'm a peacemaker, and I can certainly live with that – to me, that's a totally good thing. But to be a chicken in an arena where there will be conflict – that's not good at all. It's like being a chicken at KFC – you get eaten up. I've worked hard on making sure that when the going gets tense, I'm able to react the way I want to. I've used a lot of dedicated thinking time to rehearse my way to appropriate reactions. Proper preparation is key. Now that I have had years of experience and exposure to conflicts in my aviation/ investigation/litigation world, I'm able to handle it so it looks natural. And as I've said, I even kind of enjoy it now – but I'll readily admit that being in a conflict still feels unnatural to me, away down deep in my core.

My overabundant curiosity drives me to try to understand other people – to try to figure out what set of basic traits makes them the way they are. Why do they think what they think? Why do they do what they do? That's a big part of accident investigation – it's part of what makes accident investigation so interesting to me. You can't figure out many accidents without studying the main players involved. Almost every accident has elements of human performance connected to it. A key person to study might be a pilot, or a maintenance person, or a dispatcher, or a manager, or an air traffic controller – there are a whole host of people who might be in line to be studied during an investigation.

Whenever I need a way to put things into perspective, I have a sliding scale hard wired into my head. It's marked with 0% at one extreme, and 100% at the other. I've used it for so long now that it's automatic. Every input that comes to me gets placed on that scale, either consciously, or subconsciously. I use it in everyday life, but it's especially handy in my investigation life.

When I get an investigation input, on my scale it goes straight to 50%. The evidence will move it one way or the other. Big things – small things – they all get the same treatment. Starting at 50% keeps me from falling victim to my trusting nature. I use the same scale when I'm making investigation decisions. Should I approve a request for someone to travel? I start at 50/50 – then I think my way through it. Doing that keeps me from instantly approving something just to be a nice guy. I find it very handy to have a go-to plan for handling inputs, and the sliding scale works best for me. I've worked with people who should have a plan like mine – they're the ones who put everything at one extreme or the other right away.

It's human nature to assess and judge other people – to watch how they operate – to figure out whether their methods are more effective than yours – to assess their outcomes – basically, to compare them to yourself. We all learn from watching each other – we see things that we can incorporate, and things we want to stay away from. There are two stories that I have in my head that give me my most important markers when I'm assessing people.

Here is story number one.

There was a little girl who was five years old. She went to the refrigerator to get herself a glass of milk. As she lifted the milk container, it slipped from her hands and she dropped it. The container tumbled to the floor and broke open. Milk spilled everywhere. Her father heard her cry out, and he went towards her to comfort her and to tell her not to be upset, and to tell her that it was just an accident, and to tell her that things like that happen to everyone, and to tell her that he would help her clean it up. Her mother went towards her to express her frustration and disappointment, and to point out how this spilled milk had splattered on many other things in the fridge, and to show her that a big puddle of milk had pooled under the fridge, and to explain to her in no uncertain terms how much of an inconvenience she had caused.

Here is story number two.

At the Moncton Flying Club, we had a licensed lounge in a separate building behind the hangar. Right on schedule, a liquor board inspector showed up to inspect the bar. When the guy finished, he came over to debrief Don McClure. He reported that everything had passed inspection, and that he had given it his seal of approval. Just as he was about to leave, for whatever reason the inspector mentioned that it was good that he had found the beer taps plumbed the way they were, because otherwise he would have had to shut the bar down. Don came back with no, that wouldn't be reason enough to shut things down. And the inspector said that it would, and there would be nothing Don could do about it. And Don said that we would see about that — he said he would stay at the bar himself, and he wouldn't let it close no matter what. And the inspector said that he would call in the law — and Don said he could go ahead and try — and the whole thing escalated into a real shouting match between the two. It was a weird thing to watch. They went to war over something that wasn't even an issue.

For me, these two stories provide context for virtually everything I need when it comes to assessing people. When I'm working with an investigation team, I find it helpful to know where to place each individual on my sliding scale – the scale where I compare them to the characters in these two stories. It's not necessarily a predictor for how well they'll perform, but when I'm working with a group, I find it handy to know how individuals are likely to react when things happen.

It's the same for assessing the people you need to interview for your investigation – the ones involved in the accident. With a bit of strategic probing, they'll reveal how they operate. Again, that's not necessarily a predictor for their truthfulness or openness, but it's handy information to have.

I'll expand a bit on story number one. That's the one that I find most useful, in all aspects of life – and of course it fits perfectly in my work. The little girl didn't purposefully take the carton out of the fridge and throw it on the floor. Why would it ever be appropriate to react as if that's what she did? Why would someone's natural instinct (their immediate reaction) be to treat her as though she had done that intentionally? I can think of one answer. What if, prior to this incident, the little girl's mother had directed her (many times) to stop trying to get the milk from the refrigerator on her own – explaining that she wasn't tall enough to pick it up securely?

What I have with this simple story is my framework to assess people, and to study accident scenarios. Substitute the little girl for a pilot – the father could be a pilot's family member, or the union rep for an ATC controller – the mother could be an air regulator, or a prosecutor. What's required, of course, is an investigation. Was the dropping of the milk actually an accident? Did the mother actually warn the little girl? Perhaps the mother is just saying she had warned her in order to cover up her own initial reaction. If the mother had put in place a warning, was her warning clear enough? How did she test to make sure the little girl actually understood the warning? Did the father overreact with kindness before he knew the full circumstance? I hope that you get the idea – anyway, for me it works.

There's not much more to say about story number two – Don McClure fighting with the liquor board inspector. Being a peace-loving person, I find it particularly disturbing when I see flareups that make no sense – people arguing about things that are completely irrelevant. In accident investigation, you tend to see that happen when someone has trouble accepting that a fact is a fact – or when someone is setting up a smokescreen to hide the real issues.

I've always recognized that my way of assessing things is this: I relate each new event or situation to one or more of the particularly memorable incidents (like the two stories above) that I have stored away as reference points. Here's one of the memorable incidents that got lodged in my brain. I was maybe ten years old – I was out for a drive with my dad – we were talking about cars – we were having a really neat grown-up conversation about which cars we liked – I felt great that my dad was talking to me the same way that I had heard him talk with his adult friends. I was smitten by the look of the 57 Chev – my dad liked Fords – I told him the only Ford I liked was the T-Bird – somehow, he got a charge out of me referring to a Thunderbird as a T-Bird, and he said to me, "what's a T-Bird, do you mean Thunderbird?" – and with his question he started to laugh at me (yes, he was laughing "at" me).

At the time, I didn't react to his laughing. But that laugh has stayed with me my entire life. I found it incredibly hurtful. I'm positive my dad meant nothing by it – I'm sure it never registered with him at all. But for me, it cut really deep. That laugh told me that we hadn't been having a grown-up conversation at all. I was devastated – I was humiliated – I was deflated. That laugh told me that to him I was still a little kid, and it was perfectly fine for him to laugh at me when I made a cute comment – when I made a little kid comment.

Over the years, I've used up many dedicated thinking hours putting context to that laugh – figuring out how to use the circumstances to build a comparison frame. Like my other go-to memorable incidents, I can broaden this one out to cover a number of issues – for this one, the broadening is in the basic category of respect.

I'll use this story to illustrate how this works – here's what I concluded away back then, and what I still think. In my view, my dad should have thought his way to where he was better prepared for a situation like this – he should have thought about how his basic traits might cause him to instinctually laugh during this kind of exchange – he should have prepared himself to not laugh – his preparation should have caused him to react differently – so instead of laughing, he could have shown me the respect I deserved – and indeed, expected. On my sliding scale of measuring things, my dad came out well on the wrong side of 50% on this one.

So, this is a big component of how I operate. I use the simple frames that I've constructed from memorable happenings as starting points for making my assessments about all the various interactions. For me, it's handy to have these simple frames to start from, regardless of the complexity or intensity of the interaction.

After I got through my teenage years, and especially after I had kids of my own, I began to realize that some of my motivation comes from not wanting to disappoint my parents. They're both gone now – my dad died in 2007 at the age of 81, and my mom died in 2017 at the age of 93. I think that for most people, being motivated that way is both ingrained, and important. It can squeeze out your best effort if you let it go to work on you. I hope my kids and grandkids have motivation like that, and that they recognize how incredibly proud I am of them – I hope that when they are deciding about things, they give a passing thought to how proud I would be about their decision.

I'll share with you part of a communication I had a few years ago – this was with someone who I had worked with on a case in Europe. She had just lost her father after his battle with cancer – she knew that my dad had also died of cancer. She had been exceptionally close to her dad. This is part of what I wrote:

> The news of your dad's passing was met with great sadness here, but also with some sense of relief that his suffering finally has ended. And of course, our thoughts are with you as you pass through this stressful phase of grieving and loss. As I am sure you keep reminding yourself, it does get easier with the passage of time.
>
> What I find more and more about the loss of my dad is that he was without doubt the person with the most interest in my day-to-day activities – even the most mundane things. I still find that I miss being able to share with him the details about how I discovered I had low air pressure in a tractor tire, or a bug infestation in a tree away back in the woods – things that nobody else in the world would be interested in except my dad – simply because it is me who is sharing the story. I miss him for that – I miss hearing his mundane stories, and I really miss sharing mine with someone who really wanted to know the little details.
>
> What I take away from missing that about my dad is that it might be important to my children and my grandchildren to have me to be interested in their lives in the same way. I go out of my way to make sure that if they want to share something, I am there to be excited and keen and interested, and I will remember what they tell me and bring it up again. My son just got a new car and I went over

300

there last night to check out everything, down to the last detail. He knows I am truly interested and excited for him – that is important, I think. From your description of your dad, I expect he was keen and interested in everything in your life – maybe you will miss that the most. But you can fill the void some by upping your own game with those who are close to you and depend on you to be there for them.

As I've mentioned previously, my career path has required me to do a lot of assessing of people – that's a big part of instructing, and flight testing, and accident investigation. For all of my adult life, I've had to assess people as part of my work – to assess individuals – looking through the full range of their competencies and behavioral traits. And all that "professional" assessing is over and above the assessing I do (like everyone else does) in my everyday life.

In professional assessing, there's lots to look into: physical attributes, spatial awareness, situational awareness, judgement, motivation, honesty, self-confidence, trustworthiness, dedication, perseverance, intelligence, initiative, integrity, personality, stability, perceptiveness, flexibility, sensitivity, sensibility, focus, loyalty, assertiveness – I could go on and on.

In accident investigation, you have to figure out the exact circumstance an individual was confronted with leading up to the mishap, and then you have to figure out exactly how that individual behaved in that circumstance. But then you have to figure out why that individual behaved the way they did – you do that by studying their competencies and behavioral traits. Of course, that's easier to do when they're alive, but in accident investigation that's frequently not the case. You have to chase that down through other means, and through other people – and then you have to assess all these other people too.

In training and flight testing, it's kind of the opposite. For these people, you need to assess their competencies and behavioral traits up front, so you can predict how they'll perform later in a particular circumstance – will they be able to save the day? For students, you can build on their competencies, but if you want to do them the most good you try to help them recognize and modify any behavioral trait that will make them less successful overall. You try to point them in the right direction – thinking wise. The ones who'll be the most successful will work the hardest at understanding all their own traits – they'll figure out ways to modify any that might be undesirable.

In accident investigation, the most valuable attribute is curiosity, and the most important virtue is integrity. I've worked with many investigators over the years. One of my "0 to 100" scales has each one placed according to my assessment of how much they actually cared about aviation safety. It wasn't hard to place them. The ones motivated by safety stood out – the others revealed themselves along the way.

I'll take the ones motivated by safety every time. Here's a real-life example from the Swissair investigation. Some people on our team were uncomfortable having representatives from IFALPA (pilot union people) be part of the team. I had worked with pilot union people in the past, especially the ones from the local airlines in the Atlantic region, and I knew them to be super motivated to get safety improvements. I made sure they came aboard, and that they were able to stay engaged. They turned out to be some of our most dedicated and hardest-working team players, doing whatever was asked of them – from grunt work sorting wreckage, to designing computer wreckage tracking applications. They were major contributors.

I have been incredibly fortunate to have worked with some exceptional people. Don McClure was exceptional in so many ways. He was passionate about aviation. He gave me my start by hiring me as an instructor, and he made me his chief flying instructor. It was tough working for him, but it was a great learning experience. I don't remember getting too many compliments from him – in fact, I don't remember getting any – but reliable sources tell me that he told people that I was the most natural and instinctive pilot he had ever flown with. I'll return the compliment here – to me, Don was the very best judge of pilots.

Terry Heaslip is an exceptional investigator – in my opinion, he's the best technical investigator in the world. He and I have been investigation partners on dozens of cases since I joined AIR back in 2009. Without doubt, I have learned more about the technical side of accident investigation from Terry than from anybody else. His contributions to my career cannot be overstated – most prominently, he provided the technical underpinnings for both the Helios case, and the MH370 case.

I won't even try to list all the names of the people who were my closest comrades and allies along the way. They know who they are. I learned so much from them – we went through some incredible times together – we all learned from each other, about flying, about investigating, about life in general. We shared so much. We overcame some incredible challenges. My best memories are of the adventures, and the laughter.

In writing this book, I've searched back for disappointments and regrets. Only a few stand out. I regret that we didn't get the proper safety action out of the Air France 358 investigation. That left a gaping hole in the defence against operating near thunderstorms. More such accidents will happen – more people will die needlessly.

I was deeply disappointed in how the Helios case unfolded. Important parts of the aviation community turned a blind eye to obvious incompetence. People who should have been demanding the abandonment of the criminal charges stood silent. I had expected better. It's not too big a leap to connect the Helios case to the two disastrous Boeing 737 Max accidents that happened in October 2018 and March 2019 – two accidents that attracted worldwide attention. Helios uncovered (at least to me and my cohorts) two obvious safety issues – first, the huge safety culture issues at Boeing – and second, the inappropriate cosiness between Boeing and the FAA. Those issues could and should have been fixed back when we tried to expose the Helios fiasco. Instead, everybody was shocked to learn about them after 346 more innocent people were dead after the two 737 Max accidents.

I found the entire MH370 investigation debacle to be a major disappointment. The international aviation safety community has to do better. It's time to take the responsibility for investigating crashes involving international flights away from individual countries – away from the influences of individual governments. What's required is an international Go Team, pre-populated with the best and brightest. They must have a mandate to explore everything to do with the crash – without restrictions or outside influence. The results of their work must be reviewed openly, by a non-biased panel of respected and pre-selected individuals. That's the only way to make it work properly.

Here's a more personal disappointment. When I published my book about MH370, I laid out irrefutable evidence about what had happened to that aircraft. The evidence I present in my book is easily understandable, especially by trained investigators. I have had longstanding relationships with numerous very credible investigators, and I have to say that their lack of public support for the evidence in my book has stung me a bit. I have never asked any of them for public support – I'm not one to pressure people to go where they might not be comfortable – but I had honestly thought that more of my fellow investigators would speak up to support me in public.

When it comes to examining air crashes, there are three types of investigators, as follows:

1. INVESTIGATOR	That's a person who examines evidence to document what happened.
2. ACCIDENT INVESTIGATOR	That's a person who examines evidence to document what happened – and then asks – "Why did this accident happen to this crew?".
3. AIR SAFETY INVESTIGATOR	That's a person who examines evidence to document what happened – and then asks – "Why did this accident happen to this crew?" – and then asks – "Why would this accident have happened to me?".

I am a professional air safety investigator. To be an air safety investigator, you must complete this mission: go out and investigate to find out why, if you were faced with the exact same circumstances, this accident would have also happened to you. Then, write a report that explains to the people reading the report why this accident would have also happened to them. Then, develop recommendations that will stop this accident from happening to everyone else. If, during your investigation, you haven't yet figured out why this accident would also have happened to you, then you have not yet determined exactly what happened – you need to keep investigating. I can tell you from many years of first-hand experience that not many of the investigators out there have the information in this paragraph in their heads. Most of them don't graduate past accident investigator.

As I said previously, in school I was a terrible student. I'm still not sure why. I was smart enough, but I had no real motivation to learn what they were teaching. I'm not proud of that, because I wasted a lot of time. I've spent my whole life in catch-up mode. I especially disliked English grammar – I refused to learn the grammatical rules of English. For all of these years, I've had to write without any formal knowledge of any of those rules. I've had to rely on a simple way of writing – I just put the thoughts in my head into the simplest words I can think of, and I hope for the best, grammatically.

Sometimes I read stuff written by authors who I'm sure know the grammatical rules. You can tell, because they're able to write in a way that makes you have to think about what their words mean, or what thoughts they're trying to express, or what points they're trying to make. I think that my way of writing has its advantages in report writing. To me, it's best to keep it as understandable as you can. That's the only way I know how to write, so that's what you see in this book.

I think my lack of formal education has had its benefits in other ways in my career. Since I got so far behind in school learning, I've had to study extra hard all my life, just to try to catch up. I've tried to learn everything I could from the people I met along the way – the ones who knew more than I did – that was almost everybody.

I learned to be a pilot from some of the best pilots out there. I learned how to instruct from the top dog in the business. I stuck with instructing until I knew as much about it as anybody. I learned accident investigation from the bottom up. I've done just about every task that can be done by a field investigator. There was nothing I didn't get exposed to – I took no shortcuts. I had to learn – and to work hard – and to leave no stone unturned. That was the only way to avoid being embarrassed.

In accident investigation, dedicated thinking has a more descriptive name – it's called stump sitting time. Proper accident investigation requires lots of stump sitting time. Too many people think that activity is the best measure of progress – but it's not – your target is understanding, not activity. For accident investigation, you need curiosity, informed exploration, and stump sitting.

How incredibly fortunate for me that I was chided into raising my hand to join the Air Cadets – and that my buddy needed an extra candidate to go after a flying scholarship. Those chance happenings led me into one of the world's most interesting professions – with exposure to such incredible diversity – I've extracted technical data in a world-class lab using breakthrough technology – and I've extracted human remains from a frozen river using an axe.

There are not many professions where you get a chance to test yourself in such a variety of ways. You can be out in the wilderness – feeling alone, sitting on a stump, looking at wreckage and puzzling through an accident sequence. Or you can be on the world stage, interacting with world-renowned experts, adding your own expertise to the mix.

Back at the beginning of this book, I wrote about being in court to testify about a Cessna Caravan that crashed because it was overweight and contaminated with ice. Some of the people who heard me testify in that court told me that my life's story was interesting, and worth telling. Writing this has been a lot of work – I sure hope they were correct.

Larry at age two;
Fishing and Thinking – 1951

Larry with his grandmother and sister – 1951

CONTENTS